General Editors:

Max Beloff
*Former Gladstone Professor of Government and Public Administration
in the University of Oxford*

Gillian Peele
*Fellow and Tutor in Politics, Lady Margaret Hall, Oxford*

# Governing France

## The One and Indivisible Republic

### SECOND EDITION

J. E. S. HAYWARD

*Professor of Politics, University of Hull*

WEIDENFELD AND NICOLSON
*London*

First published in Great Britain by
George Weidenfeld & Nicolson Ltd
91 Clapham High Street, London sw4

ISBN 0 297 78235 5 Cased
ISBN 0 297 78243 6 Paperback

Printed in Great Britain by
Butler & Tanner Ltd, Frome and London

# Contents

# Tables

# Abbreviations

| | |
|---|---|
| APPCA | *Assemblée Permanente des Présidents de Chambres d'Agriculture* |
| CEA | *Commissariat à l'Energie Atomique* |
| CELIB | *Comité d'Etudes et de Liaison des Intérêts Bretons* |
| CFDT | *Confédération Française Democratique du Travail* |
| CFTC | *Confédération Française des Travailleurs Chrétiens* |
| CGC | *Confédération Générale des Cadres* |
| CGPME | *Confédération Générale des Petites et Moyennes Enterprises* |
| CGT | *Confédération Générale du Travail* |
| CID-UNATI | *Comité d'Information et de Défense – Union Nationale des Artisans et Travailleurs Indépendants* |
| CNIP | *Centre National des Indépendants et Paysans* |
| CNJA | *Centre National des Jeunes Agriculteurs* |
| CNPF | *Conseil National du Patronat Français* |
| CRS | *Compagnies Républicaines de Sécurité* |
| DATAR | *Délégation à l'Aménagement du Territoire et à l'Action Régionale* |
| DGRST | *Délégation Générale à la Recherche Scientifique et Technique* |
| DGSE | *Direction Général de la Sécurité Extérieure* |
| EC | European Community |
| EDF | *Electricité de France* |
| ENA | *Ecole Nationale d'Administration* |
| ESC | *Economic and Social Council* |
| FASP | *Fédération Autonome des Syndicats de la Police* |
| FDES | *Fonds de Développement Economique et Social* |
| FEN | *Fédération de l'Education Nationale* |
| FNSEA | *Fédération Nationale des Syndicats d'Exploitants Agricoles* |
| IFOP | *Institut Français de l'Opinion Publique* |

| | |
|---|---|
| MODEF | *Mouvement de Défense de l'Exploitation Familiale* |
| MRG | *Mouvement des Radicaux de Gauche* |
| MRP | *Mouvement Républicain Populaire* |
| NATO | North Atlantic Treaty Organization |
| ORTF | *Office de Radiodiffusion-Télévision Française* |
| PCF | *Parti Communiste Français* |
| PR | *Parti Républicain* |
| PS | *Parti Socialiste* |
| PSU | *Parti Socialiste Unifié* |
| RPR | *Rassemblement Pour la République* |
| SCIC | *Société Centrale Immobilière de la Caisse des Dépôts* |
| SDECE | *Service de Documentation Extérieure et de Contre-Espionnage* |
| SFIO | *Section Française de l'Internationale Ouvrière* |
| SNI | *Syndicat National des Instituteurs* |
| SNIAS | *Société Nationale Industrielle Aérospatiale* |
| SOFRES | *Société Française d'Enquêtes par Sondages* |
| TPG | *Trésorier Payeur Général* |
| UDF | *Union pour la Démocratie Française* |
| UDR | *Union des Démocrates pour la République* |
| UFF | *Union et Fraternité Française* |
| UNEF | *Union Nationale des Etudiants de France* |

# Editors' General Introduction

The series of which this volume forms a part is intended as a contribution to the study of contemporary political institutions in a number of countries which have been selected either for their intrinsic importance or for the particular interest attaching to their form of government and the manner of its working. While we expect that the majority of the readers of the books in this series will be students in universities, schools or other educational institutions, we also hope that the style and presentation of each volume will make it accessible to the general public as well. Indeed we should like to feel that anyone suddenly required for official or business or cultural purposes to go to one of the countries covered by the series would find the relevant volume of immediate use in understanding the governmental system in which he had to operate.

All study of government must be comparative in that the questions one asks about one system of government will usually arise from one's knowledge of another; and the distinctive features of any given system will only be highlighted by reference to a range of other political systems which work differently. Yet the generalizations to which political scientists aspire need to be based on the secure foundation of knowledge of the history, institutions and culture of a country and of how its pattern of government has been formed. By providing new volumes on the government and politics of individual countries we hope to make a modest contribution to the development of the discipline of comparative politics.

Government is not of course, something carried out for its own sake – much less something undertaken for the amusement of academics. It is an important practical activity and ultimately the criterion of success is to be found in its impact upon the lives of individual citizens. And here two vital questions need to be asked: how does a government conduct itself in regard to the citizen and what protection has he through the courts or in other ways against the possibility of arbitrary action or maladministration? In these volumes we have been especially anxious to see that these issues (which are sometimes neglected in general texts) receive substantial attention. A related central question is how the citizen can in fact make his influence felt upon the course of government both in countries which are democratic and in those which depart from the western model of liberal democracy. Such an inquiry will naturally involve a discussion of political parties, interest groups and the organs of public opinion which are the normal vehicles for conveying the views of the governed to the governors.

Although we have encouraged a balance between the formal legal and constitutional elements of a political system and the informal and cultural aspects of each country's political life, we have made no attempt to impose uniformity of treatment upon the volumes of the series. Each writer is an authority on his or her particular country or group of countries and will have a different perspective on the politics of the area in question. None would wish to see a long-established polity such as France or the United Kingdom treated in the same way as a vast and heterogeneous political society such as India which is still searching for stable political forms. Much less would it be appropriate to treat countries such as China or the Soviet Union (volumes on which will soon complement the series) in the same way as Spain or the Federal Republic of Germany. This volume, which is a second edition, comes at an especially interesting time for the study of French government and we are delighted that Professor Hayward's assessment of the French polity represents the latest addition to the series.

MAX BELOFF
GILLIAN PEELE

# Preface to the
# Second Edition

As France approaches the bicentenary of the French Revolution under the aegis of a Socialist president of the republic, this would seem to be a propitious time for a reassessment of the ways in which French politics works. The ten years that have elapsed since the publication of *The One and Indivisible French Republic* have led me to reconsider some of the views expressed as well as bring up to date the description of the French political system. Some readers did not recognize that the choice of title was done with tongue in cheek. I thought I had made it amply clear at numerous points that the *claim* to be monolithic was not to be taken at face value. The persuasive official norms are of course not to be identified with French reality, which is often anything but monolithic. It is precisely because neither the French state nor French society are highly integrated entities that it has been necessary for nearly two hundred years to present them *as if* they were united.

Having made this explicit, the old title largely survives as a subtitle, because it still seems worth according this influential founding myth pride of place. However, the new title marks the fact that, although the structure of the previous book remains largely intact, the content – by a combination of substantial cuts and even greater additions – has notably changed. The number of statistical tables has been almost halved and most of them are new. The balance of some chapters has been markedly altered. Thus, chapter seven gives more space to nationalization than to education because the post-1981 developments seem to warrant this modification. So, like French politics itself, *Governing France* is a mixture of continuity and change, whether for better or worse it will be for others to decide.

I would like to thank Miss Janet Braim and Mrs Enid Tracy

for their care and patience in typing parts of the manuscript and Lord Beloff and Gillian Peele for their constructively critical comments.

JACK HAYWARD
Hull, October 1982

# 1 The Unwritten Constitution

France has both a written and an unwritten Constitution. The written Constitution – the formal legal text – is easy enough to identify. France's unwritten Constitution is partly constituted by the debris of its numerous written Constitutions. It is profoundly affected by the experience of its numerous predecessors so that all earlier regimes have left their mark on the Fifth Republic and its procedures. Because Frenchmen expected regimes to be short-lived – indeed their Constitutions were often dismissed as periodical literature – little authority was attached to the Constitution itself at any one time. The current document was regarded as a treaty provisionally settling the allocation of power to suit the victors in a political struggle. Far from being a basic and neutral document, it was seen as only a partisan procedural device setting out the formal conditions according to which the government was entitled to rule. Thus it could not be endowed with the sacredness or permanence attributable to a Constitution where there is fundamental agreement about political values as well as about political procedures. The failure to make this distinction between prevailing institutional arrangements and the supporters of the government currently in power for France had many consequences. It meant that each regime was fragile because its legitimacy was always open to question and the duration of each regime depended on the strength of the political forces which had established it. It was impossible to institutionalize opposition because all governments tended to regard their opponents as dedicated to all-out war against the order established in the wake of the last constitutional crisis. And it created a general mood of uncertainty in the political environment.

The successful assumption of power in 1981 by a Socialist

government after twenty-three years of right-of-centre rule appears to have broken this pattern and to demonstrate the durability of the political institutions of the Fifth French Republic. The fact that the Socialist President was supported by an ample parliamentary majority suggests that, despite partisan polemics, there may be a new consensus in the French political system. Before this new consensus is scrutinized, it is necessary to situate the Fifth Republic in relation to its antecedents, so that we can assess what is enduring and what is new about the form of government that was instituted in 1958.

The main theme of this book is the perennial dialogue between French unity and French diversity, between a divided nation and a unitary state. The conception of undivided state power, inherited from the 'old', pre-Revolutionary regime, needed a new legitimizing myth to replace divine right monarchy. This founding myth infused the cold monster of state authority with the hot blood of democratic nationalism. Eugen Weber has argued that, by a flight of historical fancy, French national unity was perceived as expressing 'the general will of the French to be French, to achieve a state that was somehow historically foreordained'. This myth assumes that an integrated society can be taken for granted as the foundation for political institutions. Yet, as the selfsame historian has perspicaciously put it, 'The fact is, the French fuss so much about the nation because it is a living problem, became one when they set the nation up as an ideal, remained one because they found they could not realize the ideal. The more abstractly the concept of France-as-nation is presented, the less one notes discrepancies between theory and practice.' In fact national unity in France was a slow and painful process, of coercion, of colonization and of indoctrination. Armed force and conscription, roads and railways, the spread of state officialdom and state schools, all played a notable part in the formation of the French nation. Despite its role as a legitimizing myth, it is indispensable to recognize the French 'nation not as a given reality but as a work-in-progress, a model of something at once to be built and to be treated for political reasons as already in existence'.[1] Those exponents of French public and constitutional law who have a firm grip on political reality do not subscribe to the normative claim that the state is subsidiary to the nation but that prior state power is rendered legitimate thanks to the Jacobin conception of the national sovereignty of the people.[2] The importance of invoking the nation was that it could impart a democratic sacredness to state power and the cultural-cum-political expression of the fusion of nation with state was 'the Republic'. With this new mobilizing myth, the venerable conception of divine right monarchy could be buried, though it fought a stubborn rearguard action during the nineteenth century.

The Fifth Republic is the most recent reassertion of the authoritarian tradition in French political history, exemplified by the absolute monarchy and the Napoleonic Empires, against the regimes, such as the Third and Fourth Republics, that sought to circumscribe public power by subordinating government to an indecisive legislature that accurately reflected French diversity. During the period from 1789–99, bedevilled by civil and foreign wars, France tried out a variety of political systems, culminating in a seizure of power by Napoleon Bonaparte that concluded a decade of revolutionary experiment. The failure of the First Republic to find an acceptable institutional expression for the replacement of hereditary monarchy by popular sovereignty was to promote a search for a way of reconciling stability and effectiveness with freedom and democracy that has still not been concluded. Each of the regimes that followed left behind a legacy of constitutional experience that collectively incorporate the values which shape day-to-day French political behaviour. The First Republic's main contribution was the development of government by a single chamber Assembly elected by universal suffrage. Together with the assertion of the civil and political rights of the citizen, government by Assembly provided a continental model of liberal democracy which contrasted strongly with the parliamentary government that developed in Britain. However, the two constitutional monarchies (1815–48), the Third Republic (1870–1940) and the Fourth Republic (1946–58) sought to import and adapt the British model as the French misunderstood it. The constitutional monarchies, in particular, thought that British practice involved an active, politically implicated head of state; while the conspicuous absence of the religious, economic, social and political solidarity that allowed Britain to achieve the simplicity of a two-party system led to unstable republican government,

3

the Third Republic having reduced the president to the role of master of constitutional ceremonies. The Fourth Republic curtailed the power of the second chamber and increased the importance of the prime minister and of the political parties. However, the reversion to government by Assembly and weak coalitions that disintegrated when faced with each new controversial problem left the regime vulnerable.

The 1958 challenge to the indivisibility of the republic – could Algeria be given independence? – provided General de Gaulle with his long-awaited opportunity to 'restore the state'. This meant reverting to the Napoleonic concentration of power in the hands of the chief executive and a reduction in the ability of parliament to paralyse government. It involved a reorganization of the administrative, military and judicial system of the country in the most authentic Napoleonic style. However, it was not possible to make all the necessary changes straightaway. The direct popular election of the president was postponed until 1962 and the president's supporters in parliament and in the country were gradually organized into a party that achieved an unprecedented measure of comprehensiveness and cohesion on the right of the political spectrum.

De Gaulle resuscitated the Napoleonic plebiscite as a means of appealing to the French people over the heads of their parliamentary representatives and used it with success until the rejection of his 1969 referendum, which he interpreted as a personal repudiation. While he provided France with the remodelled political institutions of the Fifth Republic, embodying his vision of a truly sovereign state authority, de Gaulle always considered that the requirements of the state, the *raison d'état*, allowed him to infringe legality with impunity.

His contempt for constitutional restraints (except those inflicted on his opponents) provided he had public support, is clear from two comments made to a scandalized Pierre-Henri Teitgen, Professor of Constitutional Law and de Gaulle's minister of justice in 1945. 'There is France. There is the State. And then, after the higher imperatives, only in third place, there is the Law.' 'Three things count in constitutional matters. Firstly, the higher interest of the country ... That has priority over everything else and I alone am judge of it. Secondly, a longway behind, come the political circumstances ... Thirdly, and very much further behind, come legalistic matters.'[3]

Such a cavalier attitude towards constitutional propriety is anathema to Mitterrand, a lawyer by training and a man who is imbued with an appreciation of the need for legal constraints upon authority. His frequent attacks upon one-man rule derived from his fear that 'A regime without law will succumb to arbitrary power'. Quoting Article 16 of the Declaration of the Rights of Man of 1789, he asserted in a debate on the creation by de Gaulle of a State Security Court (the abolition of which Mitterrand made a top priority in 1981), '"A society in which the separation of powers is not stipulated has no constitution" and I would add that such a country ... is not a Republic either.'[4] Many believed that one of the features of French public life that has led to most criticism, the arbitrary use of state power, would improve under the presidency of a man who had a passionate commitment to the protection of civil liberties from the incursions of the agents of the sovereign power he provisionally personifies.

### The preoccupation with state sovereignty

In seeking to identify the source of legitimate political authority, Alexis de Tocqueville concluded:

It is with the doctrine of the sovereignty of the people that we must begin. The principle of the sovereignty of the people, which is to be found, more or less, at the bottom of almost all human institutions, generally remains concealed from view. It is obeyed without being recognized, or if for a moment it be brought to light, it is hastily cast back into the gloom of the sanctuary.[5]

Sovereignty was bound to be an especially sensitive issue in France, where the power to decide has always been bitterly contested. However, to single out state sovereignty as the salient feature of the French political tradition involves a great oversimplification. For France is a country of counterbalancing contradictions. It combines anarchic individualism and centralized statism. Revolutionary responses and rhetoric are coupled with the conservative traditionalism of entrenched vested interests. Instability and continuity coexist in extreme forms. Nevertheless, to clarify such familiar paradoxes, we assert the thesis that the attitude of the French élite towards politics has been dominated by a belief in the need for a strong, unified, centralized authority, capable of containing the centrifugal forces that constantly threaten the integrity of the state. It will be our task to develop and qualify this assertion.

It was the sixteenth-century French forerunner of political science, Jean Bodin, who first systematically expounded a theory of state sovereignty, a concept alien to the mainstream of medieval political thought. The sixteenth and seventeenth centuries marked a rapid modernization of the royal administration and army, the breakdown of medieval pluralism being associated with the reassertion of sovereign authority embodied in an absolute monarch. The concept of sovereignty involved a revival of the Roman Law notion of *imperium*. In the republican period it had referred to the supreme power of the citizens; in the consular period to the authority conferred on the emperor by the senate representing the citizens; whilst in the imperial period it had described the omnipotence and omnicompetence of the emperor, who was above the law. Written in a period of civil war, such as nearly a century later was to inspire Hobbes' *Leviathan*, Bodin's *Les Six Livres de la république* defended the pragmatic view of those in France (the party known as *politiques*) who argued that the state's role was to maintain order, not to establish true religion. Against the warring factions of Catholic and Huguenot, Bodin returned to the Roman Law assertion of the state as perpetual and absolute power and to the claim that the only constraint on the sovereign was his ability to limit his own sovereignty. The unique attribute of sovereignty was the power to make binding law, the sovereign's commands being entitled to unconditional obedience. Bodin's concept of sovereignty, a legal fiction formulated in the service of the nascent nation-state, an entity inclusive of all its provincial and sectional parts and exclusive of all more universal communities, was to prove influential long after his works ceased to be read.

It was Bodin who, by describing sovereignty as 'one' and 'indivisible',[6] prepared the way for the French Revolution's subsequent assertions of national, parliamentary and popular sovereignty as embodied in the one and indivisible republic. However, it required the mediation of Rousseau's *Social Contract* to transfer sovereignty from the monarch to the people, whilst reiterating that 'sovereign authority is one and singular and cannot be divided without being destroyed'.[7] Despite Rousseau's warning of the dangers of representative government and his assertion of the inalienable nature of sovereignty, the 'general will' was displaced by the people's elected deputies as the repository of national sovereignty. The principal architect of this transformation of popular into parliamentary sovereignty in 1789 was Sieyès, just as in 1799 he paved the way for Bonaparte's seizure of power. So central a figure in the establishment and demise of the First Republic's representative system of government merits a brief comment on his contribution to the French conception of political authority: the advocacy of government by Assembly.

The attack on the *Ancien Régime* was inspired by a wish to substitute a political order based on nationwide uniformity and equality for the provincial, estate and corporate particularisms and privileges that had survived as the enfeebled vestiges of feudal polycentrism. After having asserted in *What is the Third Estate?* of January 1789 that 'the right to be represented is single and indivisible', Sieyès, who proposed the transmutation of the Third Estate into a National Assembly, presented a motion in June 1789 that 'representation being one and indivisible, no deputy of whatever order or class he may be chosen, has the right to exercise his functions separately from this Assembly'.[8] He went on to develop a theory of representation to allow the Assembly to take over the people's sovereignty. It was based (like Burke's more famous British version) on the contention that the deputies represented the nation and not their constituents. The exercise of legislative power had been delegated to the Assembly by the people, whose sovereignty was reduced to the right to elect their legislators. In a speech in September 1789, Sieyès affirmed: 'The people or the nation has only one voice, that of the national legislature; it can only speak through its representatives.'[9] Thus was the threat of direct democracy *à la* Rousseau exorcized.

Sieyès' standpoint was enshrined in Title 3 of the 1791 (monarchical) Constitution which proclaimed:

Article 1. Sovereignty is one, indivisible, inalienable and imprescriptible; it belongs to the nation; no section of the people nor any individual is entitled to appropriate it.

7

Article 2.    The French constitution is representative ...
Article 3.    The legislative power is delegated to a national assembly
...

In the republican Constitution of 1793, the emphasis shifts from
the nation to the people. Its first Article proclaims: 'The French
republic is one and indivisible.' However, whilst reiterating the
principle of popular sovereignty in Article 25 of the Declaration
of the Rights of Man and in Article 7 of the Constitution, it goes
on to proclaim: 'The legislative body is one, indivisible and
permanent.' The sovereign power was successively transferred
between 1789–99 by successive *coups d'état* from the king to the
nation, from the nation to the people, from the people to the
Assembly and from the Assembly, via an attempt at a 'dictatorship of the notables' led by Sieyès, to the popular dictator Napoleon. On the 19 Brumaire (10 November) 1799, the day after
the coup, the consuls of the republic – who included Sieyès and
Napoleon – took an oath to 'the sovereignty of the people; to
the French republic, one and indivisible; to equality, liberty
and the representative system'.[10] However, Napoleon was to
establish a Caesarist regime in which, in the words of Sieyès,
concerned now to strengthen the executive against the legislature, 'authority comes from above and confidence from below'.
In 1814, shortly before he lost his imperial throne, Napoleon
lectured the legislative body on his superior representativeness,
just as in 1869 Louis Napoleon was to secure overwhelming
public support in a plebiscite shortly before the end of the
Second Empire. Such has been the pattern ever since in France:
the fragility of a power impersonating popular sovereignty.

France having attempted government by Assembly and
one-man rule, it remained for Benjamin Constant to sketch out
a liberal type of representative government inspired by British
constitutional monarchy, in which sovereignty would be constitutionally curbed. Like Sieyès, Constant supported the middle-
class reaction that led to the *Directoire* in 1795 and the installa-
tion of Napoleon in 1799. However, he spent the period 1800–
14 in outspoken opposition to Napoleon before joining him
during the Hundred Days, being charged with the task of preparing a liberal constitution. In his *Réflexions sur les constitutions* of
May 1814, Constant wrote: 'None of our constitutions have

8

assigned limits to the legislative power. The sovereignty of the people, absolute and unlimited, was transmitted by the nation, or at least in its name, as is customary, by those who dominated it, to representative assemblies. The result was the most unheard of arbitrariness.'[11] A year later, in his *Principes de politique*, Constant went on to develop a theory of 'limited and relative' sovereignty, declaring in an anticipation of J. S. Mill's *On Liberty*: even if authority is 'the whole nation, less the citizen that it oppresses, it would be no more legitimate'.[12]

The French have been both fascinated and repelled by the notion of sovereignty. It is the harbinger of modernization, order and security but also of conflict, arbitrary power and despotism. Constant pointed out how Rousseau tried to evade the dilemma of sovereignty:

Terror-stricken at the sight of the immensity of the social power he had created, he did not know into whose hands he should deposit this monstrous power and found no safeguard against the danger inseparable from such sovereignty except in an expedient that renders its exercise impossible. He declared that sovereignty could not be either alienated, delegated or represented. This was tantamount to stating that it could not be exercised; it was to annihilate the principle he had just proclaimed.[13]

This unresolved problem of the location of sovereign power has continued to bedevil French attempts at creating an effective and acceptable form of government. All these attempts have required violation in practice of the ambiguous fundamental principles, either in the direction of parliamentary omnipotence or of executive dominance. Constant gave the French a characteristic liberal warning: 'When sovereignty is not limited, there is no way of protecting individuals from governments. It is in vain that you seek to subordinate governments to the general will. They always dictate that will. . . .'[14] Unfortunately, France has been deaf to this message, liberalism having shrunk into a narrow and feeble doctrine when it reached France. Constant's ideas have ever since suffered a guilt-by-association with the July monarchy's reign of the 'absolute bourgeoisie'.

Extreme statism has led by reaction to its antithesis: the outright repudiation of the state, although this usually takes the form of inconclusive protest. It has been stressed that in France, on the right as well as on the left, in political parties as well as among pressure groups, protest is the norm.[15] It is a type of protest that is generally quietist in deed but verbally vociferous; intransigently negative, moralistically ideological and demagogically defeatist. Albert Camus' *The Rebel* provided the most celebrated mid-twentieth-century formulation of this philosophy, as had Alain under the Third Republic. In the mid-nineteenth century, Proudhon, France's greatest anarchist, gave eloquent expression to a traditional hostility towards the coercive, centralized power of sovereign governments:

To be governed is to be kept under surveillance, inspected, spied upon, directed, regimented, regulated, enrolled, indoctrinated, sermonized, checked, numbered, valued, censured, commanded, by creatures who have neither the right, nor the wisdom, nor the virtue to do so ... To be governed is to be at every action, at every transaction, noted, registered, inventoried, taxed, stamped, measured, enumerated, licensed, assessed, authorized, penalized, endorsed, admonished, obstructed, reformed, rebuked, punished. It is, under pretext of public utility and in the name of the general interest, to be placed under contribution, manoeuvered, ransomed, exploited, monopolized, extorted, pressured, mystified, robbed; then, at the slightest resistance, the first word of complaint, to be repressed, fined, vilified, harassed, hounded, manhandled, bludgeoned ...; and to crown all, cheated, ridiculed, outraged, dishonoured. That is government; that is its justice; that is its morality.[16]

This extreme distrust and defiance of authority and the consequent propensity to direct action makes Proudhon as characteristic a spokesman of the French working classes as the Fabians are of intellectual British socialism, with its reliance on gradualist reform based upon influencing a rather passive government.

Although Proudhon's practical alternative to state domination was voluntary association, the civic culture in France has been too weak to provide a viable alternative, despite the proliferation of many competing groups, each articulating the overlapping demands of a voluble and self-consciously diverse society. The 1970s surge in the number and assertiveness of voluntary associations has not overcome the habitually negative attitude towards freedom, liberty being conceived as fundamentally a matter of non-commitment, an antipathy towards authority so complete that any involvement with it is shunned.

The result has been subordination to a remote and bureaucratic authority, Frenchmen responding with free thought and servile conduct, except for occasional outbursts of revolt, such as May 1968, followed by another demonstration of their lack of capacity to participate. The Socialist president and parliamentary majority installed in 1981 are unlikely fully to live up to their promises of increased participation, partly because of the reluctance of French citizens to accept the correlative responsibilities. Ten years before becoming president of the republic, at the Epinay Congress of June 1971 at which he was elected first secretary of the rejuvenated Socialist Party, Mitterrand showed his awareness of the contending ideologies within his pluralistic, catch-all party: 'Marxists are numerous, both real and fake; there is a Proudhonian tradition bubbling over with vitality; as well as the Personalist followers of Emmanuel Mounier', representing the left-wing Catholics, who, along with the 'Proudhonians', had been active in the voluntary movement, embodying the political counter culture of 'Dissentient France'.[17] This reassertion of a pluralistic society against the all-embracing propensities of a domineering sovereign state may, with the state controlled by professed champions of self-management, encourage more constructive forms of activism than the episodic eruption of ineffectual protest.

### Institutionalizing heroic leadership: presidential impetus

After the traumatic experiences it underwent in the revolutionary decade of 1789-99 when the two main French political traditions, Jacobinism and Bonapartism took shape, France experimented with a variety of constitutional devices. For most of the Third Republic, however, despite the fact that the legitimacy of the regime was under challenge by intransigent minorities, it was possible for government to function in a routine fashion, giving full play to the representative tradition of parliamentary sovereignty. This 'representative' emphasis, by reaction against the executive and administrative domination of the *Ancien Régime* and of the First and Second Empires, was modelled on the 1792 Convention. Nevertheless, despite Sieyès' famous stricture on second chambers – if they disagree with the first chamber they are obnoxious and if they agree with it they are superfluous – the indirectly elected Senate shared parliamentary sovereignty with the Chamber of Deputies. A century after the Convention, however, it was possible for parliament to exercise its sovereignty in the social context of a bourgeoisie no longer struggling for ascendancy, but triumphant.

Although based, like Bonapartism, on the doctrine of popular sovereignty, Jacobinism had, under the guidance of Sieyès, rapidly translated this into a doctrine of parliamentary sovereignty nominally not unlike that attributed to Britain in the mid-nineteenth century. Members of the National Assembly were representative of the nation and not of their constituents. The deputies, in particular, chosen by direct manhood suffrage, were the authentic spokesmen of the popular will and the custodians of political legitimacy. Their constituents had sectional interests which were to be expounded and defended in dealings with the administration and with ministers. This was the price of re-election. The mass electorate were, however, expected passively to rely upon the notables, whom they had selected to represent them in the national parliament, to decide matters of national policy on their behalf. Thus emerged what has been dubbed the 'deputy-centred republic',[18] in which, unlike Britain, power was really concentrated in parliament. Undisciplined by party, members of the French parliament were also independent, in practice, both of a predominantly peasant electorate and of the government.

Although rent by the bitter anti-clerical and anti-militarist struggle of the Dreyfus Affair, the Third Republic had achieved, at the turn of the century, an uneasy compromise between the liberal-representative tradition embodied by the parliamentary institutions and the authoritarian-administrative tradition of the civil service. Behind the protective tariff wall erected in the 1880s and 1890s by Jules Méline, who combined the premiership with the agriculture portfolio from 1896–8, resistance to change was reinforced. The peasant, the artisan and the small shopkeeper of the predominantly small-town and rural society flourished. An anarcho-syndicalist industrial proletariat was making anti-capitalism an increasingly important issue, whilst a united Socialist Party emerged to challenge the hitherto dominant Radical Party for the left-wing vote. However, what has been described as 'the coexistence of *limited* authoritarianism and *potential* insurrection'[19] continued to characterize the prevailing style of authority in the latter half of the Third Republic. Power was concentrated in parliament, itself paralyzed by class, ideology and sectional and local cleavages. Gambetta's claim in 1875 that the new constitution would 'consecrate the union between the bourgeoisie and the proletariat' proved an illusory hope. Successive governments devoted themselves to preserving stability, the Radicals in particular acquiring a reputation for self-restraint in office that was connected with the frequency with which they occupied it. The same behaviour was required of the prefect who, as the local agent of the centralized political system, had as his prime function the maintenance of the status quo.

While universal suffrage was accepted in the nineteenth century as the fountain-head of legitimate authority, centralized authority was mediated by both administrative and representative institutions and of these the bureaucratic ones were both older and more deeply rooted. The establishment by Napoleon of the prefectoral system in 1800 was intended to be the centrepiece of a chain of command from the minister of the interior at the centre to the agents of the government at the periphery: prefects in the departments, the sub-prefects in the *arrondissements* and the mayors in the communes. The prefect was a senior official, appointed and removable by the central government, who was supposed to centralize all administrative activities in each of the country's territorial sub-divisions, directly or through his subordinates. The 'administered', as the French people came to be known – a term they accepted alongside the nobler title of citizen – however, became the responsibility of other agents of the central government, notably the field services of the ministries in Paris, which expanded with increasing public intervention. They evaded the control of the prefects, whose repressive and electoral functions became less significant than the provision of public services. The prefectoral preoccupation with preserving, in conjunction with the local economic, political and social élites, the stability of the provincial status quo, came to appear less and less suited to the changing needs of a modern society.

The stability of the French administrative substructure

tended to go unnoticed by contrast with the instability of French governmental superstructure. However, as Alexis de Tocqueville pointed out over a hundred years ago:

We have had several other revolutions in France since '89, revolutions which changed the whole structure of the government of the country from top to bottom ... Usually, in fact, the majority of the population was almost unaffected by them; sometimes it hardly knew a revolution was taking place. The reason is that since '89 the administrative system had always stood firm amid the débacles of political systems ... For though in each successive revolution the administration was, so to speak, decapitated, its body survived intact and active.[20]

While for the most part the bureaucracy helped to prop up the status quo, it had shown in the past and was to demonstrate once again in the post-Second World War period, that it, rather than the business bourgeoisie, was the main modernizing force in France.

A regime organized to minimize the impact of change postpones and accumulates a backlog of overdue business. Developments in the political system's environment make increasingly pressing demands for attention. If they are neglected, they may threaten the regime with revolt or abrupt innovation. During the ensuing crisis it is sometimes possible' to carry out the changes which the political system has hitherto rejected. The crisis might take the relatively anodyne form of a government reshuffle, the characteristic method of the Third and Fourth Republics, but it might lead to the collapse of the regime, as in the case of the settler-military revolt over the Algerian issue in May 1958. At such times, France appeals to 'one of those men who spring from events and are the spontaneous offspring of peril' as Pompidou expressed it, in presenting his general policy declaration to the Assembly on taking office as prime minister in 1962. The appeal to the heroic leader involves a reassertion of the latent need for assertive executive action within the political system to impose changes precluded by the routine operation of a representative system that inhibits ambitious reforms.

Writing at a time when France had subordinated itself by plebiscite to the *coup d'état* of *Napoléon le Petit*, Tocqueville presented a superb portrayal of his countrymen's equivocal attitude to strong leadership:

Ordinarily the French are the most routine-bound of men, but once they are forced out of the rut and leave their homes, they travel to the ends of the earth and engage in the most reckless ventures. Undisciplined by temperament, the Frenchman is always readier to put up with the arbitrary rule, however harsh, of an autocrat than with free, well-ordered government by his fellow citizens, however worthy of respect they be. At one moment he is up in arms against authority and the next we find him serving the powers-that-be with a zeal such as the most servile races never display. So long as no one thinks of resisting, you can lead him on a thread, but once a revolutionary movement is afoot, nothing can restrain him from taking part in it. That is why our rulers are so often taken by surprise; they fear the nation either too much or not enough, for though it is never so free that the possibility of enslaving it is ruled out, its spirit can never be broken so completely as to prevent its shaking off the yoke of an oppressive government.[21]

When the routine working of the political system fails, the nation turns to someone who is immune from the discredit shared by those closely identified with the *système*.

The heroic leader is usually someone who has not been involved directly in politics: a general like Napoleon or de Gaulle. On the other hand he might be a solitary rebel against the conventional political system, like Clemenceau or Pierre Mendès France.[22] It is vital for such leaders to mobilize mass support against the stranglehold of the traditional élites and of the political parties and sectional interests who have monopolized the mediatory role between the people and the government. They do this by seeking to personify an underlying national consensus, exalting national pride and stimulating hero-worship. In the early 1960s, with de Gaulle no doubt in mind, the heroic leader's freedom of action was characterized thus by Michel Crozier: 'During crises, individual initiative prevails and people eventually come to depend on some strategic individual's arbitrary whim.'[23] This style of leadership entailed a humiliatingly passive role for the Gaullists when – under a succession of party labels – they provided support for the General.

However, once the emergency is over, the heroic leader seems out of place, less an object of gratitude than a flagrant reminder of the incapacity of the political class to cope with serious problems successfully. Having fulfilled his function as 'agent of

*Governing France*

social change *in* the system and the preserver *of* the system',[24] he lacks the routine legitimacy to survive under crisis-free circumstances. He may seek to keep up a sense of impending crisis to sustain his flagging authority, as de Gaulle did by using the bogey of a return to the Fourth Republic or the threat of a totalitarian take-over by the Communists. Although the May 1968 'events' temporarily sustained him by creating the feelings of mass fear and panic peculiarly propitious to maintaining the national saviour in power, public notice of the termination of the heroic leader's task was signified in the plebiscite less than a year later.

The May 1968 crisis* represented the escalation of student unrest into an all-out attack on authority in all French institutions. Michel Crozier has argued that, because of the bureaucratic character of French organizations, change, when it finally comes, is comprehensive. 'To obtain a limited reform in France, one is always obliged to attack the whole "system", which is thus constantly called into question ... Reform can be brought about only by sweeping revolution. Reformers, in any case, cannot succeed without counting on the pressure generated by revolutionary or quasi-revolutionary movements.'[25] Another leading French disciple of Tocqueville, Raymond Aron, recalled in his study of the May 'events' that in the early 1950s he had said in a lecture: 'From time to time France carries out a revolution, but never carries out reforms.' He was corrected by de Gaulle's comment: 'France only undertakes reforms in the wake of revolutions.'[26] That this should in part hold true under the Fifth Republic, whose founder prided himself on the imperious and sovereign fashion in which he exerted his authority, by contrast with the despised Fourth Republic, is an earnest of its enduring character.

A Gaullist deputy sweepingly asserted in an Assembly debate on the 1969 referendum, that in France governments were inclined to postpone action until placed under extreme pressure:

Our citizens sometimes contribute to this awareness of the need for action by methods which should be condemned but whose effectiveness one cannot objectively deny. A few windows are broken in a prefecture or even a subprefecture; then a series of measures awaited for years, sometimes vainly demanded in the national assembly, sud-

* See below, chapter 7, pp. 218-19.

16

denly begins to be implemented. The paving stones are dug up and a few cars are set on fire: the entire French educational system is totally reformed. ... France thus progresses by reprimands that brutally bring it to its senses, at the cost of unrest which paralyses it and from which it emerges as from a dream. ...[27]

The political system excluded mass participation at the national level except of a very remote and indirect kind. Despite its modernizing rhetoric, it slowed down the tempo of economic change to preserve the social and political equilibrium, arousing frustrations not merely among student activists but in many quarters. Farmers, shopkeepers, artisans and workers were all accustomed to using extra-legal and 'outrageous' forms of pressure on government. Each sectional interest has been prepared to use a strategy of blackmail against the authorities, openly flouting the law through forms of direct action which expose the pretence of national consensus upon which the government prides itself. When they cannot repress these challenges, the authorities are compelled to surrender. At such times, recourse to negotiation, and the modest reconciliation of conflicting interests with public policy, is more effective than the promulgation of grandiloquent edicts.

The new stalemate into which Gaullism was sinking in the period 1963-8, following the double victory of autumn 1962 in which the Constitution was amended to the president's advantage and a stable majority was returned to the National Assembly, was spectacularly interrupted by the May 1968 crisis. However, instead of imparting to the Fifth Republic a new heroic impetus, it marked an interlude in the transition to a different style of political leadership. Georges Pompidou had, as prime minister, played a major part in organizing the domestic scene whilst President de Gaulle concentrated his innovative energies in the field of foreign policy. However, he emerged in the crisis as the leader capable of settling the immediate grievances by economic concessions and restoring the government's authority by a parliamentary general election, not by recourse to a presidential plebiscite. After leading the Gaullist candidates to an overwhelming victory in June 1968, Pompidou said in a complacent broadcast: 'Now we can take a breather.' The heroic leader's response to the May crisis was entirely different. He saw it as a summons to new endeavour and ten days later, when he sacked Pompidou, he is supposed to have said to him: 'Now Pompidou, you can take a breather.' However, in the referendum of 27 April 1969, a majority of the French people said that they wanted to 'take a breather' from the heroic exertions imposed upon them by de Gaulle.

The search for political equilibrium through the avoidance of conflict was the hallmark of the post-Gaullist Fifth Republic up to and including the presidency of Giscard d'Estaing. It was content to settle for an unheroic consensus based upon the general acceptance of the existing constitution and institutions. De Gaulle's successors attempted to create the national unanimity ardently pursued by de Gaulle; they acted not so much by aggressive assertions of a provocative nationalism on the international stage, as by a more discreet promotion of domestic consensus through accelerated industrial modernization in the case of Pompidou. Confronted by the consequences of bipolarization, which led in 1972 to a united left, and a presidential election in 1974 that neatly bisected the electorate, Pompidou's successor Giscard d'Estaing deceived himself into believing that the undoubtedly increasing affluence of the 1960s would ensure the permanent triumph of the liberal–conservative centre. Despite the onset of economic recession that coincided with his assumption of office as president, Giscard believed that the trend he detected would bring about a sociological centrism, based upon a broad middle class that would dwarf the socio-political forces to the left and right.

Giscard spelled out his analysis in *Towards a New Democracy*:

The fact is that France is socially on the road to unification, under the impulse of three factors which we must constantly bear in mind: the rise in the standard of living, education, and the widespread dissemination of news. Development now taking place, far from leading to a confrontation between two, strongly differentiated and antagonistic classes – bourgeoisie and proletariat – is characterized by a large, expanding, open-ended central group; its exceptionally rapid increase in numbers, its links with the other two social categories, its accessibility to both of them, as well as the modern values it stands for, means that it will gradually and peacefully incorporate within itself the whole of French society.[28]

This vision of an emerging consensus, initially coupled with a call for moderation and toleration, as well as some modest reforms, evaporated as the French economy slid in the late 1970s into recession and mass unemployment. Furthermore, the attempt to increase the strength of the centre at the expense of both right and left, would have required a change in the electoral system. As long as the two-ballot, first past the post electoral system existed, it would bipolarize the political parties into left-wing and right-wing coalitions, with those occupying the centre of the political spectrum compelled to compromise with their electoral allies. Giscard's inability to secure the electoral underpinning for his attempt to redistribute power to the centre condemned his ambitions to humiliating frustration.

The political leader who most profited from the modernization of French society – the expanding salaried middle classes, the increasing urbanization and dechristianization of much of provincial France, the 'coming of age' of the second sex – was François Mitterrand, who triumphed over Giscard d'Estaing in the 1981 presidential election and carried his Socialist Party to a sweeping Assembly majority. The most intransigent castigator of the Constitution of the Fifth Republic, against which he had published a withering polemic entitled *Le Coup d'état permanent*, was to assume its ample prerogatives with delectation. There was a gradual *rapprochement* over the twenty-three years that separated the humiliating suicide of the Fourth Republic in 1958 and the coming to presidential power of Mitterrand, the arch critic of the Fifth Republic. In 1969 Mitterrand explained: 'I voted against the Constitution more because of the context than the text, though it was debatable ... the government and Assembly (of the Fourth Republic) had surrendered the Republic.' While both de Gaulle and Mitterrand championed 'the Republic', they had very different conceptions of the relationship of its state and society components. Mitterrand recalled saying to de Gaulle at the height of the 1958 crisis: 'one can hardly base a republican regime on this one-man rule and he replied that he would not disappear without having guaranteed the survival of the republican regime.'[29] Not merely has the Fifth Republic survived the resignation of its progenitor in 1969; it has survived the long-awaited and feared swing of the electoral pendulum from right to left. The Fifth Republic yields only to the Third Republic as the longest lived political regime since the French Revolution. The latest guardian of a Constitution whose First Title, labelled sovereignty, begins: 'France is an indivisible, secular, democratic and social republic', may be more inclined than his predecessors to emphasize its secular, democratic and (especially) its social character. However, as we shall see, Mitterrand remains an intransigent Jacobin, an ardent advocate both of decentralization and of the indivisibility of the republic.

# 2 Decentralizing the Indivisible Republic

France is a state-nation rather than a nation-state. The nation is an artefact of the state. The political regime has retained a precedence over the political community that is derived from but extends far beyond its historic precedence. France is a unitary state superimposed upon a multinational society, the authority of Paris having been established under the monarchy, expanded by the Napoleonic Empires and reinforced by the Republics over *Alsaciens*, Basques, Bretons, Catalans, etc. Despite the incomparable assimilative power that France had shown over the centuries, the obsession with national unity betrays an uneasy sense that the peoples which make up France may have been swallowed but are not wholly digested. A secretary-general of the Gaullist UDR (predecessor of the RPR) could complacently recall Michelet's claim that 'French France had attracted, absorbed, amalgamated the English, German and Spanish Frances with which it was surrounded. She had neutralized each by the other and converted them all into her substance. . . . She had southernized the north and northernized the south.' However, successive French regimes have regarded the legitimacy of their authority as questionable, the monolithic character of the political and administrative state apparatus being necessary to coerce into a semblance of consensus and order the disparate and divided fragments of the national mosaic. A succession of revolutionary reconstitutions of the central authority have left it particularly sensitive when its inordinate pretensions are called into question.

This obsessive vigilance against potential dissidents is particularly associated with the Jacobins although these intransigent advocates of the one and indivisible republic initially favoured a decentralized system of local government and administration.

Because the Girondins were specifically identified with a *federalist* France, the initial Jacobin advocacy of *decentralization* became confused with the Napoleonic assertion of a deconcentrated but hyper-centralized system of local administration. Mitterrand, who was to preside over the most decentralist government since the Revolution, had in the early 1970s sought to put the historical record straight.

I am described as a Jacobin, consequently a champion of state power and the enemy of regional power. This is a two-fold error. First, it was Napoleon Bonaparte and not the Jacobins who shaped the stifling structures of contemporary France. Second, I want decentralization to be pushed to the maximum extent possible, so that decisions are taken at all the places where people live and work.

Mayor of Château-Chinon (3,000 inhabitants) from 1959–81, he admitted that he had not acquired his enthusiasm for public participation until after the 'events' of May 1968 had convinced him that 'democratic life is above all the apprenticeship for taking responsibility.'[1]

Sieyès, the leading architect and exponent of the post-Revolutionary departmental organization, commended centralized state authority on the ground that it would make France a *single whole*, uniformly submitted in all its parts to the same legislation and a common administration'. 'I know of no better means to make all parts of France into a unit and all the peoples that divide it into a single nation.'[2] At each subsequent onslaught on centralized state authority in France, the pseudo-'Jacobin' creed has been successfully reiterated. When the Constitution of the Second Republic was being drawn up, Lamennais, supported notably by Tocqueville and Barrot, sought to base the new political system on the autonomy of the commune and resigned from the constitutional committee in protest when his proposal was defeated. As Proudhon, another great victim of the Second Republic's march from the Revolution of 1848 to the *coup d'état* of 1851, put it with exasperated overemphasis: 'The commune will be sovereign or a subordinate agent, everything or nothing.'[3] This characteristic escalation into the opposite extreme to the Jacobin insurrectionary Paris Commune of 1792–4 helped inspire the ephemeral 1871 Paris Commune; after that, however, the Third Republic established the local administrative institutions which survived largely intact for nearly a century.

Before exploring the complexities of how the French system of local government works and the ways in which it has been reformed, it is necessary to explain briefly the traditional structure of French local institutions. The French Revolution established a standardized, hierarchical system of local government units, with departments (comparable to English counties) as the top tier and the prefect, located in the administrative capital, centralizing the power of the central government officials within the department. Every department was subdivided into a number of *arrondissements* (of which there were about 500), each of which was placed in the charge of a sub-prefect. These *arrondissements* were further subdivided into some 2,000 cantons, that were the constituencies from which were elected the departmental councillors. Finally, at the grassroots (corresponding in their number and size to the English parish) there were nearly 40,000 communes, whose mayors were from 1882 elected by the municipal council and not appointed by the minister of the interior on the advice of the prefect as had been the case previously. Operating outside this structure from the very start were the local personnel of the armed services, the judiciary and the fiscal and financial services of the ministry of finance. Subsequently, the field services of the expanding ministries in Paris that were established in the departments were excluded from prefectoral control. As we shall see, despite attempts under the Fifth Republic – most recently in the 1982 Act on the rights and freedoms of communes, departments and regions – to assert prefectoral control over these field services of central government dealing with agriculture, employment, public works, to name only the most important, a tendency towards functional fragmentation by service seems to be endemic.

### State idealism and comprehensive central control

National uniformity, conceived as a comprehensive code of standardized rules imposed on all and sundry by Parisian officials as the guardians of republican virtue, is the principle that is supposed to be the keynote of the relationship between the French government and its citizens. Practice is different.

The political ministers make the general rules but in implementing them the officials decide on the exceptions in particular cases. These concessions to necessity are part of a local political system which state idealists conceive as 'a kind of morality play, with the Public Interest defending the castle against a horde of savage, ruthless mercenaries of the selfish interests'.[4] To maintain the appearance of impartiality, the agents of the state take refuge in bureaucratic impersonality. They 'deal with categories and not cases'.[5] The objects of these regulations have no choice except to conform, to 'pull strings', to bribe or to revolt. It is by threatening revolt that the exceptions to the general rules are often obtained and which make centralized authority tolerable. Without such concessions to the countervailing power of the local communities, the strict interpretation of the rules would shatter the semblance of national unity which is the shibboleth on which state authority is based.

Lamennais (the unfrocked champion of papal power turned radical publicist in the 1830s), in his famous attack upon centralization, declared that it led to 'apoplexy at the centre and paralysis at the periphery'. Whilst French local authorities are subordinate parts of the administrative system of the country, the integrated prefectoral system has sought to avoid the dangers of both centralization and decentralization by deconcentrating state authority, i.e. shifting power from officials at the centre to officials at the periphery. Although ministerial directives flow from the centre, the field services of the ministries, under the aegis of the prefect, are relatively accessible. They are able to respond more quickly and enjoy a limited measure of discretion in meeting local circumstances by comparison with the functional type of field administration characteristic of Britain and the United States, where there are no prefects to personalize central authority.

The French system denies in practice that one can realistically distinguish between matters of local and countrywide concern. Particularly in an increasingly urbanized and industrialized society, interdependence is such that an integrated type of state authority is required. This conception of a comprehensive system of central administrative control based upon a hierarchical chain of command is paralleled by the integration of local and central politics. The same individuals occupy key offices at the communal level (as mayor), departmental level (as councilloror president of the departmental council), and national level (as deputies, senators and ministers), seeking to belong to the constellation of consultative institutions that encompass the decision-makers. Such a high degree of political and adminis-trative centralization was possible because it corresponded in administrative, electoral and community terms to a traditional rural partnership.

The two leaders who until 1981 dominated French local government, the centrally nominated prefect in the department and the locally elected mayor in the commune, exemplified respectively the enduring triumph of bureaucracy and demo-cracy. The authority of both prefect and mayor derived a dual legitimacy from central government consecration and local con-sent. This duality of role, involving a conflation of the Bonapar-tist and democratic ways of legitimizing sovereign power, was aimed at integrating the hierarchical imperatives of the central government and the demands of the local community. Although nominated by and absolutely dependent upon the central government, the prefect could only effectively run his depart-ment with the acquiescence of the local notables, the mayors of the communes and the departmental councillors. To win this support, he espoused their causes. He was converted into the conciliator and champion of local interests as the price for which the local leaders would curtail opposition to his authority. The prefect occupied a strategic point in the administrative system which enabled him to mediate and arbitrate between the rival claims of central government and local community.

The mayor now plays a similar role in the commune. If he is both deputy and mayor of a large town, he is usually regarded locally as the leader, with privileged access to the central government. He will be the person best capable of reconciling conflicting interests. Thus the multiplicity of government grants are not merely the instruments of central control but the result of local pressures, or as it has been described, 'the ex-change of subsidies for local votes'.[6] This has led to the pheno-menon of *saupoudrage* – the dispersion of public investment grants in egalitarian, unselective profusion, giving a little of everything to everyone – which is politically rational in the present system though economically irrational.

25

*Governing France*

A salient feature of the French type of local politics and administration has traditionally been the central claim to a monopoly of information and rationality. 'The French tend to take for granted the essential irresponsibility of local elected bodies and accordingly insist on administrative safeguards against it ...' 'If they were efficient they defied the government, if they were inefficient they endangered the safety of the state.'[7] Some 36,000 communes, whose units varied in population from under fifty to over a million people, with councils whose total membership amounted to some 460,000 people – nearly 1 per cent of the population and somewhat under 2 per cent of the electorate – were the basic areas of local administration and local pressure. The patent irrationality of such a system condemned the communes to the control and tutelage of the agents of the central government who alone could be entrusted with ascertaining and acting on the requirements of the general interest. In the words of an 1801 circular: 'General ideas should come from the centre.' At that time, the ministry of the interior was responsible for all matters other than foreign affairs, defence, finance and justice. Its prefects could act as the unquestioned embodiments of the central will. The only serious contender as the personification of central rationality was the treasurer and paymaster general (TPG) who represented the ministry of finance in each department. However, the refusal of the ministry of finance to deconcentrate decision-making and the tendency to retain a narrowly financial rather than an economic approach has prevented its field services emerging as the focus of local and regional administrative control. So, although the TPG shared in the financial supervision over the elected local authorities and collected all taxes, the prefect exercised both a political and a budgetary tutelage.

The logic of centralization, that private action must conform to a standardized state pattern, led to the proliferation of regulations to cover all acts of public life. As the type of economic rationality represented by a regionalized form of national economic planning became the official criterion for policy decisions and for allocating public funds, the old incremental improvization, the case-by-case approach was partly curtailed. The field services of the central ministries and the prefects, thanks to their control of technical and economic expertise and their

26

direct access to the decision-makers, took over the new functionof guiding local and regional economic development, conceived as part of the overall strategy determined in Paris. The myriad powers of detailed intervention, authorization, supervision and co-ordination which the prefect, in particular, possessed were mobilized for the task of reconciling the demagogic demands of the many communes under his jurisdiction, prior to negotiating on his department's behalf at the regional and national levels. However, frequently the prefect adopted the same strategy as the elected representatives of the towns and villages. He made large and irresponsible demands on behalf of his department, based on an addition of the separate claims of his constituents. These demands were backed by the threat that he would not be able to control the outbursts of discontent that would follow rejection. This left the central government free to choose between the claims made upon it and the prefect could blame Paris for the failure to meet the just requests of each and every local community. The interposition of a regional prefect between the departments and the state was aimed partly at making possible a genuine deconcentration of administration and partly at providing a regional impetus for modernization so that development rather than stability was stressed.

The acknowledged fiasco of the more ambitious aims of local government and regional reform in the 1960s and the retreat in the 1970s to a fatalist tinkering at the margin emerges from the major official study in 1976 of the problem. In its report, the commission for the development of local responsibilities (Guichard Commission) began by consideration of 'the question of the State', because the failure of the previous attempts at deconcentration and decentralization were largely due to a hazy conception of the state. As new social needs developed, it was argued, their satisfaction was 'spontaneously attributed' to the state administration. Conversely, the withdrawal of such 'collective functions' from the responsibility of the central administration was regarded as a sacrilegious 'dismemberment of the State'.[8] The Commission went on to argue that deconcentration was unsatisfactory, because it did not increase local autonomy, whether political or administrative, since no month passed without the central administration inventing new procedures for recovering from the field services the little autonomy they had acquired.[8]

The failures of the 1960s and early 1970s attempts at decon-centration were dramatically illustrated in a report by an in-spector general of administration, which demonstrated what the report on the development of local responsibilities called a 'game of hide and seek' between central ministries, between them and their field services and between state officials and the local authorities. The fragmented decision-making involved in the building of a secondary school, a relatively routine decision, strikingly illustrates the inadequacies of deconcentration in practice, with fourteen co-decision-makers taking part in a twenty-four-stage process. The twenty-two stages preceding the commencement of work on the school took two years, four times the actual time required to build the school. A less routine decision, such as building a university teaching hospital, in-volved some fifty decision-makers in a hundred-stage process, lasting about eight years![9]

The ineffectiveness of the techno-bureaucratic attempts at reform was a preliminary to the 1981 attempt at an alternative approach to dispersing power within an indivisible republic. The right, having tried to make a reality of the myth of the omnipotent and omnicompetent prefect had failed, in part because the prefects themselves did not believe in the moderniz-ing reformism they were supposed to implement; the left turned instead to the elected political leaders in commune, department and region as the driving force of decentralization. A 1970 Act of parliament had already laid down that municipal decisions would be approved by the prefect retrospectively and not in advance as in the past. At the fifty-second congress of the presidents of departmental councils in September 1981, Presi-dent Mitterrand declared that the projected decentralist re-forms would still retain an important role for the renamed prefects.

Far from being a scaled down version of our present prefects, the commissioners of the republic, free from responsibility for the day to day administration of the region and the department, no longer re-quired to undertake detailed supervision of the communes, will be able to devote themselves more successfully to seeing that laws are implemented, the state's affairs administered and the national inter-ests preserved. This is especially true because they will be in authority over all the field services of the ministries.[10]

However, though the commissioner of the republic will no longer be the executive officer of the department and the task of promoting its economic development will largely pass to the president of the departmental council (in conjunction with the mayors and the president of the regional council), this will only partly help him to perform his duties effectively.

The 1964 reforms had been specifically aimed at reconciling the traditional role of the prefect, as an agent of the ministry of the interior with the new role of deconcentrated administrative leadership. Under this dispensation, all decision-making dele-gated to ministry field services was to be concentrated in the prefecture. While the attempt to resurrect the Napoleonic model quickly failed, even the modest reforms of handing the managerial decision-making over to the prefect and confining the field services to the purely executive operations were not achieved. Instead, the prefecture was limited to a co-ordinating, 'general staff' function, symbolized by the centralization of all administrative mail. As a result, although the prefect was better informed, he usually preferred to avoid conflict at the price of giving in to the sectional bureaucratic interests. It remains to be seen whether the separation of the task of placating the local notables from that of administrative co-ordination will enable the post-1981 commissioner to provide effective administrative leadership. It will at least avoid the 'paradox in expecting the prefect, the peace-keeper and trouble-shooter, to become the promoter of dramatic change which might result in difficulties and conflicts'.[11] The latter task, in conformity with democratic principle, will be left to political leadership.

*The resurgent periphery*

(i) THE PREFECT: PREDECESSOR TO THE COMMISSIONER OF THE REPUBLIC: It is customary to trace the office of prefect to Richelieu's royal *intendants* through whom 'sovereign authority assumes the mundane guise of administrative work and royal absolutism becomes centralized administration'.[12] Whilst in England parliament was successfully asserting its right to con-trol the crown, in France a centralized administration was being established. The administrative élite is as much the salient feature of French government as the parliamentary élite has been of

British government. It was in the latter half of the seventeenth century, under Colbert, that the *intendants* became institutionalized as the administrative instrument of political modernization, the resistance to change being countered by greater centralization. During the reign of Louis xiv, the mercantilist policy of mobilizing the state's economic resources for the promotion of national power converted the *intendants* into the main agents of state economic policy, just as three centuries later de Gaulle's regional prefects were intended to spearhead the process of political and economic modernization in provincial France.

After an ephemeral revolutionary experiment in local democracy, Napoleon as first consul resurrected the Roman title of prefect to describe the 'mini-emperors' who were to rule the departments as his agents, mobilize the local resources for the central government's purposes, and ensure universal obedience to his will. The prefect was to be a heroic local leader, restoring consensus after successive revolutionary crises, imposing the changes dictated by his Paris masters, acting as an electoral agent for the parties in power, exercising a paternalistic despotism over the department allocated to him. Above all, he embodied the sovereign state's discretionary prerogative and public security powers for the preservation of law and order which were developed particularly in the 'police state' of the Second Napoleonic Empire. From the Third Republic onwards, the restraints of administrative law, the anti-authoritarian political environment, and the developing public service and welfare functions which required co-ordination rather than coercion, made the prefect less of an arbitrary hierarch and more of an urbane mediator between central and local government.

The prefect gradually became less an incarnation of central authority and more an architect of concerted action between all the prevailing social and political forces who were willing to 'play the game'. The approach was to present the general interest as not being something conceived at the centre and imposed unamended in the provinces. Rather, it was an agreed compromise, worked out with the interested parties under the guidance and leadership of the prefect. A real attempt was made to move away from chain-of-command legalism to the more informal and manipulative techniques of *animation* in a context of *participation*. The aim was to consult the field services of the ministries and the local notables on matters concerning them rather than try to command as an inaccessible and unresponsive hierarchical superior. The administrative environment is not regarded as a collection of passive subjects to be regulated, but a complex and potentially explosive constellation of 'social partners' who have to be softened up in advance and generally handled with circumspection. Their spokesmen may, as the occasion requires, be played off against each other, promised present or future benefits from public funds, flattered or browbeaten.

Compared to the more traditional, negative, regulatory functions of the prefect, the assertion of formal power is frequently neither appropriate nor feasible in the task of securing the positive collaboration on local development projects of official or unofficial 'partners'. Consequently, the prefect had to persuade, influence and manipulate through his contacts, rather than cajole, command or coerce those who have the capacity to obstruct him in his activities. In the process of conciliation and compromise, central rationality was often a casualty. It disintegrated when brought face to face with local realities. The prefect tried to reconcile his old role as the solitary, unbending, ostentatious embodiment of the sovereign state's pre-eminence with his new role as the receptive, supple, and surreptitious coordinator of public and private activities, to preserve local harmony, organize local economic development and promote the national purposes of the central government. The prefects grappled with the arduous problem of adapting their style of authority to the new norm of unheroic partnership. However, in times of crisis, the prefect was expected by the government to resume his traditional role as defender of 'state authority'.

In discharging both his functions of fostering and maintaining order and of stimulating and organizing development, the prefect needed the help of the local notables: not merely those elected to office in the departmental and municipal councils but also those elected to the chambers of commerce, of crafts and of agriculture, the leaders of business, farm organizations and trade unions. A vital aspect of being acknowledged as a representative figure was the access one was known to have to the prefect and his staff. The prefect could give the semi-official status of notable to those whom he nominated to the myriad consultative committees, the main formal channels by which the prefect communicated with his local environment. However, the prefect-made notable would be of no use as an intermediary if he did not enjoy the support of his constituents, so the choice available to the prefect was limited. He either selected the existing political, economic and social leaders as his collaborators, or, if they proved unsatisfactory partners because of their political opposition or divergent aims, discreetly sought to undermine their authority and secured their replacement by more pliable men. It is too early even to speculate realistically upon how the 1981 reform will affect the prefect–notable relationship, though it is not likely to change very much very quickly.

(ii) DEPARTMENTAL COUNCILS: To an even greater extent than is the case with the French second chamber, the Senate, the *conseils généraux* or departmental councils suffered prior to 1981 from a rural bias that not only made them unrepresentative; it also reduced their will and capacity to adapt to industrial society. It forced them into a client relationship with the prefect who, it was hoped, would secure for them the central government grants on which they were dependent to keep up appearances. About a third of French departments had reached such a state of anaemia that they were no longer capable of providing sufficiently dynamic local leadership to run their affairs. Although the Constitution of the Fourth Republic (Article 87) had stipulated that the president of the departmental council would be the head of the executive, just as mayors were in their communes, this was not implemented for thirty-five years and it was left to the Mauroy Government in 1981 to carry out expeditiously this piece of unfinished business. The legislation of Gaston Defferre, as minister of the interior and decentralization, notably the 1982 Act on the rights and freedoms of local authorities, sought to ensure that *de jure* political leadership would effectively replace the *de facto* bureaucratic leadership of the past. Article 18 of this Act provides that as well as being chairman of its proceedings, the president of the departmental council prepares and carries out its decisions. He is also responsible for levying taxes and controlling expenditure. Furthermore, he is elected for three years. Although each year he presents to the council a report on the state of the department and two months before the vote on the budget there is a guide-lines debate upon the priorities and provisions of the forth-coming budget, the president cannot be removed prior to the next departmental council elections.

The replacement of the nominated prefect by the elected president as the executive of the departmental council, and the elimination of the former's supervisory role over the latter – local decisions taking immediate effect, although they can be referred to the courts if considered illegal – has led to fears being expressed on the right of the political spectrum that there will be a danger of partisan tutelage being exercised over the com-munes. Whereas the prefect, it is argued, could be relied upon to act impartially, the mass of rural, often conservative com-munes will be dominated by the president of the departmental council who will frequently give preference to the wishes of the large, usually left-wing, towns. There could well be more pol-itical conflicts at the local level under the reformed arrange-ments; this may well be inevitable in a system that is based upon shared responsibilities, once one removes the emollient, conflict-reducing and consensus-creating prefect from a pivotal position in local decision-making. Paradoxically, the fact that by the end of 1982, following in the wake of their lost executive powers, some seventy-five members of the prefectoral corps had chosen to work for local authorities (mainly those controlled by the right), may ease centre–local tensions.

The departmental councillors are identified with the dawn of the Third Republic, the petrified structure having been estab-lished in 1871. The councillors formed a functional part of that largely pre-industrial society but like the Senate they have survived as an immobilist obstacle in a modernizing society. Their unchanging nature was reflected in repeated re-election, though less often on the first ballot, although the low poll by French standards (43 per cent abstentions in 1961, 1964 and 1967, 38 per cent in 1970, 46 per cent in 1973 and 35 per cent in 1976 and 1979) indicated that it was indifference rather than contentment that accounted for continuity. Having successfully excluded the forces of change, the departmental councils lay stranded, allowed to perform their ritual functions but deprived of real power. Until the 1981 reform, priority was given to the avoidance of conflict within the department and between it and the government, the parochial commitment to 'keeping politics out' playing into the hands of the prefect, who preferred to operate in a noncontroversial situation where administration rather than politics was on the agenda. Although subsequent legislation is to set out the new functions of the departmental council and its financial arrangements, there will be an important transfer of functions from central government to elected local council in 1983–5, decentralization replacing deconcentration to the field services of the Paris ministries. There will still need to be collaboration between the commissioner of the republic and the president of the departmental council, who will share the opulent accommodation of the erstwhile *préfecture*, now significantly renamed *hôtel du département*. In the departmental councils, they have been authorized to intervene 'to protect the economic and social interest of the inhabitants of the department' but not to invest in commercial firms. The temptation to help local lame ducks would often be irresistible at a time of severe recession, resulting in the accumulation of bad debts.

Considering how powerless these councils were, there was still a substantial measure of competition for election to membership even before the 1981 reform. In the March 1970 elections – half the cantons hold elections every three years – there were some 6,000 candidates contesting the 1,769 seats. They included 168 deputies, 75 senators and 14 ministers, as well as a dozen ex-ministers and over a hundred ex-members of parliament. There was a steady decline in the number of deputies who stood for election to departmental councils in the 1970s. They numbered 154 in 1970, 148 in 1976 and 129 in 1979. This decline is not evident among senators where the number of candidates were eighty-six in 1973, seventy-nine in 1976 and eighty in 1979. However, if we consider those elected, the number of parliamentarians has steadily increased, underlining the political advantages of combining representative office at the centre and in the locality.[13] After the 1979 departmental council elections, the number of ministers who served on councils numbered eighteen, and five of them were presidents of their departmental council. Of the hundred presidents, twenty-four were deputies and thirty-two were senators and in 1979 the right provided the president in fifty-two out of the ninety-five metropolitan departments.

Table 1 shows the growth in the Socialist vote and representation in the latter half of the 1970s at the expense of the right, especially those candidates that did not belong to a political party. Despite the fall between 1973-79 of the number of non-party candidates from 26 per cent to 21 per cent and of non-party councillors from 33 per cent to 19 per cent,[14] the traditional apolitical style was fighting a stubborn rearguard battle, especially in the over-represented rural areas. Table 1 also shows the swing to the right in 1982, which yielded the largest gains to the RPR, while on the left the main losses were sustained by the Communists and Left Radicals. The right increased the number of presidencies in metropolitan France to fifty-nine, the left being reduced to thirty-six. Consequently, the initial political beneficiaries of decentralization were not principally the Socialists who had introduced it. They had paradoxically chosen to stress national rather than local issues and the exceptionally high turn-out (70 per cent) hurt rather than helped the left.

(iii) THE RURAL MAYOR: In 1884, Waldeck-Rousseau, minister of the interior in the Ferry Government, persuaded parliament to pass two Acts that laid the foundations for the articulation of grass-roots grievances: the Act legalizing trade unions and the Act democratizing commune government (with the notable exclusion of Paris). Approximately 36,000 communes form the basic units of French local government. Each is headed by an elected mayor who personifies authority as much in his town or village as did the prefect in the department or the president of the republic in the state as a whole. At their level, they each exercise a paternalistic style of authority, purporting to embody community consensus and eschewing overt politics in favour of an uncontroversial application in particular situations of the 'general interest'. There is some uncertainty as to whether this apolitical pursuit of consensus, coupled with the legal subordination of the communes to the central government, means that the mayor and his municipal council are powerless. The large number of micro-communes, the overwhelming and increasing majority of which are too feeble in terms of population and finance to be viable as autonomous local authorities

*Table 1*
Votes for and seats on departmental councils, 1973–1982

| Party | Votes (%) | | | | No. of votes 1982 (000s) | Seats (%) | | | | No. of seats 1982 | Gains/Losses 1982/79 |
|---|---|---|---|---|---|---|---|---|---|---|---|
| | 1973 | 1976 | 1979 | 1982 | | 1973 | 1976 | 1979 | 1982 | | |
| Extreme Left | 1·0 | 0·8 | 0·8 | 0·6 | 73 | 0·5 | 0·2 | 0·3 | 0·3 | 5 | +1 |
| Communist | 22·7 | 22·8 | 22·5 | 15·9 | 2,000 | 10·6 | 13·4 | 12·3 | 9·9 | 198 | −44 |
| Socialist | 21·9 | 26·5 | 27·0 | 29·7 | 3,737 | 22·0 | 28·5 | 30·2 | 25·4 | 509 | −5 |
| Left Radical | 1·9 | 2·4 | 1·9 | 1·7 | 217 | 3·5 | 4·7 | 3·7 | 3·0 | 61 | −27 |
| Other Left | 6·4 | 3·9 | 3·2 | 1·7 | 214 | 9·0 | 5·2 | 4·2 | 2·6 | 54 | −24 |
| Ecologists | — | — | 0·5 | 0·4 | 56 | — | — | 0·1 | 0 | 0 | 0 |
| Independent Right | 14·3 | 11·8 | 10·0 | 13·1 | 1,646 | 16·8 | 14·9 | 14·9 | 18·9 | 380 | +51 |
| UDF | 19·0 | 20·4 | 21·1 | 18·6 | 2,344 | 24·9 | 23·4 | 23·3 | 23·4 | 470 | +69 |
| RPR | 12·7 | 10·6 | 12·3 | 18·0 | 2,262 | 12·7 | 9·5 | 10·7 | 16·7 | 336 | +146 |
| Extreme Right | — | 0·7 | 0·7 | 0·2 | 25 | — | 0·2 | 0·2 | 0·0 | 1 | 0 |

These ministry of interior figures should be treated with caution because of the problem of classification involved. 'Local action' and 'non-party' councillors have been allocated a particular orientation, a rather subjective exercise into which bias enters. The accuracy of these figures is always challenged by the various party organizations, as are the commune election figures.
Source: adapted from Albert Mabileau, 'Les Elections cantonales', *Annuaire de l'Administration locale*, 1980, p. 283, with additional figures for 1982.

(see Table 2), lack the competent full-time staff that would enable them to hold their own *vis-à-vis* the president of the departmental council. Although in 1980 there were over half a million (554,000) local government officials in the communes, compared with 101,000 in the departments, the basic public and private services have been deserting many communes. Thus, between 1970–80 one post office in five and one primary school in ten had been closed. By 1980 there was a state primary school in only 79 per cent and a café in only 76 per cent of communes. Three communes in five no longer have a baker's shop and two-thirds have no butcher's shop. However, medical services have improved, with doctors in one-quarter of the communes in 1980 and not merely one-sixth as was the case in 1970. Ageing populations require more medical care and the attractions of the medical profession have ensured a plentiful supply to meet this increased demand.

*Table 2*
*The number of communes according to size and population in 1975*

| Population size | Number of communes | Population (000s) | Number of councillors |
|---|---|---|---|
| Less than 100 | 4,002 | 263 | 9 |
| 101–500 | 18,729 | 4,750 | 11 |
| 501–1,500 | 8,862 | 7,341 | 13 |
| 1,501–2,500 | 1,892 | 3,614 | 17 |
| 2,501–3,500 | 821 | 2,419 | 21 |
| 3,501–10,000 | 1,321 | 7,434 | 23 |
| 10,001–30,000 | 538 | 9,047 | 27 |
| 30,001–40,000 | 120 | 4,571 | 31 |
| 40,001–50,000 | | | 33 |
| 50,001–60,000 | 109 | 14,258 | 35 |
| 60,001 or more | | | 37* |
| Total | 36,394 | 53,697 | |

*The three exceptions were: Paris, with 163 councillors; Marseille, with 101 councillors and Lyon, with 73 councillors. The number of councillors was increased in all communes with more than 500 inhabitants, especially those exceeding 30,000 in 1983.
Source: adapted from *Vivre Ensemble*, report of the Guichard Commission, 1976, Vol. II, p. 130.

Prior to 1981, rural mayors accepted the political and financial tutelage of the prefect, his 'right to review the *wisdom* and the *desirability*' of decisions[15] as a routine matter and became accustomed to consulting the field services of the ministries and the sub-prefect before coming to a decision. Thus the prefect's actual influence greatly exceeded his formal power of intervention. These formal powers were, of course, important and included the ability to suspend or dismiss a mayor; the power to dissolve the municipal council; the power to act in default; the power to check the legality of all decisions and annul them; and the right to exercise stringent control over the commune's budget, which included the right to strike out any source of revenue he deemed inexpedient or against the public interest. Such powers were used sparingly, being more effective in conditioning the local councils to accept the prefect's guidance in the knowledge that he could have recourse to coercion if necessary. He would not wish to provoke an irate municipality into collective resignation or into an embarrassing 'administrative strike', but he might dissolve the council if he believed the subsequent election would yield a more tractable majority.

The mayor, like the pre-1981 prefect, is both the agent of the central government and the representative of the local community, although he generally plays down the former role and often thinks of himself as in opposition to the state rather than as its servant. Nevertheless, in practice, thanks to the mayor's functional amalgam of politics and administration, the majority of rural mayors accept their subordination to the central government officials, particularly the sub-prefect (renamed assistant commissioner), the tax collector and the public works engineer. The commune's budget was generally drawn up in conjunction with the sub-prefect and the local tax collector, so that even in the case of this key function, government officials were able decisively to influence the taxing and spending policies of the commune at the preparatory stage. Thereby, potential sources of conflict were ironed out before the prestige of either side was risked by an open dispute. The fact that over half the staff of the communes are part-time and that the rural communes in particular lack competent personnel, compels dependence upon the central specialists who are located in their area. The countrywide network of public works engineers is particularly important. They have the dual function of advising on and carrying out, for a fee, local authority road and building projects and supervising the local authorities' public works programmes. Outside the larger towns, this places them in a monopolistic position from the technical standpoint. It also provides a powerful weapon of central control to ensure standardized service.[16] It is precisely this nexus that the reform of local government seeks to break to ensure greater autonomy for the local authorities, though in the rural areas the mayors may exchange administrative tutelage for that of the staff of the departmental council.

Under the guidance of officialdom, control is exercised by the mayor rather than the municipal council, which consists mainly of leisured notables who regard their election as a recognition of social status and economic success. The mayor runs municipal affairs in a personal manner, unlike his British counterpart. Whereas British local politics are essentially committee politics, in France 'there is no history of independent *ad hoc* authorities, with legal status and statutory powers' providing particular local services.[17] When these specific functions were absorbed into the general local authority system in nineteenth-century Britain, they gave rise to a collective, committee-based leadership, whereas in France it was the cult of personality in the shape of the mayor, the embodiment of the commune's would-be one and indivisible consensus, that became established: 'If the council is unanimously and actively satisfied with mayoral decisions, this signifies that the commune is ideally united. The municipal council's function is thus primarily symbolic. A mayor does not expect or desire the council to function as a legislative body; rather, he wants the municipal council to ratify decisions that he has already reached',[18] thereby placing him in a strong bargaining position *vis-à-vis* the other agents of the central government with whom he will have to negotiate. He can use the commune's united support to secure the satisfaction of demands made on the government, just as he uses such success in conflicts with central authority to reinforce community cohesion under his leadership. The electoral influence of the mayor also conditions local bargaining.

The close collaboration between the mayor and the prefect (renamed commissioner of the republic), reflected at the national level by the links between the thirty-thousand-strong *Association des Maires de France* and the ministry of the interior, facilitated by the many active mayors in both chambers of parliament, tends to reinforce stability at the price of inhibiting change. The strong tendency for national office-holders to combine this function with local office is popular (see Table 3), although it is regarded with less favour in the case of ministers than of deputies, especially in rural communes.* The traditional elected and nominated oligarchs in the departments and communes naturally seek to preserve the system upon which their influence is based. Until the advent of President Mitterrand, they successfully resisted attempts to reform the local taxation system and the structure of local government, notably by the government forcing an amalgamation of communes and threatening the existence of the department with the creation of a fully fledged region. Whilst within his circumscribed commune the mayor's capacity to innovate is greater than that of any elected person other than the president of the republic, he

Table 3
*The desirability of combining the office of mayor
with other local or national offices* (%)

|  | Desirable | Undesirable | No importance | Don't know |
|---|---|---|---|---|
| Departmental councillor | 61 | 15 | 13 | 11 |
| Deputy | 54 | 24 | 11 | 11 |
| Minister | 48 | 30 | 11 | 11 |

Source: SOFRES, February 1971.

seldom does innovate because he places the harmony of the community above all other purposes and fears that change will be disruptive. His leadership is therefore passive in character, except in the larger towns where developments beyond his control compel him to sponsor innovation.

(iv) URBAN POLITICS: It is important to contrast urban and rural politics because 'the traditional battle between the town and countryside ... is in many ways the fundamental division in all French politics'.[19] Each Republic has witnessed conflicts between a revolutionary, minority urban France and a mainly reactionary rural France, repeatedly summoned to restrain and

*On the interrelationship between local and national elected office, see below, chapter 3, p. 84.

repress a restless Paris commune, although the *embourgeoisement* of Paris was such that President Giscard allowed the capital its first elected mayor since 1870. Ironically, it was his leading right-wing rival, Chirac, who was elected in 1977.

Outside Paris, the demographic and industrial transformation of France since the Second World War has involved a decisive shift of population away from the generally apolitical, passive consensus of the declining rural communes to the frequently assertive, controversial politics of the urban metropolis which has accepted the disruptive challenge of modernity. Even before the liberating legislation of the early 1980s, it was not the eight officially designated counter-magnets to Paris: Lille: Metz-Nancy, Strasbourg, Lyon-St Etienne, Marseille, Toulouse, Bordeaux and Nantes-St Nazaire, which provided the best examples of urban municipal dynamism. Two medium-sized towns, Grenoble in the south-east (whose population increased by 27 per cent between 1962-8), led by Hubert Dubedout, an 'outsider' engineer turned pragmatic Socialist mayor, and Rennes in the north-west, controlled until the 1977 Socialist take-over by the right-centre, were the most striking demonstrations of what municipal leadership could achieve when freed of the toils of rural consensus politics or central red tape. They demonstrated what would be possible in a restructured local government system in which the anti-urban, anti-industrial, rural and artisan France of the 36,000 communes was finally replaced by a modern system of some two thousand new communes which have the potential for autonomous local management and development. However, so drastic a surgical operation, envisaged by techno-bureaucrats as part of a radical reconstruction of French local and regional government in which the number of regions would also be reduced from twenty-two to twelve,[20] is too 'modernist' either for the left or the right, although successive Fifth Republic governments have sought to promote some form of amalgamation between communes. Nearly half the French communes are involved in some type of joint board, notably nearly 2,000 *syndicats à vocation multiple* and 154 urban *districts*, which are piecemeal and timid attempts to grapple with the problem of reducing the number of communes.[21] Four conurbations out of the eight counter-magnets – Bordeaux, Lille, Lyon and Strasbourg – were selected in 1966 for the imposition of compulsory co-operation on adjacent communes, ranging from twenty-seven in the case of Bordeaux to eighty-seven in the case of Lille. This involved the transfer of the major financial, secondary education, transport, town planning and public works decisions to an 'urban community' council, indirectly representative of the inhabitants.

Under the Mitterrand presidency, the drive towards decentralization has led to a rival tendency to that of the earlier policy of integrating communes in the large towns. Paris was first singled out for the application of this policy, the twenty *arrondissements* being authorized to elect their own decision-making councils. (Chirac, as mayor of Paris, had already instituted non-elected, consultative bodies in the *arrondissements*.) However, under criticism for what was widely regarded as in part a political manoeuvre directed against Chirac, both mayor of Paris and *de facto* leader of the Opposition, it was decided to extend the policy of municipal decentralization to the second and third largest cities: Marseille (of which Minister of Interior Defferre was mayor) and Lyon. This controversial reform was accompanied – alongside the initial requirement that 25 per cent of candidates on lists in communes with more than 3,500 inhabitants had to be women, which was ruled unconstitutional – by a drastic change in the local electoral system in advance of the 1983 local elections. As in the case of the Paris reform, the Socialists were committed to a switch to proportional elections in the communes. This enabled minority parties to secure representation in communes with a population exceeding 30,000 whereas previously a 'winning list takes all' system prevailed. However, to ensure that there would be a majority list, providing a firm basis for mayoral authority, the system that operated in 1983 laid down that the winning list would secure half the seats plus its proportionate share of the remaining half of the seats. The other lists that secured at least 5 per cent of the vote would receive their proportionate share of half the seats. This ingenious compromise between the simple majority and proportional electoral system was applied not merely in communes with populations of more than 30,000 but in those with more than 3,500, in the hope that the left would be able to make inroads into the smaller town councils. However, the 1983 swing to the right meant that, as in the case of the 1982 departmental elections, it was the right-wing parties that were the initial beneficiaries of the decentralist policies of the early 1980s.

In the towns, as well as in the villages, power tends to be concentrated in the hands of the mayor, especially when he is both the town's deputy and mayor, like Chaban-Delmas of Bordeaux and Gaston Defferre of Marseille for decades under the Fourth and Fifth Republics. The former remained mayor when prime minister (1969–72), and the latter when minister of the interior in the government headed by Pierre Mauroy, mayor of Lille, in 1981. Despite the 1983 electoral swing to the right – which won back half of the sixty towns with a population of over 30,000 that it lost to the left in 1977 – both Defferre and Mauroy retained control of Marseille and Lille. However, Chirac achieved a clean sweep in Paris, which put paid to the attempt to allow Socialist countervailing power to emerge in some of the *arrondissement* councils. In addition, the Socialists lost bastions like Roubaix and Grenoble, while the Communist losses confirmed their continuing decline in support. So, because of the right's gains, due to national considerations, the municipal elections of 1983 meant that fewer left-wing councils could benefit from increased autonomy.

As in the rural communes, the urban mayors have an ambivalent attitude towards their relationship with the central government. On the one hand, they claim that they are at the mercy of the ministries of finance and of regional planning, the *Caisse des Dépôts et Consignations* (the major public source of loan funds for local authorities), as well as the prefect, who until 1981 could determine whether their programme would be carried out, particularly through control over grants.[22] As local authorities spend 30 per cent of civil public expenditure and while 95 per cent of the state budget is current expenditure and a quarter of local authority expenditure is for investment, it is obvious that the centre is concerned to control local expenditure closely. However, the local sense of impotence seems to vanish in practice, because it is recognized that there is scope for substantial variations in performance, depending notably upon the mayor's ingenuity. At the price of assuming a substantial debt burden, a town like Rennes can achieve nationwide renown for its achievements. Furthermore, the political complexion of the municipality influences the housing, education and tax policies pursued. This is particularly evident if one contrasts the behaviour of the 'united left' municipalities that came to local power in 1977 with that of their predecessors. Particularly though by no means only where the Communist Party has provided municipal leadership, there has been an activist rather than an acquiescent style of decision-making, in which commitment to partisan-inspired policy change e.g. provision of public housing, takes priority over reliance upon access to well-disposed central officials.[23]

The decentralization of power to the communes was a natural policy for a Socialist government to adopt, as it was the would-be innovative left-wing municipalities that had been most inhibited under the pre-1981 system. In his presidential programme as candidate in 1965, Mitterrand stressed that the communes should have greater freedom from state control and, in his last major speech before the second ballot in the 1974 presidential election, he called for a 'change in the relations between the all-powerful state and its oversized administration and citizens, local authorities and grassroots communities'.[24] Elected at the third attempt, Mitterrand was able to implement this proposal in 1981.

*The region as a focus of deconcentration and decentralization*

The rationalization of authority was, for centuries, equated with the centralization of power in France. It has since been equated with political modernization, in conjunction with a hierarchical, disciplined and functionally differentiated power structure and mass participation mediated through groups. It is argued that in divided societies, particularly those in which change is being resisted, centralization is the rational response.[25] This undoubtedly helps explain the passionate anti-federalism of the Jacobins and the subsequent resistance to any 'dismemberment' of central control by most politicians and officials. Yet in contemporary France, which has undoubtedly been traversing a period of rapid change that has provoked bitter resistance, there has been a widespread reaction against centralization as the privileged instrument of political modernization. This movement in favour of administrative deconcentration and political decentralization long preceded the May 1968 challenge to authority. No less an embodiment of the authoritarian tradition than de Gaulle espoused it in a speech on 24 March 1968, two months before his first failure to grapple with the challenge and thirteen months before his second and self-destructive failure at the referendum of April 1969. He then said: 'The centuries-old centralizing effort required to achieve and sustain [France's] unity, is no longer necessary. On the contrary, it is its regional development that will provide the motive force of its future economic power.'

Regionalist initiatives came as a result of grass-roots pressure notably from regions such as Brittany, which were suffering the consequences of rural depopulation in an extreme form. Together with the Planning Commissariat's recognition of the need to give the National Plan a regional dimension, they led to the June 1955 decrees designating what were to become the

*Table 4*
*The regions in 1975*

| Regions | Population | Départements | Communes |
|---|---|---|---|
| Alsace | 1,517,330 | 2 | 897 |
| Aquitaine | 2,550,340 | 5 | 2,276 |
| Auvergne | 1,330,479 | 4 | 1,309 |
| Bourgogne | 1,570,943 | 4 | 2,027 |
| Bretagne | 2,595,431 | 4 | 1,266 |
| Centre | 2,152,500 | 6 | 1,840 |
| Champagne-Ardennes | 1,336,832 | 4 | 1,905 |
| Corse | 289,842 | 2 | 360 |
| Franche-Comté | 1,060,317 | 4 | 1,773 |
| Languedoc-Roussillon | 1,789,474 | 5 | 1,539 |
| Limousin | 738,726 | 3 | 747 |
| Lorraine | 2,330,821 | 4 | 2,301 |
| Midi-Pyrénées | 2,268,245 | 8 | 3,018 |
| Nord-Pas-de-Calais | 3,913,773 | 2 | 1,552 |
| Basse-Normandie | 1,306,152 | 3 | 1,800 |
| Haute-Normandie | 1,595,695 | 2 | 1,417 |
| Pays de la Loire | 2,767,163 | 5 | 1,501 |
| Picardie | 1,678,644 | 3 | 2,294 |
| Poitou-Charentes | 1,528,118 | 4 | 1,453 |
| Provence-Alpes-Côte d'Azur | 3,675,730 | 6 | 960 |
| Rhône-Alpes | 4,780,723 | 8 | 2,881 |
| Paris Region | 9,878,524 | 7 (+ Paris) | 1,278(*) |
| (*) Including Paris | 52,655,802 | 96 | 36,394 |

Source: adapted from *Vivre Ensemble*, report of the Guichard Commission, 1976, Vol. II, p. 150.

twenty-one (later twenty-two) planning regions and to pioneering attempts at regional planning (see Table 4). These developments were bitterly opposed by authoritarians like Michel Debré, who in 1947 had favoured reducing the number of departments to forty-seven rather than creating regional institutions. In 1956 he argued that in France centralization was indispensable because 'the permanent tendency to weaken power, due to political and social conflicts, makes the administration the discreet but tenacious guarantor of unity, particularly through uniformity'.[26] At that stage even the regionalist champions like J.-F. Gravier, whose *Paris et le désert français* of 1947 had stimulated the reaction against centralism, did not wish to go beyond 'regional deconcentration' by 'adapting to our time a great French tradition: that of the *intendants*'.[27] The remedy was to be found in a transformation of French administration to enable it to cope with the demands being made upon government by the regional economic expansion committees and other pressure groups. Edgard Pisani, a prefect who became a senator and then a minister under the Fifth Republic, in an influential article (in the same issue of the journal that published the articles by Debré and Gravier) called for the creation, 'parallel to traditional administration ... of a specialized, dynamic and creative administration' capable of undertaking the new planning tasks. After condemning the tradition of administrative centralization, he went on to champion the need for an enterprising *administration de mission* which would take the initiative. It would not seek to be neutral. It would be ready to act in a selective way, carrying out the government's strategy without constantly 'turning to Paris to obtain authorization, funds or a guilty acquiescence'.[28]

The emergence in the 1950s of regional pressure groups in the form of regional economic expansion committees deriving their support from both local authorities and local agricultural, industrial and even trade union organizations, forced the central government to react. Its prime concern was to combine the restoration of central authority with an attempt to canalize and neutralize these new regional movements. It sought to do this by standardizing and reinforcing an administrative regionalism placed under the aegis of the regional prefect. As a leading beneficiary of this new development, the regional prefect of

Aquitaine, wrote at the inception of the regional reform in March 1964:

When one is deeply conscious of the need to preserve French unity, any provincial creation must be prudent ... Can one imagine regional commissions, having deliberative power, rejecting the National Plan in five or ten French regions and thereby preventing its application? This would mean accepting a federal type of government. It is essential, in our republic which is still one and indivisible, that the government, the expression of the will of parliament, has the power to guarantee the primacy of the national over the regional. It is its function to distinguish, within the framework of the law, what serves the general interest from what can threaten it.[29]

(As we shall see in chapter 6, the reform of economic planning and of the regions by the Socialists, without going as far as federalism, may well raise such problems.) Meanwhile, the task of recentralizing regionalism was entrusted to just such exponents of traditional administrative orthodoxy. They subscribed to the centralist conception that 'the only conceivable form of local or regional government would be a *delegation from the executive* – some members of the executive being selected as local administrators, and applying to a geographical fraction of the subjects the decisions of the general will ... it is a mere *sub-delegation* of power ...'[30]

The recognition of the need to deconcentrate sluggish, centralized decision-making, coupled with the decline of the department as the appropriate unit for such reorganized administration, led to the development of regional institutions. These had the further advantage of superimposing a more flexible instrument of public action on the existing institutions rather than trying to change them. Just as a major force for innovation at the centre was provided by the Planning Commissariat, which provoked or manipulated the ministries into a measure of modernization, in regional matters an equally small, but high powered and more overtly politicized 'parallel administration', the *Délégation à l'Aménagement du Territoire et à l'Action Régionale* (DATAR) or Regional and Spatial Planning Delegacy,* was the architect of reform from its creation in 1963. DATAR's success depended heavily upon its direct link with the prime

---

*See below, pp. 190–1.

minister (until a minister delegate for planning and regional development was interposed in 1967 and then abolished in 1972, when DATAR was for a while attached to the ministry of public works and housing under Olivier Guichard) and also by the close political ties between its first head, Guichard, and President Pompidou. In conjunction with the ministry of administrative reform, DATAR played a leading part in the preparation of the March 1964 decrees that reasserted executive supremacy in the shape of the regional prefect. However, it was felt necessary to proclaim in the general instruction on the application of these decrees that the department remained 'the normal unit of administrative management and would even extend this function through an increase in deconcentration, regional reform being confined to a strictly limited and particular sphere and not diminishing the role and vocation of the department'. The prefects were informed of their duties as follows: 'To impart a stricter unity and greater cohesion to administrative action, all the powers of the state in the department are concentrated in your hands. You will thus be able fully to exercise your vital role of stimulation, general direction and co-ordination of public services in the department.'

The regional prefect, who combined this function with being prefect of the department that contained the regional capital, was given the task of co-ordinating and directing the work of the departmental prefects in the field of regional development planning. This involved the preparation of the regional segment of the National Plan, working through the regional administrative conference. The other prefects and the treasurer-paymaster general were represented on this body, the heads of the various ministerial field services attending when matters directly concerning them were discussed. The regional prefect was helped in this task by a small general staff of senior civil servants (called in Pisani fashion a *mission*) under a sub-prefect who was the regional prefect's main economic adviser and executant. Their task, within the framework of the central government's directives, was to work out and seek to impose a regional rationality upon what could and did all too easily degenerate into an allocation of public investment funds between departments on an unselective and piecemeal basis.

Finally, to curb the threat represented by regional pressure groups and the opposition parties, Guichard ensured administrative supremacy by refusing to set up either an elected regional council or an elected regional executive to counterbalance the power of the regional prefect. Instead, regional economic development commissions (REDC) were created, composed of mayors and departmental councillors (25 per cent), interest group representatives (50 per cent), and prefectoral nominees (25 per cent), exercising only feeble consultative functions. Of the initial 924 REDC members, 72 were deputies, 53 senators, 202 departmental councillors and 286 mayors (bearing in mind, however, the overlap between these categories). Leading political figures, such as Jacques Chaban-Delmas in Aquitaine, Antoine Pinay in Rhône-Alpes, René Pleven in Brittany, François Mitterrand in Burgundy, Edgar Faure in Franche-Comté, Maurice Faure in Midi-Pyrénées and Pierre Pflimlin in Alsace, were elected REDC presidents. They became impatient when they discovered how little influence they could exert. The result was rapid and widespread disenchantment with what had purported to be a major step in reorganizing central–local relations but which in practice consolidated the position of the department and its traditional head, the prefect.[31]

It required a major upheaval to transform a situation in which the minister of the interior, addressing the members of the prefectoral corps in June 1964, could reassure them: 'The only possible hierarchy in our provinces is the prefectoral hierarchy and at its foundation, in the department, the prefect still remains in charge, the only person responsible.' The 1969 referendum proposal to elevate the region to a constitutionally recognized part of the governmental system was conceived by de Gaulle as an answer to the May crisis of 1968. It was profoundly ironic that in 1969 the French government should simultaneously prepare to celebrate the bicentenary of Napoleon's birth and to dismantle part of the centralized administrative system identified with him. However, this apparent contradiction quickly dissolved as it became clear that behind the rush of propagandist rhetoric about promoting 'popular participation', 'direct democracy', decentralization and autonomy, the prefects were not only to remain in charge; they were to be buttressed with powers deconcentrated from a megalocephalic administrative system that had proved in the crisis to have attained the pathological

condition of paralysis at the centre and apoplexy at the periphery. The real aim of Gaullist neo-regionalism was to constitute a deconcentrated administrative system under the regional
prefect that would be more capable of recognizing, resisting and
reducing revolutionary discontents. Like Louis-Napoleon a century earlier, in his 1869 attempt to 'liberalize' an autocratic
system, what purported to be decentralization was in fact a
disguised reinforcement of central control. In the prophetic
words of Odilon Barrot: 'It is the same hammer that strikes but
the handle has been shortened.'

Under the proposals that were defeated at the April 1969
referendum the functions of the new regional authorities were
to be restricted to prevent them, in the words of the minister
mainly responsible, 'venturing along the dangerous path of
federalism'. The local authority lobbies were assured that the
powers acquired by the region would be exclusively at the
expense of the central administration, being primarily an extension of their existing regional planning role through a more
resolute 'transfer of technocrats' than had hitherto been undertaken. This deconcentrationist view of regional reform was
reflected in the financial arrangements which retained the traditional features of a reliance upon specific central grants, central
approval of borrowing and a budget drawn up by the regional
prefect, making it unlikely that regional councillors would
abandon their 'public assistance' complex of dependence upon
the central government and its nominees. The rejection of a
directly elected regional council in favour of a tripartite composition of *ex-officio* deputies, representatives of local authorities
and of the major organized interests, was also calculated to
ensure that the representative element in regional politics remained under the tutelage of the administrative component.

The culmination of this administrative and centralist emphasis was the selection of the regional prefect as the undisputed
executive authority. The most curt dismissal of the idea of an
elected regional executive came in parliament from the ex-civil
servant prime minister, Couve de Murville: 'The French nation
was, through the centuries, shaped by the central government',
monarchical and republican, culminating in the proclamation
by the 1793 constitution ... of the one and indivisible republic. Napoleonic administration, still ours today, gave permanent practical

application to this assertion of principle. None of this, which constitutes French political reality, has been to my knowledge challenged by anyone. The best proof is that few deny that in the new regional bodies, executive power can only be conferred on a prefect chosen by the central government because he alone is able to ensure not only effectiveness in action but also conformity with the general interest as against the private interest.[32]

That the spirit of Couve de Murville's claim was accepted by the bulk of French political and economic *notables* was made clear by the fact that in the preliminary consultation on regional reform, 80 per cent of them replied in favour of the regional prefect exercising the executive power, whilst only 11 per cent favoured entrusting it to the president of the regional council. The traditionally diffident and dependent clientele of the prefect continued to regard him as the manifestation of the 'one and indivisible' sovereign central authority which, in the French political culture, was considered alone capable of maintaining order, resolving disputes and taking decisions.

Under the retrograde regional reform adopted by parliament in 1972, the regions were not given the status of 'territorial authorities' like the communes and departments. They were mere 'public establishments' with specific functions primarily concerned with national planning. The twenty-two regional councils were composed of all the deputies and senators of the region and an equal number of local authority representatives chosen by the departmental council and by the commune councils. (The *ex-officio* inclusion of national politicians in the regional councils was in flagrant contradiction with the professed desire to avoid politics, but it was a natural consequence of the close interrelationship of national and local politics in France and the UDR's desire to overcome its weakness outside parliament.) The regions' modest financial resources – not to exceed £2 per inhabitant – principally came from the driving licence revenue. Regional economic, social and cultural committees replaced the REDCS. The regional prefect remained in managerial command.[33]

Appropriately enough, the major reform of 1982 toppled the regional prefect from his pivotal role as head of the regional executive. As in the case of the reform in the departments, the president of the regional council replaces the regional prefect as the executive head, the regional commissioner of the republic being confined to a role of administrative co-ordination, although he is responsible to all ministers, especially the prime minister, rather than the minister of the interior as hitherto. In particular, although the 1982 reform did not set out the functions and financial arrangements of the new regional councils (to be dealt with in subsequent legislation), they inherited the regional prefect's powers of allocating regional development aid; they could become shareholders in the regional development bank in their area or in urban development joint public-private enterprises. They were allowed to play a much more active role in the industrial rescue of local firms and in making tax concessions to attract new firms or encourage existing firms to expand. The regional councils will play a far more active part in the national planning process (as we shall see in chapter 6) and genuine regional plans will be prepared rather than the regions having to accept a regionalization of the National Plan. The councils will be protected from surreptitious central tutelage, previously exercised through regulations communicated by each ministry through circulars and instructions to its field services, the worst and most dangerous offender being the finance ministry's treasurer (TPG). However, they will be subject to *ex post facto* budgetary control by regional chambers of accounts, cases being brought by the regional commissioner of the republic, to ensure that the councils do not engage in *ultra vires* expenditure with impunity.

The first election to the regional councils take place in 1984. Following the 1981 general election, the left secured control of a majority of the mainland regional councils, thanks to sweeping gains made by the Socialist Party in the National Assembly. Whereas prior to 1981 thirteen regions had a right-wing president, eight a Socialist president and one was headed by a Communist, after 1981 the Socialists controlled thirteen councils, the rest of the twenty-two remaining in right-wing hands. The composition of the consultative economic and social committees (ESCS) has been changed, giving trade unions equal representation with employers (at least 35 per cent each) while other representative bodies have up to 25 per cent of seats and only 5 per cent are government nominees. ESCS can range in size from forty to one hundred and ten members, who serve a six-year term. These committees, representative mainly of socio-occupational groups, had been previously weighted in such a way as to act as a pro-right-wing countervailing influence to left-wing councils. Seventeen ESC presidents came out in support of Giscard d'Estaing in the 1981 presidential election, which did not endear them to the Socialists. Furthermore, whereas they were previously automatically consulted on all matters before the regional council, the ESCs now only retain the right to be consulted on planning and the preliminary guidelines to the budget. On other matters, the president of the regional council will decide whether he wishes to have the benefit of their views, although the ESC can volunteer its advice on its own initiative. These reforms were strongly criticized by the right-wing deputies and senators, who secured an explicit reaffirmation of the 'unity of the republic'. However, although the regions are now local authorities on an equal footing with the departments, they are still seen as both unions of departments and competitors with them because the wish to reduce the number of tiers of government might in the future threaten the existence of the department.

The boundaries of the regions have not been altered for the present, despite strong representations, notably in Brittany, which was envious of the fact that Corsica was promised a special Assembly and a greater measure of autonomy than that accorded to all other regions. In addition to an Assembly elected for five years, Corsica will have both an economic and social council and a cultural development council, as well as six regional economic development agencies. The Socialist *rapporteur* of the Corsica Bill – which became law in 1982 after successfully surviving reference to the Constitutional Council – felt called upon to quieten right-wing fears by declaring: 'The indivisibility of the Republic is in no way threatened when the authority concerned derives its powers from the state, which can always withdraw them.'[34] The Council's decision significantly reasserted the indivisibility of the republic and appeared to rule out any move towards federalism, not that such a move was contemplated. So, the founding myth of the French republic remains intact.

Characteristically, the press and parliamentary debate over regional reform was dominated by the fear that it represented a real threat to the unity of the state and the nation. Under opposition pressure, the authorization given to frontier regional councils to engage in co-operation on a regular basis with adjacent foreign regional authorities (inserted at the behest of the Senate) was made subject to the approval of the government, on the grounds that otherwise it would threaten national unity and allow the president of the regional council to play a part in the country's international relations: The amendments to the Bill on the rights and freedoms of the communes, departments and regions generally restricted the decentralist dynamic imparted by its author, Gaston Defferre. However during its decades in the provincial wilderness, the left had shed many of its centralist shibboleths,[35] so much so that Prime Minister Mauroy could describe the local and regional reform as a 'quiet revolution' that would be retrospectively recognized as 'the great achievement of President Mitterrand's term of office'.

# 3 The Representative Mediators

At the heart of French political culture there lies a tension between a passionate attachment to personal liberty, conceived as the absence of control by authority, and an intense feeling of dependence upon state power, source of protection and favours in a harshly competitive world. Although there is a great and growing variety of voluntary associations in France, the civic culture lacks vigour because liberty is conceived primarily in personal and negative terms. Freedom is fundamentally a matter of noncommitment, not the opportunity to promote common aims by joint endeavour. So, despite frequent exhortations to increased participation, most Frenchmen remain obstinately ambivalent in their attitude towards increased political involvement. As a perceptive analyst of French political psychology has observed:

On the one hand, people would like very much to participate in order to control their own environment. On the other hand, they fear that if and when they participate, their own behaviour will be controlled by their co-participants. It is far easier to preserve one's independence and integrity if one does not participate in decision-making. By refusing to be involved in policy determination, one remains much more free from outside pressures.[1]

The practical consequence is subordination to a remote and impersonal bureaucratic authority, resulting in the characteristic French combination of critical private thought and servile public conduct. Except for occasional spasms of revolt that shake French society to its foundations, most Frenchmen are content to seek refuge in parochialism, securing a personal enclave of freedom in an over-regulated world.

This introverted individualism is, however, extended to em-

brace the family, traditionally reinforced by the importance of
the family firm, farm and shop in the French economy. This fact
has led some observers to make the sweeping claim that

> there are only two important social entities in the life of a Frenchman,
> the family cell and the state. Intermediary institutions, whether they
> be schools, clubs, trade unions or political parties, count for no-
> thing.... Politics are perceived as essentially a question of private,
> individual conscience.... The Frenchman reserves his judgement and
> often voices his disagreement... but ends up by accepting and obeying
> the central authority.[2]

This assertion needs to be seriously qualified by reference to the
political role of intermediate organizations, rooted notably in
the occupational, educational and ideological sub-cultures,
which exercise formative influences on the individual's political
behaviour. Precisely because most Frenchmen 'want to be left
alone so that they will not have to change' and believe that
'organization means power and power means the oppression of
the individual',[3] they leave it to the skeletal trade unions and
occupational associations to express their class-consciousness
and wage the class conflict that is a datum of their daily experience. They have relied on the Catholic Church and the Communist Party to express their rival value systems in well-organized mass movements, historically rooted in particular parts of
the country. Education is an important link between the influences of social stratification and ideological indoctrination, the
public–private school split being markedly correlated with
cleavages in the political culture.* However, none of these
movements attract more than a minority of active members.

Public opinion surveys can help us ascertain why the French
people tend to combine a fairly high measure of interest in
politics with a sense of alienation from party politics and the
desire to take part in other forms of political action. There was
greater and more sustained interest in politics in the 1970s than
was evident in the 1960s. Table 5 indicates that those who are
more interested in politics are men rather than women; the
middle-aged rather than the young or the old; senior executives
and white collar employees rather than farmers or manual
workers; the better educated; those who support the left-wing

*See below, chapter 7, pp. 207–12.

*Table 5*
*The adult's interest in politics, 1977* (%)

| | Strong | Moderate | Weak | Not at all |
|---|---|---|---|---|
| All | 19 | 44 | 21 | 16 |
| *Sex* | | | | |
| Men | 26 | 50 | 15 | 9 |
| Women | 12 | 39 | 26 | 23 |
| *Age* | | | | |
| 18–24 | 16 | 50 | 23 | 11 |
| 25–34 | 23 | 47 | 18 | 12 |
| 35–49 | 21 | 43 | 21 | 15 |
| 50–64 | 17 | 49 | 20 | 14 |
| 65+ | 17 | 34 | 22 | 27 |
| *Occupation of head of family* | | | | |
| Farmers, farm workers | 7 | 46 | 35 | 12 |
| Shopkeepers, artisans | 18 | 40 | 26 | 16 |
| Senior executives, industrialists, professions | 36 | 45 | 12 | 7 |
| White collar employees | 25 | 53 | 16 | 6 |
| Workers | 14 | 43 | 22 | 21 |
| Retired, not working | 17 | 38 | 20 | 25 |
| *Education* | | | | |
| Primary | 9 | 37 | 27 | 27 |
| Higher primary | 21 | 41 | 17 | 21 |
| Secondary | 28 | 45 | 20 | 7 |
| Technical and commercial | 19 | 56 | 16 | 9 |
| Higher | 35 | 49 | 12 | 4 |
| *Party preference* | | | | |
| Communist | 33 | 48 | 13 | 6 |
| Socialist | 22 | 51 | 18 | 9 |
| Republican | 16 | 44 | 27 | 13 |
| RPR | 22 | 56 | 19 | 3 |

Source: SOFRES, *L'Opinion française en 1977*, 1978, p. 221.

parties and the RPR compared to the relatively uninterested
supporters of the Republican Party. When this general expression of interest is probed with a question on what constitutes

good citizenship, this is identified much more with relatively passive behaviour. Even though more than one reply was allowed, keeping informed about public life (59 per cent) and voting regularly (51 per cent) rather than joining a trade union or professional association (11 per cent), still less a political party (5 per cent) was the response. This finding is further confirmed by the fact that only 67 per cent would regard as serious the abolition of trade unions and professional associations. This figure falls to 55 per cent in the case of political parties, though in both cases left-wing supporters take a much more serious view, Communists especially in the case of trade unions, Socialists particularly in the case of political parties. While 24 per cent claim to belong to a trade union and 6 per cent to a political party, these proportions climb to 43 per cent and 22 per cent among those who are very interested in politics. Other polls show that there is public support for direct democracy (especially on issues like the location of nuclear power stations) particularly by frequent recourse to national (35 per cent) and local (29 per cent) referenda, though 27 per cent (especially the young) conceive it as involving a more active role for consumers, tenants and parents associations, while 21 per cent (particularly workers and left-wing supporters) would like the regular consultation of workers in the place of employment.[4] Such data suggest that we should ask whether political socialization, the way young people acquire their political attitudes and values, has special features in the French context.

Young French people have usually been described as apolitical because it was not appreciated that they attach a different, activist connotation to 'politics' from that of their elders. Because 'politics' is generally associated in France with party electoral competition, operating in traditional, time-honoured ways with which the young often find it difficult to identify, they are less inclined to reply positively when asked if they are interested in politics. For example, between a quarter and a third of the 18–21 age group (particularly women and especially in large towns) do not register to vote, which is about three to four times the number of those over 21 who do not bother to go to the *mairie* to place their names on the electoral register. Those aged 18–21 that register are more inclined to vote than those aged from 22–35, after which the rate of electoral abstention stabilizes at a low level. Adolescents and young adults (in the age group 16–23) are much more likely to take part in a demonstration (especially adolescents) or a general strike (particularly young adults), than those who are over 23, 244though they are much less likely to say they are interested in politics. They are also markedly more willing to engage in violent, insurrectionary action, generally more inclined to be alienated from the politico-administrative system, hostile to the police and generally favourable to revolutionary change.[5] While the 'events' of May 1968 gave spectacular expression to the revolt of young students and workers, it is important to be aware of the fact it reflected a deep-seated propensity to direct action rather than recourse to representative mediation, which we shall see is not an attitude that disappears with full induction into adult society. In the trial of strength to which both organized and unorganized categories of the French population frequently have recourse, no holds are barred, though some groups find it expedient to behave in ways that entitle them to be officially regarded as 'insiders', respectable and responsible spokesmen of well established sectional interests or causes. Just as at the local level, where the representatives of officially recognized organizations achieve the status of *notable*, 'insider' groups are admitted to a social partner–public policy maker relationship. Such groups are regarded as partners of government, in contrast to the dissentient politics of the disreputable and disruptive 'outsider' groups, like the environmentalist and anti-nuclear groups, that have a strong appeal to those on the threshold of adult political activity.

Such outsider groups have played an innovative role by vociferously expressing new kinds of social demand which the established political and administrative institutions and the insider groups have neglected or repressed. The reluctance to acknowledge new issues by the organizations that monopolize official channels of mediation between society and the state has meant that ideologically inspired voluntary associations have been able to overcome institutional inertia and thrust unwelcome issues onto the public policy agenda. Helped by the mass media, which generally welcome 'newsworthy' activities, environmentalist pressure groups have, for example, been able to arouse first public and then élite opinion in France, playing a crucial role at the initial stage of the policy process: problem identification. Such outsider groups may widen their attack from particular issues to a general onslaught upon the unjust and oppressive nature of the capitalist-statist system, at which point they tend to be confined to a role of peripheral, impotent protest, losing in effectiveness as their ambitions grow.[6] The field of effective public action is left to those groups that provide services for particular clienteles and are willing to collaborate, and to the public or private experts whose claim to a share in decision-making is based upon their command of some indispensable specialist skill. Between them, the spokesmen of special interests, with their claim collectively to represent the many publics that the citizen identifies with (most intensely when it comes to dealing with down to earth, daily concerns), and the experts who have the knowledge required to implement public preferences, have invaded spheres of policy-making hitherto denied them. The consequent problems of representation and defence of the public interest can be examined through the massive but unobtrusive proliferation of consultative bodies, which have collected like barnacles around the bulk of official decision-making bodies with the extension of government intervention particularly into the economic and social problem of industrial society.

## Bilateral consultation and direct action

Politics has been defined as 'the art of perceiving contradictions, either to elude or surmount them'.[7] The attraction of consultation to governments is that it offers the possibility of working out agreed solutions to problems instead of relying upon the controversial assertion of public power, even when decisions are legitimized by a parliamentary majority. Rather than appear to be imposing their will upon a minority, governments seek to obtain the consent of the interested parties. Because the liberal democratic ideology forbids formal representation of these interests in legislative assemblies, they are 'consulted' outside the parliamentary process. Parliament formally sanctions legislation, but the compromises are generally worked out in advance between the minister's brains trust and the interested parties. However, to the extent that their 'advice' and 'consent' is valued and accepted – and the attainment of unanimity is an important aim of such pivotal aspects of government activity as national and regional industrial intervention, in which parliament plays a minimal role – acts that are legally unilateral become ratifications of bilateral agreements. The environment of government is raised from the subject status of the 'administered' to that of fully fledged partner, and certain acts require the 'reciprocal consent' of the government and of the interested parties. Inability to obtain such consent explains the failure of an incomes policy in France. The traditional distinction between advice and decision-making is not erased but it is blurred.

The main motives for creating consultative bodies are to improve communication within the administration and to avoid or smooth over conflicts with the administered, once they are well enough organized to conquer or to be groomed into the status of consultative partners of government. To undertake complex and rapidly changing functions, particularly in the economic sphere of planning development and provision of public services, the government's administrative officials need to acquire information and to correct their own departmentalism by co-ordination. The sources of information may be experts within the public service like the Council of State, interested parties, or specialist 'sponsor' ministries like research and industry or agriculture, which rely heavily on information (including statistics) from trade associations or farm organizations. In these latter cases, 'regular and organized advice from outside the bureaucracy is considered indispensable for a balanced relationship between power and knowledge'.[8] Within its own administrative system, 'horizontal' agencies like the Planning Commissariat or DATAR were created to provide interdepartmental co-ordination in the preparation and implementation of public policies. They cut across existing hierarchies and establish negotiating and bargaining committees on which the various ministries' representatives can iron out their conflicts as they do with the administered. Particular ministries, like the government in general, have to recognize that they cannot simply issue edicts without consulting those affected. They must attempt to secure their agreement through persuasion, helped by offers of support (including financial support) and backed by the ultimate threat to impose a decision. The mutual concessions made in the confidential atmosphere of close and continuous relations between senior administrators and the officials of major, well organized interests, reduce the controversial character of many issues. Recourse to parliament is avoided except to register agreements made elsewhere.

It is extremely difficult to ascertain even approximately the number of consultative bodies that exist in France, and even more so of those that are in any real sense active. In the early 1960s there appear to have been about 4,700 consultative bodies at the national level: 500 councils, 1,200 committees and over 3,000 commissions, not counting the numerous sub-committees and working parties which they spawn. Furthermore, locally, the most conservative estimate is an average of about a hundred consultative bodies per department. So, not counting the regional bodies that developed in the 1960s, there were then at least some fifteen thousand parent consultative bodies in France.[9] This suggests that consultation is more highly institutionalized in France that it is in other countries. At the national level, most of these bodies are attached to a particular ministry. Thus in 1957 the ministry of finance had over a hundred and thirty consultative bodies attached to it, of which eighty involved interest group representation. Mere numbers are not a very useful indicator because consultative bodies are seldom abolished even when they cease to function. At the local level, a study of sixty-eight consultative bodies attached to the prefecture of the Drôme department in 1962 indicated that eight did not meet at all; thirty met only once, fourteen twice, and sixteen three or more times (one meeting on twenty occasions). It is not possible to obtain a less crude measure than frequency of meeting of the number of really effective consultative bodies. In any case consultative bodies that are influential at one time may be short-circuited at another; somnolent committees may suddenly be resurrected to help deal with a crisis and subside into inactivity thereafter.

Given the traditional suspicion of any encroachment of private interests on public prerogatives, and the tendency of some civil servants to regard consultation as an extension of the historic duty of vassals to advise their feudal lord, a firm grip is generally maintained by the government and its officials over the consultative process. They seek to control the choice of members but since the practice was instituted in the case of the National Economic Council in 1925 (forerunner of the present Economic and Social Council) of selecting after nomination by the 'most representative organizations', the interest groups have acquired effective control over their representatives. However, the government can alter the numbers from each organization and swamp the body with its own nominees. The dominant part usually played by civil servants (or ministers in the case of the more important committees) can be inferred from the fact that they usually occupy the key posts of chairman and *rapporteur* on behalf of the consultative body and are selected by the consulting authority. At the departmental level, the commissioner of the republic's staff monopolize the *rapporteur* function and supply the secretariat. The commissioner is *ex officio* chairman of all administrative consultative bodies but he often delegates this task to his secretary-general who in turn may pass it on, in less important cases, to a division head. At the national level, members of certain *grands corps* occupy most of the key posts: councillors of the Court of Accounts and inspectors of finance in economic matters, councillors of state and polytechnicians in other matters. So, consultative bodies depend mainly upon the administration to be created, to operate, to reach conclusions and to have them carried into effect. Depending on whether the consultative body is expressing a view on a project that has already been worked out in some detail following a decision, or is asked to make more or less detailed proposals in a matter on which the government has not yet made up its mind, it will be involved either in what is primarily a public relations exercise or in helping in the preparation, implementation or interment of policy.

However, over and above the institutionalized channels of communication provided by these consultative bodies, the leaders of the major interests meet members of the executive, sometimes the president of the republic and prime minister but more frequently members of the ministerial *cabinets* (i.e. personal staff) of their sponsor departments. Rather than the calm, concerted action which one would expect from an elaborate consultative system such as we have described, these meetings often occur as the result of a crisis in which some category of Frenchmen has decided to take the law into its own hands. The outburst of discontent usually takes almost everyone by surprise, although it is clear thereafter that a strong sense of grievance has been building up for some time and has been ignored by the authorities. They often try to shed the responsibility on to the shoulders of the organizations representing the group concerned. Even if one makes allowances for the fact that the channels of communication between interest group leaders and their rank and file (not to speak of the mass of the unorganized) are generally poor, part of the blame undoubtedly lies with the executive, which tends to deal with a problem only when it is vigorously and unavoidably pressed. By multiplying consultative committees whose powerlessness means that they are unlikely to resolve conflicts, the government encourages each sectional interest to respond to its unilateral decisions by uncompromising obstruction, which only confirms the government in its belief that change has to be imposed.

Under the Fifth Republic, the farmers of Brittany and the south-east have been celebrated for their recourse to direct action in defence of the status quo, resisting the impact of an agricultural revolution that drove three million farmers and labourers from the land between 1954–75 and reducing their share of the working population by two-thirds from 27 per cent to 9 per cent. All groups are prepared to resort to such blackmail against governments. Because French governments, in the state idealist tradition, refuse to negotiate with organized interests, they are forced to surrender to them when they cannot suppress their demands. In the trial of strength, the groups seek to extract concessions, not to overthrow the government. In its turn, once the crisis is over, the government seeks to make the groups revert to the status of subservient clients. Direct action by farmers takes the form of obstructing roads with farm vehicles or unsaleable farm produce, coupled with violent confrontations with the police sent to deal with them. The main purpose is to discredit the government by forcing it into repressive actions that would win public sympathy for the farmers. These tactics paid dividends in the early 1960s. Until the coming of a Socialist president in 1981, the farm organizations (especially FNSEA) preferred to develop a corporatist relationship with successive governments; since then they have reverted to direct action.

Shopkeepers and artisans have refused to pay taxes or social security contributions, attacking tax inspectors and tax offices. The Poujadist movement of the 1950s, which resorted to direct action against the forces of economic development which were 'rationalizing' the self-employed out of existence, was revitalized in the late 1960s by CID-UNATI (the defence committee of shopkeepers and artisans) led by Gérard Nicoud. After extracting numerous concessions from the government, the CID achieved the twin triumphs of an early release of its leader from prison and the creation of a new, small-business ministry of trade and crafts in 1972. Since then its influence has waned.

It is not only the self-employed lower middle class that has resorted to this type of direct action. Although the trade unions have called one-day general strikes as demonstrations to get the government to exert pressure on the employers to secure collective bargaining in the private sector, or better wages and conditions of work in the public sector, in 1936 and 1968 there were extended general strikes, combined with occupation of the factories, which correspond to the strategy of blackmail referred to above. Factory occupations became a standard response in the 1970s to the closures that were a frequent consequence of the economic recession. After years of fruitless attempts to influence educational policy, the students in May 1968 nearly precipitated the downfall of the regime when they adopted in their extreme forms the tactics of violent confrontation with the police and occupation of their place of work. Accustomed to an authority that seems congenitally incapable of negotiating a compromise, some groups feel that there is little alternative to forcing total surrender after suffering severe repression. Joseph Martray, former leader of the Breton regionalist pressure group CELIB, wrote in 1962, following the concessions won by the farmers' direct action: 'This state, which prides itself on its authority, has shown us that it is only moved by force.... The responsibility is entirely the government's which procrastinates, promises, cheats and defers as long as it is not faced by an irresistible pressure ... until it has no choice except between repression and capitulation.'[10] Thus, the behaviour of French pressure groups is explicable as the symmetrical response to the style and behaviour of executive authority in France, although the latter has itself been conditioned by past experience of group behaviour. However, times have changed since 1789 and 1871. The revolutionary tradition has been diluted into a propensity to direct action. Such action seems better suited to extracting short-term, piecemeal concessions than to securing the long-term welfare of categories of citizens who depend on sustained action within the framework of an overall strategy.

*Peak interest group organizations and multilateral consultation*

Although it has been a long road from the status of outlaws to that of industrial statesmen, the major French economic interest groups have only achieved a rather limited degree of recruitment and cohesion. This fact is connected in part with belated industrial development as well as the tendency to split along ideological lines. The peak organizations are characterized first, by their tendency to press their own case directly rather than through the weak political parties. Even in the case of the Communist-dominated CGT, where the major French trade union is in a subordinate yet symbiotic relationship with the Communist Party, its industrial activities have been more effective in challenging the capitalist regime and achieving benefits for the working class than have its strictly political activities. The interrelationship between the PCF and the CGT is a complex compromise between the Leninist rule that the trade union must be controlled by the party and used to further its ends, and the 'syndicalist' apolitical tradition of the CGT enshrined in the Amiens Charter of 1906. Whilst no more than about 10 per cent of the CGT members are also members of the PCF, they are generally the most active union members and are elected to posts of responsibility at all levels of the CGT, including its constituent federations. As well as providing the general secretary (Henri Krasucki since 1982) and most of the headquarters staff of the CGT, half the executive committee are PCF members, Krasucki belonging to the politbureau. Even when they lack a formal majority, the PCF members are able to exercise effective control thanks to the 'fellow-travelling' diffidence of others. The CGT can be relied upon to act as the PCF desires, there being no instance of anything other than tactical divergence between them.[11]

Secondly, in the absence of effective opposition parties to aggregate the demands being made on the political system, the various peak interest groups seek to fulfil this role, and in the process take over part of the function of political opposition. However, this is a hazardous task because each major interest is itself so divided that it is very difficult for them to attain a common viewpoint. The CGT with about 1.5 million members represents about half the total trade union membership but has to face competition from three other general unions: in order of size, the left-wing socialist CFDT, the right-wing socialist *Force Ouvrière* (FO), and the residue of the Catholic CFTC, as well as the executive staff union, the CGC. Apart from the open split among the trade unions, almost all French peak organizations have great problems of internal cohesion. French business manages to preserve the semblance of a fragile 'confederal' unity through the *Conseil National du Patronat Français* (CNPF), but some medium and small businesses look to the vehement SNPMI led by Gérard Deuil, whose intransigence secured 15 per cent of business suport in 1982. Yvon Gattaz, who became president of CNPF in 1982, has sought to give it a more assertive role in dealings with both government and trade unions. The CNPF has usually been paralysed by the pursuit of quasi-unanimity, evading controversial issues that might split the organization or formulating policies that it does not attempt to enforce on its members. The Grenelle Agreement of May 1968 that helped to end the general strike forced them to take a more authoritative line. It was negotiated between the leaders of the trade unions and the CNPF under the chairmanship of the prime minister, the CNPF leaders being compelled to make substantial concessions without authority from their member organizations. This helped to bring about the 1969 reform in the CNPF, representing a step towards the centralization and concentration of power in the hands of peak organization leaders.[12] Governments in Britain and France have encouraged this redistribution of power within interest groups so that these leaders can acquire sufficient authority to enter into binding commitments that will subsequently be honoured. Given the highly decentralized and dispersed character of French interest groups, in which the rank and file retain much of the initiative and 'leadership from behind' is the rule, this process of shifting power to the top is a relatively slow process, not least in the business world. For the foreseeable future, autonomy will continue to take precedence over planned strategy and freedom of action over united action.

Thirdly, the executive is so powerful under the Fifth Republic that the peak organizations are more like pressured groups than pressure groups. While the government and administration seek to increase group prestige and status to use them as agents for their policies, they do not want them strengthened to the point where the interest groups can threaten the authority of the government. In France, successive governments have struggled with the problem of carrying through an agricultural revolution in which the protected, subsistence peasant farm would be mechanized and enlarged into a competitive, capitalist farm producing for the market. To achieve this, they had to overcome the opposition of the traditional farm organizations: the FNSEA (the main peak organization, of which about half French farmers are members, embracing thirty-six product organizations, notably the powerful cereals, meat, milk, wine, fruit and vegetables and sugar-beet associations) and the chambers of agriculture, elected on a departmental basis, whose presidents formed the APPCA. These organizations have the support of the influential *Amicale Parlementaire Agricole et Rurale*. However, the direct action tactics used in 1959–61 led the prime minister and notably the new minister of agriculture, Edgard Pisani, to use the 'young farmers' of the CNJA to carry out a policy of modernizing agriculture in close consultation with amenable farm leaders who 'got to know the Hôtel Matignon (the prime minister's headquarters) better than certain ephemeral fourth republic premiers'.[13]

Michel Debatisse, a former general secretary of the FNSEA and leader of the CNJA, who above all personified the policy of semi-corporatist ties, himself became minister for food industries during the Giscard presidency, appropriately enough for the arch advocate of the policy of integrating a select few of the farm population into an industrialized agriculture in the 1970s and 1980s. The FNSEA leaders having been accused of excessively close collaboration with right-wing governments, a rival, Communist-influenced organization, the MODEF, emerged as the champion of the family farmers threatened by the prospect of absorption into the industrial proletariat and abandoned by the FNSEA to their fate. It has been encouraged by the Mauroy Government at the expense of the FNSEA which, as a result, has encouraged mass farm demonstrations, in marked contrast with its acquiescent style in the 1970s.

The problem of what sort of stance an interest group should assume *vis-à-vis* government or other groups has presented particularly severe problems to the trade unions. Their leaders seem to adopt contrasting types of behaviour, depending upon whether they are collaborating with government or business organizations in consultative bodies discussing policy matters at the summit, or are engaged in conflict with them at the office or factory level when discussing the immediate issues of concern to their members: wages and working conditions. The committee room is the sedate context of consultation, but until 1968 employer refusal to engage in collective bargaining meant that strikes, demonstrations and clashes in the streets and at factory gates were the staple of industrial life. The union leader's activities on numerous national consultative bodies are 'time consuming and burdensome for organizations whose human resources are limited. Yet they seem to take first priority, since the political and social status they give union leaders permits them to be well informed and to exert a certain amount of bargaining power ...' This apparent summit 'collusion' with government and business feeds the traditional anarcho-syndicalist suspicions that the rank and file are being betrayed. So 'workers distrust the militants; the militants distrust the leaders and refuse to give them [the] means to build responsible organizations. Weak unions try desperately to maintain the façade that enables them to speak in the name of an active, aggressive and unruly working class.'[14]

A major argument in favour of institutionalizing the government–interest group dialogue in an economic council, such as has existed in France since 1925, is that it offers the opportunity of substituting multilateral for bilateral bargaining, increasing the opportunity to work out comprehensive compromises. It provides the context in which the interest groups can learn from each other what they want; they discover from the government on what terms they can obtain it; they may work together, where this proves feasible, to secure it. It formalizes consultative procedures which have developed haphazardly to meet specific situations, with consequent gaps and overlapping. It also enables the differential access of interest groups to the decision-

making authorities to be corrected, hence the historical fact that
the demand for interest group representation in this form originated with the CGT at the end of the First World War.
Whereas other groups had their own informal and unobtrusive
opportunities to influence policy, the trade unions had no such
privileged access to government. The Council has not fulfilled
the hopes of early advocates of functional representation, who
looked to such bodies to provide 'an element of sustained research, thought and formulation of policy ... more public than
a lonely thinker, more continuous, pressing and representative
than a royal commission, more in touch with the vital elements
of industry and society than political parties, less suspect than the
creations of the "lobby", more sedate and objective in its deliber-
ations and less given to sudden fears of partisanship than the
political assembly.'[15] However, it has made the spokesmen of the
peak organizations better informed about the broad economic
and social issues and encouraged them to place their demands
realistically in the context of the national capacity to fulfil them.

The Economic and Social Council reports and makes
recommendations on matters referred to it by the government
or takes up issues on its own initiative. It works primarily
through seven sections, dealing respectively with planning and
short-term economic policy; finance; social affairs and industrial
relations; industry and trade; regional development and public
works; agriculture; overseas economic expansion and co-operation. To each section are attached representatives of all the
council groups together with ten nominated section specialists
who serve for a maximum of two years and do not participate
in the plenary sessions or vote in the full Council meeting.
Council members serve for five years and it is up to the organization selecting them to decide whether or not to renew their
nomination for further terms. They receive two-thirds of the
parliamentary salary, some paying back part of this to their
organization. Nearly one-eighth of the CGT's income in 1965
was derived from this levy, just as the Communist Party used to
derive an important part of its income from its parliamentary
representatives when these were more numerous. One-seventh
of the CFDT's income is received through a similar levy. Seats on
the ESC thus provide a concealed subsidy to financially weak
peak organizations.

The Council's amalgamation with the Senate into a new second chamber was part of the package of proposals that was defeated at the referendum of April 1969. The groups represented on the ESC were almost unanimously hostile towards this attempt to integrate them more fully into the decision-making process, although the new Senate was to lose its legislative power and became a consultative body. Even though the title of Senate was to be retained, Alain Poher, the Senate president, could legitimately claim that it was not the ESC that was being abolished but the Senate. This failure of institutional integration marked a major rebuff for Gaullist attempts at incorporating the trade unions into a political system in which class conflict was to be eliminated in favour of consensus.

Subsequent attempts at developing corporatist ties with the working class were swept aside with the development of a credible 'united left' alliance between the Communists and a rejuvenated Socialist Party from 1972. Although it took nearly ten years, the election of a Socialist president, supported by a Socialist parliamentary majority, with the Communists reduced to the role of junior partner, put an entirely new complexion on trade union–government relations. Even though Communist Party support was dispensable in parliamentary terms, the presence of four Communist ministers in the Mauroy Government meant that the CGT – still the largest union with some 1·5 million members in 1982, despite its slow, long-term decline as shown in Table 6 – would be on its best behaviour. (Table 6 underestimates the importance of FO because it is concerned only with

*Table 6*
*French trade unions and private sector works committee elections, 1966–78 (%)*
*Workers (and sometimes employees)*

| Trade union | 1966 | 1968 | 1970 | 1972 | 1974 | 1976 | 1978 |
|---|---|---|---|---|---|---|---|
| CGT | 57·8 | 55·6 | 53·9 | 51·4 | 49 | 47·9 | 44·9 |
| CFDT | 19·0 | 19·5 | 20·2 | 19·4 | 19·4 | 19·8 | 21·1 |
| FO | 8·0 | 7·8 | 7·4 | 7·6 | 8·1 | 9·0 | 9·6 |
| CFTC | 2·2 | 2·9 | 2·6 | 2·6 | 2·6 | 2·6 | 2·6 |
| Other | 3·0 | 4·8 | 5·9 | 6·2 | 6·1 | 6·5 | 5·7 |
| Non-TU | 10.0 | 9·4 | 10·0 | 12·8 | 14·3 | 13·9 | 15·7 |

Source: *Le Monde*, 8 October 1978. For the 1975, 1977 and 1979 results, see *Le Monde*, 25 May 1982, p. 23.

private sector elections. In the civil service, the teachers union,
FEN, wins about a third of the votes, the CGT and FO about a
fifth and the CFDT about an eighth of the votes. One must also
bear in mind that only a fifth to a quarter of the employed
actually belong to trade unions.) The decline in support for the
CGT, as measured by elections to industrial disputes tribunals,
has continued, its vote decreasing sharply from 41·4 to 36·8 per
cent from 1979 to 1982, while the CFDT and FO marginally
increased their support to 23·5 and 17·8 per cent respectively.
While the CFDT and FO are closer in many ways to the
Socialist-led government, reflected in the fact that both general
secretaries belong to the PS, they have been more concerned to
assert their independence as trade unions. The CFDT, in particular, has influenced many of the reform proposals of the
Mauroy Government but it has resisted Socialist-style incor-
poration and the siren call of 'social compromise' as the price
of public policies, most of which its leaders broadly approve.[16]

## Polarized pluralism: class and 'catch-all' parties

The highly abstract character of most French political commitments, based on divisive ideologies as well as a rarefied consensus
expressed in loyalty to the republican state, encourages a divorce between the individual's behaviour as the member of an
interest category or group and his partisan or electoral behaviour. He frequently votes for a candidate who supports the
government against which he will violently demonstrate, and
then meekly votes for the same candidate at the next election.
This has made it more difficult for French political parties to
channel interest group demands. Despite attempts to keep the
interest groups free of direct partisan entanglements in France,
the distinction between political parties and interest groups is
only clearcut in countries with disciplined two-party systems
where each is likely to gain office. In a multipolarized party
system such as existed in France from the early days of the Third
Republic until 1962, those parties, for example the Communists,
which were generally excluded from office were reduced to the
*de facto* status of pressure groups; while pressure groups –
peasants or shopkeepers – could become the backbone of a

political party, as occurred with the conservative CNIP and the Poujadist UFF under the Fourth Republic.

Moreover, parties and interests tended to be more closely connected in a multipolarized party system. First, the narrower electoral appeal of each party encouraged closer ties with a specialized clientele and greater identification with a particular cause. It also allowed more scope for interest group manoeuvre, especially where two or more parties competed for the same voters. Thus the Catholic school lobby could rely on several right-wing parties to compete for its backing, whilst the secular-ist school lobby had the Communists, Socialists and Radicals competing for its support. Finally, the would-be all-embracing PS and RPR were wide open to pressure group influence in a similar way to the undisciplined 'catch-all' parties of the United States. However, they were more resistant to group pressure than were the weakly disciplined and non-ideological Fourth Republic parties of the centre and right who formed most of the coalition governments from 1947–58.

The traditional French multipolarized party system tended either towards immobility or disorderly change, maximizing demands on the political system but providing unreliable sup-port for the government of the day. The unified political super-structure superimposed by a centralized state authority upon a society with deep and complex divisions led to a 'mixture of deference and distrust' towards authority, while a retarded industrial development led to political claims outstripping socio-economic changes, which, when they did come in the form of class-based mass movements, were not properly integrated into the established institutional and political structures.[17] However, the Fifth Republic has been characterized by a pro-cess of bipolarization, on the right in the 1960s and on the left in the 1970s, which, despite setbacks, has led to stable majorities supporting governments in parliament since 1962. Although it has been exceptional for one party to secure an overall National Assembly majority (1968–73 and since 1981), party-based coal-ition government has taken a long step forward in France. Whereas elsewhere, in Western Europe and North America, political parties have been regarded as suffering a decline in public confidence, a weakening of party organization and a smaller role in the political process, in France, albeit from a low level, there has been a marked improvement in the standing of political parties.[18]

The strength of the party organization has increased where it used to be weak. Leadership has become personal rather than collective. Parties exercise more central control over the selection of candidates and there is greater voting cohesion of each party's parliamentary representatives. Party alliances in local and national elections are increasingly identical. Although no rival has managed to become a mass party on the scale of the Communist Party, membership has become larger and more active in these other parties whereas, paradoxically, the Communists have not been able to sustain past high standards of militancy and activism. Public confidence, as measured by mass identification with a political party and electoral turnout, has been more equivocal. While there has been an impressive increase in party identification among those where it was traditionally weak – women, younger and right-wing voters – there has been some recent decline in voter turnout, notably in the 1981 National Assembly election, though it remains high by comparison with most other western democracies. However, it should be noted that nearly 10 per cent of the potential electorate do not bother to register at the town hall, so the turnout figures are rather flattering.

While political marketing is a highly public activity, the acquisition of the resources to pay for it, party finance, has always been an obscure area. The major parties have had to secure increasingly large sums to meet the costs of modern political and more especially electoral activity. The treasurer of the RPR's predecessor disingenuously declared that 'The role of treasurer in a political party is a curious one; like a commercial enterprise there are takings but there are no goods for sale'.[19] For the parties on the right, in power for nearly a quarter of a century, it was possible to rely upon both public and private money: the 'special funds' available to the government and contributions from business organizations. The latter were often 'laundered' by buying services from fake firms of consultants, though payments in cash are frequently made. Business is more inclined to contribute to specific election expenditures rather than to finance the running costs of the political parties. On the left, there is more information about sources of party income, although some areas remain shrouded in a certain mystery. In the case of the Communist Party (which had the same treasurer from 1950–82), it claimed that in 1979 it derived 40 per cent of its income from subscriptions (amounting to 1 per cent of the wage of each member) and 20 per cent from the lion's share of the salary or pensions of Communist members of the national and European parliament, the mayors of large towns and departmental councillors, the party receiving the salary and paying its representative a skilled worker's wage. The loss of half its Assembly seats in 1981 was thus a severe blow, involving a loss of nearly twenty million francs income. Socialist members of parliament make more modest contributions to party funds, though like the Communist Party the Socialist Party's control of many local authorities enables it to acquire the services of large numbers of full-time officials who are on the municipal payroll. With Britain, France continues to pay a concealed price through the proliferation of corrupt practices for refusing to follow the Federal German Republic in arranging for institutionalized public financing of political parties.

As far as the place of parties in the political process generally is concerned, their electoral role is increasingly prominent, party leaders conducting national campaigns on the basis of elaborate party programmes at the expense of the past reliance upon local ties and the personality of the candidate. The role of parties in the Assembly has been made more effective by the reduction in the number of groups from ten in the 1950s, to six at the start of the Fifth Republic and four since 1978. The Socialist group alone secured nearly 60 per cent of the seats in 1981. Despite the pretence that the president of the republic is above any party – leading all the major candidates except the Communist to resign their party posts prior to a presidential election – he is increasingly recognized to be a partisan figure, strengthening the party nature of French government. The parties out of power are increasingly inclined to see themselves as an Opposition or alternative government, which helps to canalize protest into conventional institutional channels. Paradoxically, it is the Fifth Republic, whose founders made deadly play with the discreditable activities of the Fourth Republic parties, that has witnessed the consolidation of parties as the principal vehicles through which competition for political office

*Table 7*
*National Assembly elections in France, 1946–81*
(i) *% of votes cast*

| | Communists | Socialists | Radicals | MRP | Independents /PR | | Gaullists/ RPR |
|---|---|---|---|---|---|---|---|
| | | | Centre | | | | |
| June 1946 | 26·2 | 21·1 | 11·5 | 28·1 | 12·8 | | — |
| Nov. 1946 | 28·6 | 17·9 | 12·4 | 26·3 | 12·9 | | 1·8 |
| June 1951 | 26·4 | 14·8 | 13·0 | 13·1 | 12·5 | | 20·9 |
| Jan. 1956 | 25·5 | 15·5 | 12·8 | 11·3 | 13·9 | | 4·3 |
| Nov. 1958 | | | | | | | |
| 1st ballot | 18·9 | 15·5 | 11·5 | 11·6 | 19·9 | | 17·6 |
| 2nd ballot | 20·7 | 13·7 | 7·7 | 7·5 | 23·6 | | 26·4 |
| Nov. 1962 | | | | | | | |
| 1st ballot | 21·7 | 12·6 | 7·5 | 8·9 | 9·6 | 4·4 | 31·9 |
| 2nd ballot | 21·3 | 15·2 | 7 | 5·3 | 7·8 | 1·6 | 40·5 |
| March 1967 | | | | | | | |
| 1st ballot | 22·5 | 18·8* | | | 17·9 | | 37·8 |
| 2nd ballot | 21·4 | 24·1* | | | 10·8 | | 42·6 |
| June 1968 | | | | | | | |
| 1st ballot | 20·0 | 16·5 | | | 10·3 | | 43·7 |
| 2nd ballot | 20·1 | 21·3 | | | 7·8 | | 46·4 |
| March 1973 | | | | | | | |
| 1st ballot | 21·5 | 21·2 | | | 13·1‡ | | 36·4 |
| 2nd ballot | 20·6 | 25·1 | | | 6·1‡ | | 46·2 |
| March 1978 | | | | | | | |
| 1st ballot | 20·6 | 22·6 | | | 21·5 | | 22·6 |
| 2nd ballot | 18·6 | 28·3 | | | 23·2 | | 26·1 |
| June 1981 | | | | | | | |
| 1st ballot | 16·2 | 37·5 | | | 19·2 | | 20·8 |
| 2nd ballot | 7·0 | 49·2 | | | 18·6 | | 22·4 |

(ii) *Seats in the National Assembly*

| | Communists | Socialists | Radicals | MRP | Independents /PR | | Gaullists/ RPR |
|---|---|---|---|---|---|---|---|
| | | | Centre | | | | |
| June 1946 | 153 | 129 | 53 | 169 | 67 | | — |
| Nov. 1946 | 183 | 105 | 70 | 167 | 71 | | 6 |
| June 1951 | 101 | 107 | 95 | 96 | 98 | | 120 |
| Jan. 1956 | 150 | 99 | 94 | 84 | 97 | | 22 |
| Nov. 1958 | 10 | 47 | 40 | 56 | 129 | | 206 |
| Nov. 1962 | 41 | 66 | 43 | | 55 | 37† | 233 |
| Mar. 1967 | 73 | 121 | | | 41 | 44† | 201 |
| June 1968 | 34 | 44 | 13 | | 31 | 64† | 296 |
| March 1973 | 73 | 102 | | 34‡ | 30 | 55 | 183 |
| March 1978 | 86 | 115 | | | 123 | | 154 |
| June 1981 | 44 | 285 | | | 64 | | 85 |

* Includes some Radicals, e.g., MRG, since 1967.
† Independent Republican group led by V. Giscard d'Estaing, part of UDF since 1978.
‡ Reformers, made up of the Democratic Centre in alliance with some Radicals until 1978; thereafter UDF.

*Table 8*
*Changes in support for the Communist and non-Communist left, 1967–78 (%)*

| Socio-occupational category | Men | | Women* | |
|---|---|---|---|---|
| | PCF | *Non-PC Left* | PCF | *Non-PC Left* |
| Self-employed: | −7 | −2 | −2 | +7 |
| Farmers | −6 | −6 | 0 | +1 |
| Small Shopkeepers | −2 | −5 | −7 | +15 |
| Artisans | −9 | +9 | 0 | +11 |
| Bourgeois (including senior management) | 0 | +2 | 0 | +10 |
| Salaried middle class: | 0 | +17 | +3 | +14 |
| Secondary and higher education teachers | −2 | +3 | +11 | +16 |
| Primary school teachers | +5 | 0 | +2 | +3 |
| Administrative staff | −2 | +22 | −1 | +10 |
| Office employees | +2 | +16 | −2 | +21 |
| Technicians | −4 | +22 | +8 | +14 |
| Workers: | +6 | +12 | +4 | +15 |
| Foremen | +12 | +9 | −12 | +26 |
| Skilled | +5 | +9 | +6 | +13 |
| Unskilled | +4 | +19 | +6 | +13 |
| Shop workers and domestics | −1 | +14 | −1 | +7 |
| All | +2 | +10 | +3 | +12 |

* Classified according to occupation of head of the family
Source: Capdevielle *et al*, *France de gauche vote à droite*, 1981, Paris, p. 255.

is conducted. Table 7 represents a simplified perspective on how the major French parties have fared since the end of the Second World War.

The most spectacular feature of these figures is that, within the emerging double duality of both left and right, the Socialist Party has succeeded during the 1970s in overhauling the Communist Party in terms of its popularity to the point that in 1981 it secured more than double the votes won by its ally and rival. While the distorting effect of the electoral system gave the Socialists about a hundred seats more than they would have won on a proportional representation basis, this should not mask the historic character of their achievement. Table 8 shows that, even before the 1981 triumph, there was a five to one greater increase for the non-Communist Left among male voters, four to one in the case of women. The main Socialist gains were among lower-middle class employees, clerical workers and technicians, as well as unskilled manual workers.

The reasons for the secular decline and current crisis of the Communist Party are both domestic and international. The PCF has been too inclined to looking eastward and backward for inspiration, becoming – by contrast with the Italian and Spanish Communists – retro-communist rather than euro-communist. Under the guise of 'proletarian internationalism', the PCF remains wedded to the 'real socialism' of the Soviet Union and its satellites, resulting in the endorsement of the military take-overs in Afghanistan and Poland. The PCF has been deliberately prepared to pay a heavy domestic price for this guilt by association because it believes that the world balance of power is shifting decisively in favour of the Communist bloc and this will ensure the global triumph of their cause.

Within France, the PCF behaves like an organization that has triumphed over its revolutionary purpose. Despite the tactical semantic subterfuge of casually abandoning the Marxist principle of the dictatorship of the proletariat for reasons of electoral expediency, it clings resolutely to the Leninist principle of democratic centralism in its internal organization and has given up expulsion of dissidents in favour of hypocritical 'self-exclusion'.[20] The PCF has failed to resolve its fundamental dilemma: whether to resort to a reformist alliance of 'unity without struggle' or a sectarian breakaway of 'struggle without unity'. It has ineffectually and brutally zig-zagged from competitive conflict with the Socialists (in 1968–9, 1974–5 and 1977–81) to collaborative co-operation (1971–4, 1976–7 and after 1981), though between the signature of the Common Government Programme in 1972 and the joint attainment of power in 1981 the balance of power shifted decisively from the Communists to the Socialists. Part of the reason for this shift, involving a loss of a quarter of the PCF's previous electoral support in 1981, has been inept leadership by Georges Marchais, who was nevertheless resoundingly re-elected as general secretary in 1982 at the party's twenty-fourth congress. The PCF's loss of influence has been devastating, both among intellectuals with the decline of Marxism's erstwhile hegemony and among workers with the recession in the CGT's dominance. The PCF has lost touch with the rapidly evolving French society of the 1960s and 1970s, losing its sense of identity and of direction, condemned to a modest share of power in a government they entered 'on their knees'. It nevertheless remains almost the only party to present manual workers as parliamentary *candidates* (129 out of the 133 who stood in the 1981 National Assembly elections) though, like the Socialist Party, teachers now represent the largest single category among its *deputies*.[21]

Although it has suffered the humiliation of being compelled to join a Socialist-dominated government out of weakness, provisionally becoming the fellow-travellers of the PS, the PCF remains a force to be reckoned with, especially outside parliament. At its twenty-fourth congress in 1982, it continued to claim over 700,000 members (the reality is nearer 500,000) organized into 27,500 cells – one-third in the workplace – grouped into over 3,000 sections.[22] (About half the cells are inactive by rigorous PCF standards.) The PCF continues to govern the majority of provincial towns in tandem with the PS. In 1977 they won 349 out of the 605 towns with between 9,000–30,000 inhabitants (156 having a Communist mayor and 193 a Socialist mayor) and 155 out of the 221 towns with over 30,000 inhabitants (72 having a Communist mayor and 83 a Socialist mayor).[23] This provides both parties with tens of thousands of councillors spread throughout the country, enjoying access to the resources of the local councils they control. These councillors are even more important to the Socialists than they are to the Communists, if only because they constitute a much larger proportion of the 200,000 total party membership. They provide the bulk of the activists on whom the leadership rely.

The PCF and PS are each headed by a party secretariat, seven members for the PCF which interlocks with the political bureau of twenty-one members, and fifteen full and twelve assistant secretaries for the PS interlocking with a twenty-seven-member executive committee. Appropriately for mass parties, they are led by a general secretary for the PCF (Georges Marchais) and a first secretary for the PS (Lionel Jospin), though the real PS leader is President Mitterrand, PS first secretary from 1971–80. Many of the leaders and members of the PS formerly belonged to the *Parti Socialiste Unifié* (PSU), which also contributed much to the self-management ideology that has enabled the PS to differentiate itself from both state socialism and reformed capitalism, offering a distinctive ideology and programme that freed it from the legacy of its predecessor, the discredited SFIO. This influx helped the new Socialist Party (which, as one of its leaders (Pierre Joxe) put it, was formed by addition rather than division) to attract working class and Catholic supporters that gave it a wider appeal and contributed to its rapid expansion after 1971.

Before turning to the parties of the right, one should stress that despite the Socialist Party's attraction of increased support from Catholics, religious affiliation rather than class origin remains the best guide to political preference and voting behaviour. The socio-cultural matrix of beliefs and values which has since the French Revolution been reflected in the ideological sub-culture of Roman Catholicism and secularism (whose most extreme manifestation is communism) has led to a polarization of political attitudes that is strikingly exemplified by the figures in Table 9. Most of the 1970s swing to the (Socialist) left is due to the rapidity of dechristianization that France has been experiencing; those that remain regularly practising Catholics still overwhelmingly support the parties of the right. It would seem that 'one does not change political loyalties while remaining in the Church but rather in distancing oneself from it'.[24]

While social class is a less accurate predictor of political behaviour than religious affiliation. Table 10 demonstrates how party support varies as between occupations. The extreme left draws its support disproportionately from students, middle-managers and white collar employees; the Communists from manual workers; while the Socialist and Left Radical voters tend to be a cross-section of the electorate. The Environmentalist vote clearly comes disproportionately from students, higher

*Table 9*
*Party preference and religious practice of Catholics in France* (%)

| Catholic religious practice | PSU Extreme Left | Communists | Socialists/ Left Radicals | Right |
|---|---|---|---|---|
| Regularly practising | 0 | 4 | 15 | 81 |
| Irregularly practising | 2 | 11 | 28 | 59 |
| Non-practising | 3 | 24 | 33 | 40 |
| Non-religious | 9 | 36 | 34 | 21 |

Source: Based on SOFRES, *L'Opinion française en 1977*, p. 129.

and middle managers. On the right, both the UDF and the RPR do particularly well among housewives and the retired, the former also scoring best among farmers while the latter has greater appeal to small shopkeepers and artisans. The 1981 first ballot presidential contest between the UDF leader, Giscard d'Estaing, and the RPR leader, Jacques Chirac, revealed some interesting contrasts between their electorates. Giscard's vote came disproportionately from women; it regularly increased with the voter's age; he attracted more manual workers and retired people than Chirac, who did markedly better among

*Table 10*
*Socio-occupational profiles of party electorates, March 1978* (%)

|  | PSU/ Extreme Left | Comm- unists | Socialists/ Left Radicals | Environ- mentalists | UDF | RPR | All |
|---|---|---|---|---|---|---|---|
| Farmers | 2 | 2 | 4 | 4 | 10 | 7 | 6 |
| Small-scale industry and shopkeepers | 4 | 1 | 4 | 3 | 5 | 9 | 5 |
| Big business and professional | 2 | 1 | 1 | 2 | 3 | 3 | 2 |
| Higher managerial | 7 | 2 | 5 | 12 | 4 | 3 | 4 |
| Middle managerial | 19 | 9 | 10 | 16 | 6 | 5 | 10 |
| Employees | 14 | 10 | 13 | 12 | 8 | 8 | 10 |
| Workers | 16 | 31 | 20 | 9 | 7 | 10 | 16 |
| Other employed | 3 | 3 | 5 | 3 | 4 | 5 | 4 |
| Students | 11 | 2 | 2 | 12 | 2 | 1 | 1 |
| Housewives | 17 | 20 | 19 | 22 | 26 | 25 | 21 |
| Retired | 5 | 14 | 16 | 4 | 25 | 24 | 20 |

Source: Based on J. Capdevielle *et al*, op. cit., p. 246.

farmers, small shopkeepers and artisans; and appealed more to practising Catholics while Chirac had greater success among non-practicing Catholics. The opinions of the two electorates on a wide range of issues were very similar, except when it came to judging the record of the outgoing president, Giscard, though Chirac's supporters were more inclined to regard the left–right distinction as being out of date.[25]

While Giscard's election to the presidency in 1974 was widely regarded at the time as heralding the long-awaited demise of Gaullism, this did not occur for two major reasons. He was unwilling to institute proportional representation and dissolve the Assembly, which would have placed him in a far better position to reconstitute a centrist alliance and reverse the process of bipolarization. So, unlike Mitterrand, who immediately after his election as president in 1981 dissolved the Assembly and secured a Socialist majority, Giscard, who had reassured the electors in 1974 that, unlike his opponent, he had a ready-made parliamentary majority, became its prisoner. Furthermore, his most loyal supporters were divided into several parties, consisting of his own Republican Party, the former Christian Democratic Centre of Social Democrats and the right-wing remnants of the Radical Party. They adamantly refused to merge their identities even when they desperately formed the *Union pour la Démocratie Française* (UDF) just before the 1978 general election, to counterbalance the weight of a resurgent neo-Gaullism led by Jacques Chirac.

It was largely thanks to a betrayal of the Gaullist candidate by Chirac that Giscard was elected president of the republic in 1974. Rewarded with the office of prime minister, Chirac quickly seized control of the UDR from the nerveless grasp of the Gaullist barons and carefully prepared what he hoped would be Giscard's succession. When it became clear that Giscard intended to succeed himself, Chirac in 1976 resigned office and reconstituted his party under the title of *Rassemblement pour la République*.[26] Its *raison d'être* is to help him win the presidency. From 1977–81, Chirac waged cold war on Giscard, while nominally remaining within 'the majority'. Having won control of Paris, Chirac managed to secure Giscard's defeat in 1981 but not his own election. He has taken advantage of the failure of centrism to assert his claim to the leadership of the anti-Socialist Opposition as the preparation for the next presidential election, at which he intends to fulfil his all-consuming ambition. Chirac seeks to personify what he chooses to call 'the republicans' against 'the marxists', it being a rule in twentieth-century France for leading conservative politicians to deny that they are right-wing. Against a France divided by class conflict, Chirac, unable to assume the disguise of the 'majority' label, holds out the vision of a republic united under his leadership. Whilst awaiting 1988, Chirac had to be content in January 1982 with being re-elected RPR president with a 99 per cent majority at a party congress from which the symbols of the party's past were banished: the photos of de Gaulle and the cross of Lorraine were nowhere to be seen, so as not to dim the splendour of the new candidate-saviour. Having played the role of kingmaker for others in 1974 and 1981, Chirac clearly intends to contend for kingship himself in 1988.

## Parliament and the legislative process

Laws are only one way of making rules and far from being the most important in terms of the volume of rule-making. The traditional pattern was a single rule-maker, the monarch, 'assisted or curbed ... by trusted advisors', and 'For more than nine-tenths of recorded history, legislatures, as collections of individuals with authority to make laws, simply did not exist'.[27] While legislatures in the liberal tradition have been primarily devices for controlling and curbing executive power, the coming of democracy has meant that the state intervenes much more comprehensively and intensively. Although the volume of legislation has consequently increased absolutely, it has declined as a proportion of rule-making as a whole because most decisions are either taken informally, formally delegated by the legislature to others e.g. the bureaucracy, or are pre-empted by interest groups, political parties, the bureaucracy and the judiciary. Most of the legislative work is in any case done outside parliament at the pre- and post-legislative stages of policy formulation and policy implementation in which parliamentarians usually play only a modest part. The advent and the decreasingly inhibited intrusion of television and opinion polls have weakened parliament's previous quasi-monopoly over political communication and representation of the people. However, one should not exaggerate the decline in the role of the French parliament, even though it may be more important in influencing rulers rather than making the rules. The power to amend legislation had meant that from 1967–77, while the government put down 12 per cent of the amendments, accounting for 22 per cent of those carried, and Assembly committees put down 39 per cent of the amendments (59 per cent of those carried), deputies proposed 49 per cent of the amendments, of which only 20 per cent were carried. The success rate of government amendments was 82 per cent, committee amendments 67 per cent and by deputies only 17 per cent.[28] While parliament is a convenient way for governments to correct the consequences of hasty drafting, incorporate late concessions to interest groups and enact its own afterthoughts, it is the place where the compromises made are legitimized.

The virtues of legislation are often overrated. As Winston Churchill said in the House of Commons in 1934, 'Most bills ... cost money, lose votes, create officials and worry the public.'[29] In the traditional French conception, a deputy is primarily a local representative, the spokesman for local grievances and the source of local patronage. Deputies find that too many of their electors regard them essentially as intermediaries – 'social workers', 'commercial travellers', 'ambassador in Paris to defend local and private interests' – rather than fulfilling important national functions.[30] Whilst local connections are vital for candidates of the old-style centre parties, which give them *ex-post facto* party endorsement, they are less significant for the centralized and well-organized Communist and RPR parties whose 'parachuted' candidates subsequently attempt to acquire a local identity. The reversion to single member constituencies in 1958 has encouraged the constituency-orientation of the deputies. In contrast with the clear British demarcation between local and national politics, the two are intimately related in France. Both local and national office must be held concurrently if the politician is to play his role as privileged mediator between the mass public and the political or administrative executive. Mayors who are also members of parliament spend a large part of their time in their constituencies. Even when in Paris, deputies and senators are busy contacting ministries on behalf of their councils and constituents, so that absenteeism has been a major problem, both on the floor of the house and in the committee work of both chambers.

Table 11 indicates the contrasting strength of the various parties in the two chambers in 1982. Under the Fourth Republic, the French suffered from 'government by Assembly'. Fleeting ministries were overthrown by shifting majorities. Because the Fifth Republic's attainment of stable government based upon a loyal majority since 1962 was not anticipated, the constitution makers devised a series of draconian curbs on the Assembly's powers over legislation, finance (dealt with in chapter 6), the executive and constitutional amendment. The con-

Table 11
Composition of the French parliament, 1982

| Groups | National Assembly | Senate |
|---|---|---|
| Communist | 44 | 23 |
| Socialist* | 283 | 69 |
| Democratic Left | — | 39† |
| Centre Union | — | 67 |
| Republican | — | 52 |
| UDF | 63 | — |
| RPR | 87 | 41 |
| Non-party | 11 | 13 |
| Total | 491 | 304 |

* The Left Radicals are attached to the Socialist parliamentary group in the Assembly, while the rump of the Radical Party forms part of the UDF.
† Includes 13 Left Radicals.

stitutional limitations on parliament's legislative power are numerous. Article 34 specifies the subjects on which parliament may legislate. On some matters parliament is entitled to 'make rules' and in others it can fix the 'fundamental principles'; but Article 37 states that all matters not enumerated in Article 34 are part of the government's regulatory power and need not be submitted for parliamentary approval. The executive's decrees and orders are now on a separate but equal footing with the laws enacted by the legislature.* Furthermore, Article 38 provides that parliament may delegate its legislative power to the government which makes ordinances. This occurred in 1967 when the government had a slender parliamentary majority and wanted to carry through unpopular social and economic reforms. Ordinances were, however, again used in 1982 by a government having a large majority but wishing to proceed quickly to deal with increasing unemployment, notably by reducing working hours.

To prevent parliament from 'meddling excessively' in government, Article 28 restricts the length of parliamentary sessions to less than six months annually. The Assembly held about one hundred and forty sittings a year just before the Second World War. This increased to over two hundred under the Fourth Republic but before 1981 fell to about one hundred and forty

* Regulatory *decrees* emanate from the president of the republic and prime minister. Regulatory *orders* are issued by lesser executive authorities.

sittings under the Fifth Republic. An example of the rushed legislation that results is provided by a comparison between the Acts reducing conscription to one year in 1928 and 1970. The Third Republic Bill was presented in August 1926. After being examined by the standing committee, it was discussed in the Chamber of Deputies eight times between June 1927 and January 1928. The Fifth Republic Bill was decided upon by the government on 3 June 1970, examined by the Assembly's defence committee from 4 June, by the Assembly itself on 9–10 June 1970, and by the Senate on 25 June, becoming law after a conference committee on 29 June. Because of its ambitious legislative programme, the Mauroy Government has made extensive use of its right (under Article 29) to summon special sessions of parliament to deal with a specific agenda. The government (under Article 48) controls the parliamentary agenda and uses it to give priority to its own bills. There has been a consequential fall from nearly 30 per cent in the Fourth Republic to about 13 per cent in the Fifth Republic of the private member's bills' share of all legislation adopted. Non-government legislation (four-fifths of which is initiated by deputies) is much less likely to be enacted. Although the overall average 'success rate' from 1970–77 was about 10 per cent, this varied from 15 per cent in the case of the 'Gaullists' to 4 per cent for Communists. All parliamentary groups (other than the UDF) insist on giving prior approval to private member's bills and proposed amendments. The proportion of private member's bills initiated by senators increased from 11 per cent in the 1969–73 legislature to 38 per cent in the Giscardian period 1974–80, but the advent of a Socialist Assembly majority has made a fall in this figure likely.[31] There is no equivalent of Opposition 'supply days' which in Britain allow the government's opponents in the House of Commons time to debate a subject of their choice. In France they must put down a censure motion.

Other changes in procedure and organization were devised to incorporate features of the British parliamentary system which strengthen the executive. Government bills are discussed in the form presented by government, not, as was the practice (and still is in the United States), as amended by the relevant parliamentary standing committee. In major debates the minister speaks first but on other occasions the traditional practice is adopted of the committee's *rapporteur* opening the debate, being followed by the minister who explains whether he accepts or rejects the committee's proposed amendments. They generally speak from their specially reserved seats at the front of the Assembly. Through Article 44 of the Constitution, government legislation can escape the 'death by a thousand cuts' which the Assembly used to inflict on executive-sponsored bills under the Fourth Republic by insisting that its legislation be voted *en bloc* and unamended. This device has frequently been used to restrain the government's own supporters from voting for electorally popular amendments at the instance of pressure groups.

Before the establishment of the Fifth Republic, governments tended to follow the lead of parliament and this meant primarily the chairmen and *rapporteurs* of the twenty or so specialist standing committees, approximately one for each government department. The Fourth Republic situation has been described as follows: 'The standing committees were the central feature of French parliamentary procedure. All Bills, before the House debated them, went to the committees, which killed the majority and redrafted the remainder.... It was through its committees above all that parliament asserted legislative and encroached on executive power.'[32] Ministers (see Table 12) and officials did and do appear before them (though ministers require the prime minister's permission, and some ten officials a year, with the minister's permission, do testify), but they do not hold elaborate public hearings on the American model, nor do they have a comparable investigatory staff. The number of standing committees in both chambers was reduced to six by Article 43 of the Constitution but they remain more specialized, on the American as contrasted with the British pattern. They are, in the Assembly: (i) finance and economic affairs, the most powerful committee and the one which attracts the best-calibre parliamentarians; (ii) foreign affairs; (iii) defence; (iv) constitutional, legal and administrative affairs. These four committees have some sixty members each, but (v) production and trade, covering all industrial, labour, transport and housing matters; and (vi) cultural, family and social affairs, including education, health and the social services, have over one hundred and twenty members each.

87

*Table 12*
*Private hearings of ministers by National Assembly standing committees,*
*1972–6*

| Year | Finance | Foreign | Defence | Law | Production | Cultural | Total |
|------|---------|---------|---------|-----|------------|----------|-------|
| 1972 | 11 | 5 | 6 | 7 | 10 | 17 | 56 |
| 1973 | 11 | 6 | 6 | 9 | 17 | 23 | 72 |
| 1974 | 22 | 18 | 3 | 10 | 16 | 25 | 84 |
| 1975 | 17 | 12 | 14 | 19 | 16 | 28 | 106 |
| 1976 | 16 | 16 | 4 | 9 | 16 | 27 | 88 |

Source: Based on P. Loquet, *Les Commissions parlementaires permanentes de la V^e République*, 1980, p. 245. Senate committees held comparably numerous hearings.

The 'winner takes all' principle has been followed in the matter of committee chairmanships and attempts to allow the opposition parties at least one post have failed. Thus prior to the 1981 election, the chairmanships were shared between the UDF and the RPR, while since then the Socialists hold five posts and their coalition partners, the Communists, one. Whereas under the Fourth Republic, such chairmanships were a stepping stone to ministerial office, the opposite has been much more frequent under the Fifth Republic, both because ministers more often do not come from parliament and because committees prefer an ex-minister at their head to facilitate dealings with the government. Deputies and senators spend far more time in parliamentary committees than in full session, the chairman of the law committee (which examines more legislation than any other) pointing out in 1981 that 'in full session you only see the last hundred metres. All the work of reflection has already occurred and public opinion is all too often unaware of it.' Because legislation depends so much upon anticipating the problems likely to be experienced in its implementation, committees have become increasingly concerned with examining those that will apply the law before it is enacted.

The Constitutional Council is charged by Article 41 with the task of acting as the executive's watch dog against any attempt by parliament to recover its old power to harass the government, and it has assiduously done so. Nevertheless, usage has undermined a number of the new rules of parliamentary procedure, notably in the failure to restrict either the reading of speeches or their length, or to check on attendance and make salary deductions for absenteeism. The attempt was made to replace the traditional practice of 'interpellation' – a question that is debated and concludes with a vote of confidence – by the innocuous House of Commons' device of the private member's motion and by oral questions. Since 1974 some three hundred 'questions to the government' are put each year on Wednesdays, without advance notice, when parliament is in session, the time being divided equally between deputies of the majority and of the Opposition. (All ministers are present, Wednesday being the day on which the Cabinet meets.) To call them 'questions' is something of a misnomer, as they consist of a speech by the questioner to which the minister replies with a speech. 'Oral questions without debate' are dealt with on Fridays (when most deputies are in their constituencies), allowing two minutes each to the questioner and the minister, followed by five minutes each for supplementary comments on both sides. Written questions, directed most frequently at the minister of finance, were in use before the establishment of the Fifth Republic and have increased in importance as a source of information, especially when parliament is not in session. They are increasingly popular (the distribution between ministries being indicated in Table 13), the number climbing from 3,506 in 1959 to 12,617 in 1977. Although they are supposed to receive a reply within a month, this seldom happens and in 1977, 41 per cent of written questions had to wait for over three months for a reply.

Finally, in the matter of restraints on parliament's legislative power, by Article 45 of the Constitution the government has secured the means to break a deadlock between the Assembly and the Senate by supporting the Assembly version or by using the Senate to block the wishes of the Assembly when these conflict with the government's will. Under the Fourth Republic, the Assembly insisted on the last word only in 1 per cent of bills between 1954 and 1958. Despite the fact that the Senate was controlled by the government's opponents, from 1958–68 the two chambers were able to agree on 96 per cent of the 829 acts of parliament passed. Of the seventy-eight bills (9 per cent) that went to a conference committee of the two chambers (seven members from each) in that period, agreement was reached in forty-five cases, leaving only thirty-three disputed bills in which the government imposed the Assembly version. Of these, twenty-one bills only met with Senate opposition because the

*Table 13*
*Ministries replying to written questions in the National Assembly, 1969–79* (%)

| Ministry | 1969 | 1974 | 1979 |
|---|---|---|---|
| Finance | 24 | 16 | 17 |
| Health | 5 | 10 | 14 |
| Education | 12 | 12 | 12 |
| Agriculture | 7 | 7 | 6 |
| Interior | 5 | 6 | 6 |
| Labour | 1 | 8 | 5 |
| Transport | 2 | 1 | 5 |

Source: Based on P. N. Huu, 'L'Evolution des questions parlementaires depuis 1958' in *Revue française de science politique*, xxxi/i, February 1981, p. 174. Only ministries replying to at least 5 per cent of questions in 1979 have been included.

government refused to accept *some* of the Senate amendments (for example, the Agriculture Guidelines Act of 1960, the Finance Acts of 1962 and 1966, the 1964 Broadcasting Act) or had insisted on an *en bloc*, unamended approval. This left twelve bills (notably three on the atomic programme in 1960, 1962 and 1964, the 1963 creation of a State Security Court, the 1967 Act authorizing the government to reform the social security system by ordinance, and the 1968 Act ratifying these ordinances) on which the Senate felt it had to express its total disapproval. The Senate had always acted expeditiously in considering bills from the Assembly and delays that have occurred in implementing the acts, often passed in a few days, are due to the slowness with which the necessary detailed decrees are issued. The July 1966 Act on the health insurance of the self-employed, voted in twenty days, took two and a half years to be implemented by decree and was then the cause of a violent series of demonstrations by those affected, necessitating a new Act in 1969.

The Pompidou presidency marked a transition between the senaticidal hostility of the de Gaulle presidency – culminating in his resignation following the defeat of the referendum proposal to amalgamate the Senate with the Economic and Social Council – and the harmonious benevolence of the Giscard presidency. The centrist majority in the Senate, even though there was no UDF parliamentary party as such, reflected the presidential views far more accurately than the UDR/RPR-weighted majority in the National Assembly. Whereas under the Pompi dou presidency 85 per cent of bills were approved without convening a conference committee, 11 per cent being agreed after one and 3 per cent being finally decided by the Assembly alone, from 1974-80 bills approved without a joint committee fell to 79 per cent, those agreed after one rose to 20 per cent, and only in less than 1 per cent of bills did the Assembly have the last word.[33] This period of harmony was rudely disrupted by the election of a reforming Socialist majority in the Assembly, the Senate feeling itself to be an encircled bastion of the Opposition. The Bill to reform regional and local government met all-out opposition from the Senate, which virtually sought to replace the Defferre proposals with an entirely different Bill. Its failure did not deter the Senate from taking an equally intransigent line over the Mauroy Government's nationalization proposals. Use was made of the senators' right to refer what they regard as unconstitutional proposals to the Constitutional Council, but though the Nationalization Bill was delayed and the cost of compensation increased, the government's Bill went through. In 1982 an increasing number of government bills were purely and simply rejected by the Senate. Even during the amicable Giscardian period, the Government was often inclined to require the Senate to consider bills as a matter of urgency and the Assembly did not consider all the Senate's amendments. Only those which its seven representatives on the conference committee select are included in the final draft to be ratified. It is to be expected that such practices will continue to be resorted to frequently.

The constitutional rules (Article 49) enforcing government accountability to parliament are based upon the presumption* that the Assembly majority will be precarious and needs to be bolstered up by procedural devices. The main one is the provision that the government is deemed to have retained the Assembly's confidence unless a censure motion is carried by an absolute majority. The same is true, paradoxically, when the government makes the adoption of a bill an issue of confidence. This device was frequently used (thirty-four times by the fifteen-month Mollet Government of 1956-7 and twenty-three

---

* An exception arises when the prime minister, usually on assuming office, seeks approval of the government's programme or of a general declaration of policy, when a simple plurality is necessary.

times by the ephemeral forty-day Edgar Faure Government of 1952) to secure a debate, reject hostile amendments and carry a bill under the Fourth Republic. Under the Fifth Republic only opponents vote on censure and confidence motions. From its parliamentary supporters, the government does not seek explicit, positive confidence but implicit, negative acquiescence. This helped the Government, which in 1967–8 had only a tiny majority in the Assembly, to survive thanks to a procedural device that counted all non-hostile votes as tacit votes of support. This draconian safeguard has been superfluous throughout most of the Fifth Republic because stable Governments have been supported by a loyal majority in the Assembly. There has been a polarization of the inconsistent government supporters (which amounted to over half the deputies until the 1962 dissolution of the Assembly following the defeat of the Pompidou Government by a vote of censure) into the rival blocks of a majority of consistent supporters and a minority of consistent opponents. The 1981 election gave the Socialist-Communist coalition a more than two to one majority in the National Assembly (327 to 150 in 1982), though it was in a clear minority in the Senate (105 to 186).

Parliament's role in amending the Constitution (under Article 89) has been curtailed by requiring that the proposed amendment must either be passed by both the Assembly and the Senate before being approved by a referendum (the most difficult procedure and not used), or by both chambers meeting jointly and carrying it by a three-fifths majority. (Characteristically, the latter procedure applies only to constitutional amendments proposed by the government.) However, anticipation of senatorial opposition led de Gaulle twice to adopt a third, unconstitutional, method of amendment by referendum alone, invoking Article 11 concerned with 'the organization of the public authorities'. After his success in 1962 on the issue of the popular election of the president of the republic, de Gaulle sought to repeat his feat in April 1969. It resulted in defeat and resignation. This result makes recourse to Article 11, bypassing parliament, unlikely as a method of constitutional amendment in future. Furthermore, it restored the prestige of the Senate, opinion polls showing that, in February 1969, 38 per cent wanted a more important role for the Senate, 27 per cent a retention of the status quo, and only 7 per cent a reduced role, with 28 per cent not replying. The Chaban-Delmas Government fully reintegrated the Senate into the legislative process after a prolonged period of ministerial boycott in the 1960s. While the composition of the Senate may be made more representative of urban areas, its basic features and functions are likely to remain unchanged by the Socialist majority in the 1980s.

Domestic policy-making in France was, until the Fifth Republic, closely linked with legislation. However, the decline of laws or acts of parliament in favour of executive decisions, associated with the subordination of law-making itself to the government, has made it unrealistic to expect parliament to recover more than a fraction of its old power and prestige. We have seen that there has been an increasing tendency for the government to negotiate directly with the interest groups, the subsequent settlement being sanctioned by the prime minister or president. Because 'both the integration of interests and the legitimization of policy decisions now take place outside parliament',[34] the interest groups have partially displaced the political parties as the representative mediators between the people and the government, which has successfully acquired a quasi-monopoly of formal policy-making. However, the May 1968 crisis demonstrated that to avoid the accumulation and explosion of public grievances, parliamentary representatives may provide the 'feedback' that is indispensable to long-term political stability. It indicated the dangers of provoking extra-parliamentary opposition when proper opportunities are denied for the parliamentary expression of opposition. Unlike its predecessors, the left-wing parliamentary majority elected in 1981 is less inclined to leave the political and technobureaucratic executives to manage as best they can with the inadequate mediation of the interest group élite.

# 4 Making and Implementing Government Policy

*The political executive*

Before Pompidou succeeded de Gaulle as president of the re-public, anyone who had predicted that the new president would not merely maintain but accentuate the subordination of the prime minister to him would have been regarded as indulging in eccentric humour. Mitterrand equally surprised everyone by his uninhibited readiness to exert his presidential powers to the full. 'The institutions were not designed with me in mind. But they suit me' was the way he ironically put it.[1]

Between 1944 and 1946, before the Fourth Republic was established, de Gaulle was both president and prime minister, so there was no problem of ensuring that the two leaders of the political executive worked in harmony. Thereafter, until his return to power in 1958, it was the premier, responsible to parliament and not the head of state who was in control of government. Clemenceau expressed the traditional Jacobin standpoint when he declared: 'There are two things in the world for which I have never seen any use: the prostate gland and the president of the republic'; but the extreme left-wing champions of the view that the president of the republic should be reduced to a figurehead did not get their way under the Fourth Re-public. Vincent Auriol (president from 1947 to 1954) used his constitutional position to the full. Through his selection of the prime minister, his chairmanship of the council of ministers and his intervention particularly in foreign, defence, colonial and judicial matters, he preserved the regime from the Communists and Gaullists, provoking the latter into criticizing him for exceeding his powers. Auriol's successor, Coty, legalized the transition from the Fourth to the Fifth Republic by inviting de Gaulle to form a government in May 1958 and threatening parliament with his resignation if it did not approve of his nominee for the premiership. De Gaulle himself frequently used the threat of resignation to get his way, until April 1969 when it led to his downfall.

At the outset of the Fifth Republic, the allocation of responsibilities within the bicephalous executive was declared by Chaban-Delmas to be between the president's exclusive policy sectors of foreign, defence and post-colonial affairs, deriving from his supreme responsibility as protector of national integrity and independence on the one hand and the mass of mundane, domestic political concerns on the other. The latter were the subordinate responsibility of the prime minister who, in conjunction with the other ministers, prepared, co-ordinated and implemented policy decisions. The president intervened only when a matter impinged on his own sphere (for example the cost of defence) or had assumed crisis proportions (his refusal to devalue the currency in 1968). This distinction corresponded to the 'ontological one between the interests of France and the concerns of Frenchmen'.[2] It was reflected in the long tenure of office by Maurice Couve de Murville (foreign affairs) and Pierre Messmer (defence) and the fact that matters within this exclusive presidential sector were not discussed in Cabinet, which merely heard statements from those responsible for carrying out the president's orders.

However, although de Gaulle was content to reign rather than rule over large areas of public policy, he had made it clear that he did not accept any such limitation as was implied by the notion of an exclusive presidential sector. At his press conference of 31 January 1964 he asserted that 'the indivisible authority of the state is completely delegated to the president by the people who elected him' and in his *Memoirs of Hope* he contrasted 'the supreme office of head of state, responsible for the fate of the nation ... and the secondary role of the prime minister, whose function it is to run the executive, to direct current policy and to deal with day-to-day contingencies'. His claim to supreme and uncircumscribed power was defended by Prime Minister Pompidou in an Assembly debate in April 1964 at which this interpretation of the Constitution was challenged by Mitterrand. Pompidou admitted that there had been an 'evolution' since 1958 in the role of the president (notably since the 1962 constitutional amendment providing for the direct election of the president by the people), but reminded the Assembly that as early as 1946 de Gaulle had proclaimed at Bayeaux that 'executive power should emanate from the head of state'. He presented the relationship of president and prime minister as one based upon 'a close identity of views', policy being decided jointly between them and then discussed with the whole government.[3] When he succeeded to the presidency some five years later, Pompidou proceeded to assert in his own right the presidential pre-eminence he had attributed to de Gaulle. He preserved all the president's prerogatives. The relationship with the prime minister established by his predecessor, which as premier he had formulated as 'to the president of the republic the major policy decisions, to the prime minister the price of milk', was accepted as normal.

After six months in which the new president, with characteristic caution, took a grip on the situation, Pompidou bluntly reasserted the primacy of presidential power: 'I have conducted the affairs of France with the help of the prime minister and government I appointed. My first decision was to devalue.' From 1969–72 Chaban-Delmas accepted the Pompidou interpretation of their relationship, denying that his 1959 conception of a presidential sector was intended to be more than a provisional assessment of a situation that was bound to change. In January 1970 he put it thus:

Our constitution has an Achilles heel. This weakness can be summarized as the requirement of close, almost intimate relations between the president of the republic and the prime minister, between whom mutual trust must be complete ... [The latter's] subordination should not be rigorous or rigid. ... They must work together, it being understood that the final decision lies with the head of state ...

The conservative parliamentary majority being mainly concerned with the preservation of the status quo, the policy embodied by President Pompidou was hostile to the 'new society' programme of Chaban-Delmas. The latter was forced in June 1970 to acknowledge that it was the programme put forward by the successful presidential candidate, legitimized by popular vote, that authorized the president to 'give directives to the government, which was responsible for carrying them out'. On the same day, President Pompidou lauded the fact that France was 'a strong state, where the authority of the president of the republic, elected by universal suffrage, guarantees the stability of governments and the unity of leadership'.

What was less expected was that François Mitterrand, who in his 1964 debate with Pompidou had stoutly defended an interpretation of the Constitution that favoured the prime minister who was responsible to the Assembly as head of the executive, should by 1981, when he was elected president, adopt a 'Gaullist' conception of his office. Some six weeks after taking office, he asserted 'I will exercise in all their plenitude the powers conferred on me by the constitution. Neither more nor less. Both the government and I know the meaning of the tenth of May'; while a year later he asserted that, as far as the work of government was concerned, 'I have not only approved but willed it and I am fundementally responsible for it.'[4] Since the direct election of the president – and Mitterrand had already made this clear in the way he conducted the 1965 presidential campaign, his personal policy choices and proposals becoming the basis for future government action – his political supremacy, sanctified by the legitimacy conferred by universal suffrage, was a fact. Whereas Gaston Defferre abandoned his presidential candidature in 1965 because he failed to secure formal party support, Mitterrand had managed without it, going as far – ten years later, after his election as the Socialist Party's first secretary in 1971 and his second presidential candidature in 1974 – to declare: 'The PS is not a party. It is a radiance (sic) linked to my person.'[5] In a debate with Chaban-Delmas, one of the rival presidential candidates in 1974, Mitterrand made clear that he accepted that the president had become what in 1978 he was to describe as 'the absolute master of all the decisions of the executive power'. As early as 1974 he said of the president: 'I wish him to keep all his authority so that he can guide France on matters of major concern', though he immediately added: 'But I donot want him to replace all the institutions or all the citizens.'[6]

By the time of the 1981 campaign, it was categorically asserted and accepted that it was Mitterrand's programme, not that of the Socialist Party, that constituted the 'charter' of the future Mauroy Government. Mitterrand had also made clear, as early as the 1974 election, the basis on which he would select his prime minister and government: 'I will choose him from among the Socialist deputies, from the members of my parliamentary group. I need a man in whom I have friendly confidence, the certainty of his competence, as well as being exactly on the same wavelength. . . . Afterwards the government will be formed, as Pompidou put it, to reflect the presidential majority.'[7] This was, of course, exactly what happened in 1981, even to the point, as he declared in 1965, that he would appoint an interim government after dissolving the National Assembly, although in fact he took these two steps in the reverse order![8] The continuity in perception of the presidential role, at a time when there was so striking a discontinuity in the holder of the office, should not lead us to overlook the fact that by dissolving the Assembly Mitterrand achieved the objective, fixed by that ardent opponent of presidentialism Pierre Mendès France in *A Modern French Republic*, of securing a coincidence of view between the legislative and the executive. This was made possible by the left winning control of the presidency before it won control of the Assembly, so that the prime minister could simultaneously be responsible to both president and the Assembly.

The extent to which the French public have tended to identify the president and the prime minister is shown by the convergence and divergence in their popularity since 1959.[9] In a first phase (1959–63) the president's overwhelming superiority in public esteem was indicated by an average gap of 29 per cent between his standing and that of the prime minister. This was the period when de Gaulle was moving towards an Algerian settlement, followed by his triumph over parliamentary opposition to the direct election of the president. Once the spotlight shifted from ending military entanglements and institutional reform to domestic, social and economic policy, President de Gaulle's popularity declined. The spring 1963 sharp fall in presidential popularity followed the failure of de Gaulle's personal 'requisition order' to force striking miners to return to work. As the president rather than the prime minister was personally blamed for the unsuccessful and authoritarian conflict with the coal miners, the gap between their respective popularities fell from 32 per cent in autumn 1962 to 17 per cent in spring 1963. This second phase lasted from 1963 until spring 1967, via the 'desacralization' of de Gaulle at the December 1965 presidential election when he was forced to a second ballot. Over this period, the average gap in popularity between president and prime minister fell from 29 per cent to 16 per cent. The third phase does not begin, as one might expect, with the May 1968 events. The further decline in the president's popularity started in the latter half of 1967, the gap falling to 13·5 per cent. The very narrow victory in the March 1967 general election, the rise in unemployment and unpopular social security reforms were factors that foreshadowed the May 1968 events via a decline in the president's popularity. From autumn 1967 to spring 1969, when he resigned, de Gaulle's popularity remained at 55–6 per cent but the gap with the prime minister narrowed to 9·5 per cent in the year before his departure, owing to an improvement in the premier's standing. When former prime minister Pompidou became president in 1969, the gap at first narrowed further in 1970 to 3 per cent, the responsibility for the acts of the political executive being attributed almost equally to president and premier, but in 1972 the gap reopened following Prime Minister Chaban-Delmas' fall from public favour when it was revealed that he had managed to avoid paying income tax for a number of years. This reopening of the gap heralded the prime minister's dismissal in July 1972 and his replacement by Pierre Messmer.

The period of the Giscard–Barre presidential–prime ministerial tandem, which endured from 1976 until the presidential election of 1981, provides an excellent opportunity to observe how the institutional duality of the French political executive was received by public opinion.

Though at the beginning of 1977 – shortly after Barre took office – his rating was close to that of Giscard, the number of the discontented quickly exceeded the satisfied by margins far in excess of the president's rating. Thus in May 1977, Barre's 'deficit' was 16 per cent as against Giscard's 6 per cent and the dissatisfied consistently exceeded the contented right up to the 1978 general election (3 per cent in February), falling briefly below the contented in April, only to recommence the ascent to new heights of unpopularity. In September 1978 and June 1979 Barre's 'deficit' was 29 per cent, whereas Giscard had a 'surplus' of 12 per cent and 4 per cent. By the time the president had plummeted to a 4 per cent 'deficit' in September 1979, dissatisfaction with the prime minister had reached the record deficit for the fifth republic of 31 per cent (57 per cent dissatisfied as against 26 per cent satisfied)! If one takes the average quarterly figures, the popularity gap between president and prime minister significantly widened. In 1977 they were 4, 5, 7 and 11 per cent; in 1978 they increased to 11, 15, 19 and 16; modestly continuing this late 1978 reversal in early 1979 with percentages of 15 and 14.[10]

Though there was some subsequent relative recovery for Prime Minister Barre in the run up to the 1981 presidential election, the gap narrowing to an average 13 per cent in 1979–80 and 12 per cent between September 1980 and April 1981, this owed more to a loss of support by President Giscard than any gain in popularity by Barre. The failure of the president to replace his prime minister before the 1981 presidential election meant that he could not shift on to the shoulders of his anti-populist prime minister the blame for the rising unemployment they had been unable to prevent. The early months of the Mitterrand presidency were marked by an unprecedented situation: the prime minister was slightly but consistently more popular than the president.[11] This was undoubtedly in part due to the personality of Pierre Mauroy, whose down-to-earth geniality contrasted strongly with his deliberately anti-populist predecessor. His 'social democratic' image appealed especially to right-wing voters. However, this disparity also reflected the willingness of President Mitterrand to allow his prime minister to act as the leader of the Socialist majority in the National Assembly and the head of the government, whilst making it clear that ultimate control remained firmly in his own hands. By 1982, the normal pattern had re-emerged, Mitterrand being more popular than Mauroy, though for both the honeymoon period had ended, the disatisfied exceeding the satisfied.

Even though the annual presidential postbag of 250,000 letters suggests that the French public looks to him to solve their problems, there is a danger of overemphasizing the 'presidential' character of the Fifth Republic, just as there is a danger of exaggerating a trend towards party government, associated with the emergence of a majority party or stable majority coalition of parties in the Assembly. A dominant president and a dominant party, respectively controlling the executive and the legislature, with the latter loyal to the former, are essential to the smooth working of a hybrid type of political regime like the Fifth Republic. However, the prime minister has a key role in maintaining agreement between the president, government and party coalition in the Assembly. Giscard, who had criticized de Gaulle's 'solitary exercise of power', claimed in a television interview in November 1975 that he had no desire to govern France on his own. This was prudent in a perverse country where, he acknowledged in characteristically sour fashion, 'Many of the French believe that for France to be in good health, all that is needed is a good president and, naturally, the good president is the one they do not have'. At the start of his seven-year term, his successor has been able to exert the power of the presidency in uninhibited fashion because he has enjoyed the support, not merely of a loyal prime minister and an Assembly majority but also of public opinion.

*The president of the republic*

The president's dominant position, from a constitutional standpoint, has been based upon eight traditional presidential powers (most of which have been transformed from formal into real powers) and seven prerogative powers, not requiring ministerial countersignature and made on his own nonaccountability (barring an unlikely impeachment for high treason). His prerogative powers are:

(1) The appointment and dismissal of the prime minister, dismissal not being stipulated in Article 8 but assumed by de Gaulle when he secured the resignation of both Debré in 1962 and Pompidou in 1968 when neither had been defeated in the Assembly, and when he retained Pompidou in 1962 despite his defeat. As president, Pompidou dismissed an undefeated Chaban-Delmas in 1972.

(2) The right to send messages to parliament, which was used in October 1962 to announce the referendum on the election of the president by universal suffrage.

(3) The right to call a referendum on nonconstitutional modifications of the organization of government or for the ratification of treaties, nominally at the 'request' of government or

parliament. Article 11 was invoked illegally in 1962 and 1969 because the constitutional procedure (Article 89) gave either parliamentary chamber veto power.

(4) The right, with certain restrictions, to dissolve the Assembly (Article 12) which was decisively used in 1962, 1968 and 1981.

(5) The right to nominate one-third (including the president) of the Constitutional Council and to refer matters to it (which has been left to the prime minister). President Mitterrand chose a former general secretary of the Socialist party (1944–6) and president of the League of Human Rights (1958–75), Daniel Mayer, as president of the Council in 1983.

(6) He assumes emergency powers under Article 16 of the Constitution when he considers that there is a serious and immediate threat to political institutions *or* national independence *or* territorial integrity *or* the implementation of the country's international commitments *and* the normal working of constitutional government and administration is upset. The president takes 'whatever measures are required by the circumstances' for as long as required to meet the crisis. Foreign or civil war are the circumstances envisaged and Article 16 was invoked during the April 1961 Algerian 'generals' insurrection. The revolt collapsed within a week but de Gaulle retained emergency powers for over five months.

(7) On the basis of Article 15 designating the president head of the armed forces, a 1964 decree gave him the sole and awesome right to decide on the use of France's strategic nuclear force.

The traditional powers of the presidency, which de Gaulle and his successors have extended to the point of universal oversight of policy, are:

(1) The appointment and dismissal of ministers, nominally at the prime minister's request.

(2) The president is chairman of the Council of Ministers, which is now the effective Cabinet. Its decisions are prepared by three types of interministerial meetings, the most important of which, the interministerial councils, meet at the Elysée under his chairmanship.*

(3) The president promulgates statutes, signs all ordinances

* See below, pp. 116–17.

and some decrees and can refuse or delay signing provided the
government is willing to accept responsibility for his actions.

(4) Under Article 52, the president is empowered to negotiate and ratify treaties and has directly controlled foreign policy
and diplomatic dealings, notably in breaking off EEC negotiations with Britain in 1966, agreeing to resume them in 1970 and
bringing them to a successful conclusion in 1971.

(5) He is commander-in-chief of the armed forces and presides over the national defence committee. Mitterrand, for example, has asserted his 'wish to control directly and personally
everything affecting the country's security'.[12]

(6) The president appoints to a wide range of senior judicial,
administrative and military posts, including councillors of state
and judges, ambassadors and senior officers, commissioners of
the republic and rectors (who control the field services of the
ministry of education), the divisional heads of ministries and
the heads of certain nationalized industries. In the six months
following the election of Mitterrand to the presidency, a
hundred of the six hundred posts in this category changed hands
(not counting the new appointments arising from the banks and
firms nationalized in early 1982) giving rise to 'spoils system'
criticisms of an *Etat PS* following earlier criticisms of an *Etat-
Giscard*.[13]

(7) The president is 'protector of the independence of the
judicial authority' (Article 64), appoints and presides over the
higher council of the judiciary and exercises the right of reprieve. (The higher council advises the president on his use of
the power to reprieve and on senior judicial appointments.)
Pompidou as prime minister persuaded de Gaulle to reprieve
General Jouhaud, sentenced to death for his part in the 1961
'generals' insurrection, by threatening to resign. As president,
Pompidou reprieved all those sentenced to death until his November 1972 decision to send two men to the guillotine. Mitterrand appointed Robert Badinter (like him an ardent abolition-
ist) as minister of justice with the result that the death penalty
and the guillotine were consigned to the chamber of horrors as
an early priority of the Socialist government in 1981.

(8) The president can initiate an amendment to the Constitution at the 'request' and with the countersignature of the
prime minister. If he chooses, he can submit such an amend-

ment, after it has been carried in both chambers, to a joint session of parliament where a three-fifths majority renders a referendum unnecessary. Constitutional amendments of parliamentary origin must go to referendum, a procedure unpopular with parliamentarians and therefore unlikely to be used, leaving the initiative in the hands of the president.

To help the president discharge these wide-ranging responsibilities, there is a small president's office which has often been regarded (owing to journalistic exaggeration) as the real government. The official ministers are in charge of day-to-day administration and the preparation of proposals whose fate will ultimately be settled by the president, who frequently relies on the privy counsel of his own personal collaborators. This has inspired the savage dictum that France, like Britain, has a 'shadow cabinet' but in her case it is in office.

The key figure in the 'court politics' revolving around the president's office (consisting of thirty-four civilian and eight military staff) who sees the president frequently each day, is the head of the general secretariat. Unlike his predecessors under the Fifth Republic, Pierre Bérégovoy – Mitterrand's first choice – was not a senior civil servant or the graduate of a *grande école*. He exemplifies the major contrast between Mitterrand's presidential staff and that of his predecessors: they are a predominantly partisan team, many of whom worked for years with Mitterrand in the Socialist Party. Whereas 90 per cent of de Gaulle's *entourage* and 89 per cent of Giscard's staff were senior officials, in Mitterrand's case it is one-third. On Bérégovoy's appointment as minister for social affairs and national solidarity in 1982, he was replaced by Jean-Louis Bianco, a senior civil servant with close ties to the Socialist Party although not formally a member. The secretary-general to the presidency is the president's main link with the prime minister, being present at their regular meetings each Tuesday morning and at their brief chat just before the Wednesday Cabinet meeting. He is one of two non-ministers who attends Cabinet (the other being Jacques Attali, who became responsible in 1982 for summarizing Cabinet proceedings for the press), whose agenda he prepared with the secretary-general to the government, attached to the prime minister. The President's secretary-general has under his direct authority twenty-three people, of whom the most imme-

diate are an assistant secretary-general, the president's spokesman, his constitutional adviser and press attaché. There are
twelve functionally specialized advisers who report to the president through the secretary-general. In 1982 they dealt with
African affairs (particularly France's former colonies there, Guy
Penne acting as the president's personal emissary); bilateral
diplomatic agreements; the international economy; the French
economy and planning; industry and nationalization; energy;
computers; small-scale business; agriculture; health and social
security; justice; relations with parliament. There were seven
*chargés de mission*, of somewhat lower status, dealing with: relations with parliament; industrial relations and women; culture
(two old personal friends of Mitterrand); education; Third
World affairs; repatriates (mainly a legacy of France's Algerian
past). Most of these members of the office, who have a hectic
seventy-hour work week, do not enjoy personal access to the
president, sending their reports to him through the secretary-
general.[14]

Two other important parts of the office are headed by men
directly responsible to the president. Firstly, there is the director
of his private office, who – with a staff of six – in addition to
managing the Elysée palace (known familiarly as the '*château*')
deals with nominations to and the reform of state radio and
television, as well as links with private big business. Secondly,
there is his special advisor, Jacques Attali, who for many years
has been Mitterrand's 'ideas man', especially in the national
and international economic sphere. He has the task of reflecting
on the medium and long-term problems, such as new technology
or the structural causes of inflation, all too often neglected by
politicians preoccupied with immediate issues, as well as preparing the president's position for international summits involving European, industrialized or 'North–South' countries. However, the president also keeps in close touch with the leaders of
the Socialist Party who are not members of the government: the
first secretary, Lionel Jospin – his personal choice for the office
– and the leader of the Socialist parliamentary group, Pierre
Joxe. These two attend the regular Wednesday lunch at which
the prime minister and secretary-general of the presidency are
also present.

Even less than his predecessors does Mitterrand allow his

personal staff to stand between him and the members of the government, particularly those who run the key ministries or have close personal ties with him. While only the prime minister is seen at a regular time, he has meetings with the ministers of the interior, finance and foreign affairs at least once a week. He is less inclined than his presidential predecessors to deal directly with senior civil servants, leaving it to his staff to work with members of a particular minister's private office or even by-pass them by going directly to the official dealing with the problem. It is a rule that the president's staff do not rely exclusively upon the recommendations of the minister concerned or his private office. This is one of the reasons why the president's staff has, in the past, consisted predominantly of senior civil servants, able to call upon an 'old boy' network with whom they can check the proposals coming from the minister. One of the problems of a Socialist presidency has been that with a president and prime minister who have not come through the *grandes écoles* and with staffs that include far fewer members of the *grands corps*, it has been more difficult to secure smooth collaboration among their advisers and between them and the rest of the political and bureaucratic executive.

To ridicule the accusation that he had exercised presidential power in a 'personal' and 'solitary' fashion, de Gaulle, at his September 1965 press conference, reviewing his first seven-year term and preparing his re-election, gave a statistical summary of his numerous political contacts in the libidinous tone of Leporello's catalogue song in *Don Giovanni*. He had convened the Cabinet 302 times and interministerial councils 420 times. He had received the prime minister 505 times and other ministers 2,000 times. He had seen the presidents of both chambers of parliament 78 times, the chairmen or *rapporteurs* of parliamentary committees or party groups over 100 times and senior civil servants and interest group leaders some 1,500 times! Giscard's non-ministerial contacts in 1975 involved about 200 people, of whom 24 per cent were politicians, 22 per cent were civil servants, 13 per cent trade union officials and 11 per cent businessmen, without counting meetings with foreign statesmen and ambassadors.[15] Mitterrand likewise receives many visitors. Whatever the temptation to exaggerate the influence of the president's inner circle and without denying that occasionally particular advisers have exerted great influence, this is very much the exception rather than the rule, especially on major policy matters. It is with his ministers, particularly his prime minister, that the president usually takes his decisions.

## *The prime minister*

Although after 1820 the premiership was occasionally separated from other governmental posts, it is only since 1934, when the nucleus of a prime minister's office was established at the Hôtel Matignon, that it has become customary for the premier to hold no other office. The transition lasted throughout the Fourth Republic, when four premiers were also foreign minister, three finance minister, two minister of defence and two minister of the interior. It is only since the inauguration of the Fifth Republic that the prime minister has clearly emerged as the minister who, under the president and as long as he retains his confidence, is in undisputed control of the government. However, he still has to reckon with the finance minister, who can challenge the prime minister's control and overall co-ordination of government policy. In 1952, Pinay refused Edgar Faure's offer of the finance portfolio on the grounds that the office should be held jointly with the premiership. When he became premier forty days later, he combined the two offices. His conflicts, as minister of finance in 1959, with the president and prime minister led to a paralysing period of 'work to rule' and to his replacement in January 1960. In fact, the main architect of the so-called 'Pinay-Rueff Plan', involving the devaluation of the franc and the abolition of farm price indexation, to which so much of the credit for the success of economic policy at the start of the Fifth Republic has been attributed, was de Gaulle's economic adviser Roger Goetze. A former director of the budget division within the finance ministry, Goetze was able to work closely with it and impose, thanks to the president's support, policies to which Finance Minister Pinay was adamantly opposed.[16] In 1962 the prime minister was strengthened by the transfer of the Planning Commissariat from the minister of finance. To reduce conflicts, it would also be necessary to transfer the key budget division from the finance ministry to the prime minister but this might be regarded as making him too powerful for the president's comfort. President Mitterrand, for example, ensured that there was, under the finance minister's authority, a separate minister of the budget in the Mauroy Government, Laurent Fabius, who was personally loyal to him, which enabled the president to be informed from the inside of conflict between his prime minister and his finance minister, for conflicts there have been. As we shall see, the prime minister lost control of planning in 1981 when a minister of national and regional planning was appointed in the rather numerous Mauroy Government.

During the early years of the Pompidou presidency, the energetic Chaban-Delmas exerted himself to increase the power of the premiership, which had suffered an eclipse under Couve de Murville, a passive and impassive tool of the presidential will. The main instruments of the prime minister's resolute effort from 1969 to 1972 to mobilize the government for the fulfilment of his 'new society' programme were the two parts of the prime minister's office: the general secretariat of the government and his personal staff. The former, inspired by the British Cabinet office, has the vital task of co-ordinating the heterogeneous and proliferating responsibilities accumulated by the prime minister under successive republics. Its staff of about thirty prepares and circulates the agenda of the Cabinet and the various interministerial committees, together with relevant documents, for example draft bills or decrees, preparing notes for the prime minister alone, informing him about the matters that are to be discussed. The secretary-general attends Cabinet meetings and keeps its minutes, notifying all concerned of the decisions taken. Those who have to carry them out are required to send him copies of all their instructions so that his staff can follow up the implementation of Cabinet decisions for the prime minister. All draft legislation and decrees must be sent to the secretariat who check that all concerned have been consulted. The secretary-general consults the Council of State (and occasionally the Economic and Social Council) before sending the proposals to all ministers prior to the Cabinet meeting which will examine them. The secretariat makes the necessary arrangements with parliament each week for discussion of the government's legislative programme and receives the bills passed so that they can be signed by the president. It also arranges for written and oral parliamentary questions to be answered. Finally, it collects and publishes a large amount of information, a task fulfilled by the central office of information in Britain.

Under President Giscard, the government's programme was formally fixed at six-monthly intervals by public *lettres directives* to the prime minister. However, this is misleading if one does not bear in mind that the programme was first worked out by the secretary-general to the government with the prime minister, so that the prime minister had a major hand in drafting his 'orders'. Consequently, while the procedure ostentatiously appeared to emphasize the primordial role of the president in setting the policy guidelines, the practice was less presidential. Mitterrand has discontinued the procedure and has allowed the prime minister to announce the government's half-yearly programme of action, which in February 1982 was drafted jointly by the director of the prime minister's personal staff and the assistant secretary-general at the presidency.

The first year of Mitterrand's presidency was characterized by the closest political duumvirate at the head of the executive that the Fifth Republic had yet witnessed. For, despite the rivalry between their teams of personal advisers, which seems to be endemic to the Fifth Republic, they had the advantage of a decade (1971-81) during which they, for the most part, worked closely together inside the Socialist Party leadership as first secretary and second-in-command. They were able to transpose a party government tandem into an arrangement for the smooth running of the French state. Compromise came easily to them as they shared the same partisan wavelength. While the prime minister stayed close to the president's electoral commitments, the president preferred to leave many day-to-day matters to be settled by the prime minister, discouraging most ministers (but not the finance minister, Jacques Delors) from appealing against his decisions. It has been estimated that some 90 per cent of conflicts are settled by the prime minister. If the president becomes involved, the decision is taken at their weekly Tuesday working breakfast or by telephone.[17] However, economic, foreign and defence policies have usually involved the president and his staff closely, so it is important to maintain harmonious relations with the prime minister and his staff.

Prime Minister Mauroy's personal staff is large, even bigger than that of the reforming Chaban-Delmas, numbering over fifty official members and many more unofficial members. Because both his staff and that of President Mitterrand include fewer members of the senior civil service, they often do not enjoy the 'old boy network' links that customarily facilitate the close collaboration that is indispensable. Furthermore, Mauroy's staff itself is divided between those like Michel Delebarre, who has been director of his *Nord* regional council staff and secretary-general of Lille municipality preserving his links with his power base; those like Marie-Jo Pontillon and Roger Fajardie, who provide links with the Socialist Party organization in general and his faction in particular; and those like Robert Lion, director of his staff until 1982, and Bernard Brunhes, his adviser on social and industrial relations matters, who represent the traditional senior civil servant 'specialists'. Despite herculean attempts by the secretary-general of the government and the director of the prime minister's staff to coordinate and monitor the work of the prime minister's office, it has acquired a reputation for disorder. In part, this was due to the cracking pace imposed by the desire to fulfil electoral promises as quickly as possible; in part to the difficulty of working in cramped conditions, the Hôtel Matignon not being suitable to accommodate the large numbers crammed into it. However, the main problem would appear to be Prime Minister Mauroy's preference for interminably talking about problems rather than resolving them and an allergy to reading written reports. The result has been a dramatic 50 per cent increase in the number of interministerial meetings chaired by the prime minister, which had already grown remarkably during the Giscard presidency at the expense of the interministerial councils, chaired by the president. In part this reflects the increasing role of the prime minister – particularly since Chaban-Delmas' premiership – at the expense of most of the other ministers, a tendency that has led to collisions with the finance minister, unaccustomed to being subordinated to the prime minister in practice.

To ease the burden on the prime minister, whilst allowing him to retain an oversight of certain especially sensitive or residual areas of responsibility, he delegates a number of his functions to two junior and three senior ministers attached to him. The latter are the minister delegate for relations with parliament, the civil service minister who supervises the embryo civil service department created in 1945 to unify and manage the public service, and lastly the minister for women's rights. Of the two junior ministers attached to the prime minister in the Mauroy Government, Jean Le Garrec was particularly important, partly because he was close to Mauroy politically and personally, partly because of his responsibility for the extension of the public sector, a subject to which we shall return in chapter 7.

The prime minister's ability to exert occult as well as overt influence is exemplified by having at his disposal 'special funds', which in 1982 amounted to 31 million francs, officially intended to finance secret service activities. However, a former minister of President Pompidou estimated that 80 per cent of these 'secret funds' were used for political purposes.[18] In a country where party finance is, as we have seen, an especially murky subject, the fact that the prime minister controls substantial funds for which he does not have to account, puts him and his party in a strong position. However, he does not monopolize the use of such funds, which are shared with other members of the government. In 1981, each month ministers of the highest rank, *ministres d'état*, received 30,000 francs, other ministers received 20,000 francs and junior ministers were allocated 10,000 francs. Futhermore, certain ministers – interior, defence, finance and external relations – have their own 'special funds', so that this source of occult influence is at the disposal of the government and not only the prime minister.

## The government

How does one become a minister and achieve preferment under the Fifth Republic? Traditionally it was parliament that provided the source of recruitment but in the name of the separation of powers, a principle characteristic of American presidentialism, Article 23 of the Constitution renders 'incompatible' simultaneous membership of the executive and the legislature, although ministers remain responsible to the Assembly in accordance with British parliamentarism. The intention was to reduce the incentive to government instability attributed to deputies out of office seeking to become ministers so that they could attain the prized life-long status of ex-minister. This explanation of government instability under the Fourth Republic has been seriously undermined but it was a popular view when the constitution was drafted. However, insofar as government instability was due to the resignation of ministers in the Cabinet, the current arrangements were intended also to make it more difficult for ministers to remain active in politics after resignation because they could not retire to the backbenches unless they did so within a month of being appointed to office.

Initially it seemed that parliamentarians would be replaced by 'non-political' super-bureaucrats and it is certainly the case that many key posts have been held by career officials. However, there was a steady increase in the number of ministers sitting in parliament at the time they acquired office; 60 per cent in the Debré Government (1959–62); increasing from 64 per cent to 83 per cent in the four Pompidou Governments (1962–8); reaching 97 per cent in the Couve de Murville Government (1968–9)[19] and 100 per cent in the Chaban-Delmas Government. However, in cases like those of Couve de Murville and François-Xavier Ortoli, it was as officials that they established their claim to office. They only acquired a parliamentary seat as a gesture to the traditional electoral basis of ministerial legitimacy. Somewhat surprisingly, the two Mauroy Governments of 1981 included a large number of non-parliamentarians, thirteen out of forty-three in the first and fourteen out of forty-four in the second. Even more significant were the posts held by some of these ministers: Delors at finance, Claude Cheysson at external relations, Robert Badinter at justice occupied three out of the top five in the pecking order. Furthermore, important ministries like industry (held until 1982 by Pierre Dreyfus, former head of Renault) and foreign trade (Michel Jobert, former foreign affairs minister under Pompidou) were also held by men who had never been elected to parliament, while the most senior of the four Communist ministers (Charles Fiterman at transport) had lost his seat to a Socialist in 1981. This reversion to a style reminiscent of de Gaulle's presidency suggests that for Mitterrand, having the confidence of the popularly elected president is more important than being directly elected by the people oneself.

Although constitutionally compelled to resign their parliamentary seats in favour of their substitutes, ministers have successfully circumvented the spirit of the incompatibility rule. They seek re-election at every opportunity, even when it is clear that they will not themselves occupy the seat because they will be ministers. They maintain close contact with their constituencies, openly boasting of the advantages they can procure for their constituents thanks to membership of the government. Their replacement generally resigns to enable them to be re-elected to parliament immediately should they lose office, as in the case of Jacques Chirac in 1976. Finally, when a substitute has died, the minister has stood at the by-election and then handed the seat over to his new replacement, as in the case of Chaban-Delmas in 1970. The link between legislature and executive has proved too difficult to sever and the Fifth Republic practice has marked a partial reversion to a more parliamentary type of relationship based upon the interpenetration of government and parliament. However, ministers seldom attend parliamentary debates except to preserve their bills and their share of the budget more or less unscathed. It is recognized that the real threat to the government comes, in France as in Britain, not from parliament but from the people at the next general election.

Apart from the distinction between senior and junior ministers, there is undoubtedly a 'pecking order' distinguishing the major ministries: finance, external relations, defence, interior and justice, from the minor ministries: health, transport, cultural affairs, postal services, ex-servicemen and even labour, which tend to be regarded as 'stop-gaps' when making Cabinet appointments. In between are the major spending ministries: education, agriculture, industry, town planning and housing, together with the minister for relations with parliament. The personal political weight of each office holder is important, so that although transport is not an important ministry in its own right, when it was held by the senior Communist minister and second-in-command of the party, Charles Fiterman, it rose in importance. Another, somewhat different example showing the effect of the coalition character of French governments, is represented by the fact that among the ministers of the highest rank of *ministres d'état* in 1981 were not only leaders of the Socialist Party's coalition partners, Fiterman (PCF) and Jobert (president of the tiny *mouvement des démocrates*) but also three

Socialist ministers. Two of these latter owed their status to the fact that they represented major factions within the Socialist Party – Michel Rocard in charge of national and regional planning and Jean-Pierre Chevènement in charge of research and industry – rather than the importance of their departments.

1981 brought about an important change in the way in which Cabinet meetings were conducted. During the presidencies of de Gaulle, Pompidou and Giscard, except on the rare occasions when their views were invited, ministers were expected to confine their remarks to matters concerning their own departments. If they wished to express an opinion on other issues, they tended to speak privately to the president of the republic. Under Mitterrand the Cabinet has ceased to be a rubber stamp for decisions taken by interministerial or interdepartmental committees. Discussion is much less inhibited, certain ministers, such as Michel Rocard, coming well briefed to speak on almost all matters on the agenda, though it is true that as the minister responsible for planning he could argue that virtually everything discussed impinged upon his functions. The prime minister usually speaks at the end of the discussion on each item but it is the president who sums up. Thus there can be said to be some return to a genuine sense of collective responsibility, thanks to the greater participation of ministers in the taking of decisions outside their own ministerial responsibilities. However, junior ministers only attend when invited but are collectively told what transpired by the minister of justice. Table 14 indicates that President Mitterrand has acted in a way that public opinion, particularly on the left, wished him to go.

*Table 14*
*Who should set the guidelines of national policy?* (%)

|  | *All voters* | *Right* | *Socialist* | *Communist* |
|---|---|---|---|---|
| President | 39 | 55 | 37 | 24 |
| Government | 49 | 35 | 55 | 65 |
| No reply | 12 | 10 | 8 | 11 |

Source: Based on May 1976 Publimétrie poll in R. Muraz, *La Parole aux français*, 1977, p. 169.

*Interministerial co-ordination*

The complexities of modern government require co-ordination between the divisions of ministries, between ministries and with the non-governmental 'partners' of the administration, before a matter is ready to be dealt with by the Cabinet. The administrative 'in-fighting', the patience, cunning and determination necessary to secure a minimum of co-operation and agreement even within ministries that tend to be agglomerations of introverted specialist divisions, each jealously protecting its own assigned area of responsibility, results in such extreme compartmentalization that it is vital to bring all concerned round a table to achieve a reconciliation of rivalries that threaten to paralyse action. The logic of an administrative system based on the watertight separation of sub-systems, pursuing their own particular policies up to the point where they need the sanction of a higher authority, requires the preparatory work to be done as secretly as possible. To be in a strong bargaining position when the time comes for interministerial negotiations, the scheme should be presented in a fully worked-out form. At this highly politicized level, decisions will not necessarily be made on the merits of the case but in relation to the political weight, expertise and support that the protagonists can muster.

After the Second World War France attempted to imitate the British system of semi-permanent cabinet committees to fulfil the function of co-ordinating policy preparation prior to consideration by the government as a whole and by the Council of Ministers. However, with the exception of the national defence committee, this arrangement did not survive under the unstable coalition governments of the Fourth Republic. A more flexible system of *ad hoc* interministerial meetings quickly developed. They are basically of three types. First, there are *interdepartmental committees* composed of senior civil servants, held at the prime minister's residence at Matignon, usually with a member of the prime minister's personal staff as chairman. These interdepartmental meetings are organized and staffed by the general secretariat of the government which receives the proposals to be discussed from the sponsor ministry's interministerial relations section. It circulates them to the ministries concerned. Before the meeting, each ministry prepares its case carefully. It will be represented by a member of the minister's personal staff, accompanied perhaps by senior officials and experts. The representatives of the minister of finance (though the budget and treasury division spokesmen are not necessarily in agreement) have great influence, with power to brake but not veto proposals. The meeting is concluded by the prime minister's representative summarizing the discussion and, if agreement cannot be reached, transmitting the proposals for decision at the *interministerial committee* level.

Here it is the prime minister himself who is usually in the chair. Although senior civil servants may attend, they speak only when invited to do so by ministers who will have received an account of the discussions in the interdepartmental committee. The interventionist Michel Debré took a leading part in developing the interministerial committee as the premier's main instrument for resolving disputes and working out proposals that substituted a governmental for a departmental viewpoint on any given problem. One or two members of the president's staff are present to report to him on the proceedings.

If agreement is not reached or if the president so decides, an *interministerial council* is summoned. This is the most exclusive of co-ordinating bodies, usually consisting of a few senior ministers who meet at the Elysée under the chairmanship of the president, although very senior officials such as the planning commissioner are sometimes in attendance. Under de Gaulle, interministerial councils were the place where projects were launched; interministerial and interdepartmental committees being where they were worked out in detail and the Cabinet where they were formally approved. President Pompidou held only 60 interministerial council meetings compared to 427 interministerial committee meetings from 1969-74, the latter being especially numerous from 1969-72 when Chaban-Delmas was premier. The more interventionist style of President Giscard led to a change, with 140 councils being held from 1974-8 as compared with 269 interministerial committee meetings chaired by the prime minister. However, this was compensated for in part by the increased frequency of interdepartmental committee meetings of officials at the prime minister's office, with some 100 meetings a month and 1000 a year during Chirac's premiership.[20] There was a spectacular increase in the number of such interdepartmental committee meetings in the early months of the Mauroy Government, with an unprecedented rate of 481 such meetings from the end of May to October 1981, accompanied by a halving of the number of interministerial council meetings.[21]

Ministers frequently attend interministerial council meetings accompanied by one to three members of their private staff and senior officials or may be replaced by a member of their staff. On average about five ministries are involved in such co-ordinating bodies and the tendency for a presidential observer to be present has fluctuated from one-sixth of meetings under de Gaulle, to a half under Pompidou and a third under Giscard. Under Pompidou, industrial and energy policy was the sphere in which the largest number of such co-ordinating meetings were held but there has been an increasing proliferation of subjects dealt with in this way. Legislation often only provides the framework within which the precise solutions to problems have to be settled in detail. As a result, Jean-Luc Bodiguel argues, 'administrative co-ordination has replaced juridical co-ordination'.[22] Furthermore, senior officials in the ministries become disgruntled with the fact that whereas they were able previously to decide matters, these are often discussed and amended by the co-ordinating bodies, slowing down decision-making and leading either to interdepartmental compromises or the superimposition of a decision by the prime minister or a member of his staff. In part, this is due to the need to ensure that a large and cumbersome government apparatus works with a minimum of cohesion. It also reflects the desire of the prime minister to compensate for his subordination to the president by centralizing control over the other ministries, which requires a gargantuan appetite for work.

### The techno-bureaucratic executive

At the peak of the interministerial co-ordination pyramid is located the small informal nucleus of power at the highest levels of the French state. However, this nucleus of decision-makers needs the support and assistance of an outer circle of senior officials and specialists whose minimal function is to prepare the data on the basis of which the fundamental choices are made.

They devise ways of carrying policy choices out and may actually decide many issues, not necessarily unimportant ones, which the overburdened political executive explicitly or by omission delegates to them. There is a peculiarly close connection in France between the suffrage-made political leaders and the school-made techno-bureaucrats, who by their training and experience are indispensable collaborators in administering things and governing men. Both the political and techno-bureaucratic executives have increased their power under the Fifth Republic at the expense of the Assembly, but it is not always clear where the influence of the one ends and that of the other begins.

The concept of techno-bureaucracy represents a conflation of the traditional notion of a body of officials characterized by hierarchy, permanence, professionalism and *esprit de corps* within a disciplined and centralized organization, and a more recent emphasis upon the specialist skill of the expert who has acquired knowledge necessary to making and carrying out political decisions. Both the bureaucrat and the technocrat claim to exercise power in a rational way; but whereas the bureaucrat is primarily a routine administrator, relying upon conventional wisdom to 'muddle through' by adjusting conflicting interests and enforcing rules in an impersonal manner, the technocrat seeks systematic innovation calculated to increase efficiency, based on assessments of the future rather than loyalty to the past. The technocrat purports to reduce partisan political conflicts to the serene scientific dimensions of a series of equations. Presented in this caricature form, it is difficult to see how two such contrasting 'ideal types' can be combined. Although the French administrative élite does not represent a complete fusion between bureaucrat and technocrat, the prestige acquired along with specialist knowledge in training, following on the close ties born of a common social and educational background, culminating in an organization into exclusive corps, has created a distinctive type of public official who commands both specialist skills and a general, all-purpose competence. However, bureaucratic general competence takes priority over any technocratic pretence to expertise, if only because the former allows the 'frictionless movement between the summits of the vertical hierarchies that constitute the bulk of the governmental structure'.[23]

Far from being content to apply rules rigidly, as is the custom of the mass of civil servants, the techno-bureaucrats offer informed advice and leadership without which the political executive would be unable to induce the file-bound officials to undertake new tasks using new methods. Some ministers have rejected both the bureaucratic and technocratic approach as equally statist and preached reliance upon the economic rationality of the market. However, this goes so much against tradition that despite the revival of economic liberalism in France, attempts to end what a former minister had dubbed 'administrative totalitarianism' have so far proved ineffective.

Bureaucrats tend to stress a political rationality based upon the attainment of consensus through a piecemeal and incremental process of mutual adjustment. Short-term improvization rather than medium and long-range planning predominate. By contrast with this prosaic approach, there is a 'heroic model of policy-making'. Aims are explicitly stated and the means to implement them are systematically tested by the criterion of efficiency. The assumption is that the best solution can be identified by technical calculations rather than through political argument. Alongside the transition from legislature-centred Fourth Republic, there has been a shift in emphasis within the higher administration from the consensus norms of political rationality to the efficiency norms of economic rationality. However, owing to the difficulty of reorganizing the traditional administration, the new technocratic norms have found expression in entrepreneurial, *ad hoc*, 'parallel' or 'missionary' agencies which seek to circumvent obstruction by the ministries. Though prototypes of such bodies were created under the Fourth Republic, notably the Planning Commissariat and the Atomic Energy Commissariat,* they became more common, especially in the early years of the Fifth Republic.

The tendency of the techno-bureaucrat partially to supersede the politician and the civil servant is reflected in each minister's personal staff (usually from ten to twenty in size), who provide the crucial link between the political and administrative executive, playing a part corresponding to that of both junior ministers and permanent secretaries in Britain. The absence of permanent secretaries from most French ministries means that

* Discussed in chapters 6 and 8 respectively.

the task of co-ordinating and directing the work of the various divisions has to be undertaken by the minister's *cabinet*. In the Fifth Republic, the fact that decision-making has become a more exclusively executive matter has meant that the key members of the minister's staff are not the parliamentary attachés but the aides borrowed from the civil service who are concerned with preparing, co-ordinating and supervising the implementation of policy. Consequently, they work closely with the offices of the president and the prime minister and other ministerial staffs.* The impetus to reform has frequently been secretively originated by the minister's personal staff. They are then faced with the problem of securing the support or acquiescence of other parts of the executive, of the official and unofficial representative bodies and of the mass public. It is at this point, where the products of competitive examination and competitive election may come into conflict, that the senior officials' conviction that their rationality is equated with the public interest is exposed to the most searching test.

### Public servants or corporate masters?

After a 1930s preoccupation with domination by finance capitalism in the shape of the 'two hundred families' who elected the court of the Bank of France and a 1950s concern with rule from the 'house without windows' or government by Assembly, the 1960s were characterized by a dual concern with personal rule by the president and by an interlocking directorate of senior civil servants. Behind the impressive figure of de Gaulle, the heirs to a secular tradition of administrative power were deemed to have resurrected their dominance of a century earlier in the administrative empire of Louis Napoleon. Whilst the president as head of the political executive personified the state, it was the military, administrative and judicial agents of the executive rather than the people's representatives, the deputies, who were most closely identified with the state.

It is not easy to separate myth from reality in seeking to ascertain where, in a complex process, decisive influence has been exerted; still more difficult to generalize when practice varies over time and depending upon the issue involved. Cath-

* On ministers' personal staffs, see below, pp. 127-30.

erine Grémion takes the view that frequently 'it is the politicians that, by providing the support and, where necessary, the driving force, become the auxiliaries of the administrative officials of the central decision-making network who combine possession of the initiative, continuity of action and responsibility for the practical formulation of decisions.'[24] Bernard Gournay adopts a more classical approach, putting a different construction upon the same facts. Rather than senior civil servants – especially the staff attached to ministers – imposing their will upon the minister, the latter 'implicitly or explicitly delegates his power to them. For a minister, the fundamentals of a proposal are more important than its practical details.'[25] So, when he is requested by the president or prime minister to take up a problem or chooses to do so on his volition or after pressure from an organized interest, he asks a member of his staff to take the matter in hand, collect information and advice from other ministries, organize meetings of officials within the ministry, serve on an interdepartmental committee, represent the minister at interministerial committee meetings and even prepare draft proposals. The informal nucleus of senior officials can, however, only partially compensate for ministers that do not have strong policy views and the determination and skill to steer them through the politico-administrative shoals. The omnipresence of the administrative élites should not be confused with their omnipotence.

The six hundred or so senior civil servants who occupy the most important administrative posts are not at odds with the general public when they consider themselves the most permanent manifestation of public power and the best protectors of the public interest. However, because the legitimacy of authority is conferred by universal suffrage, the senior civil service usually do little more than maintain the routine working of the political system in the absence of political direction. They can preserve continuity but they seldom implement change. This was clear from the paralysis, as far as important innovations were concerned, during the periods of governmental crisis under the Fourth Republic. It also partially explains the enthusiasm of many senior civil servants for the Fifth Republic. It has enabled them to act within a more secure political framework.

However, if the National Assembly is castigated as a 'house

without windows', the administration has also been criticized as an impersonal, Paris-centred élite, superimposed upon field services that are in direct contact with the problems but are denied the discretion to adapt the rules. This self-reinforcing bureaucratic system is based upon a vicious circle in which poor communication between the administration and the administered does not lead to corrective action because of the lack of an efficient feedback process. The field services, who have the necessary information, cannot decide. Their hierarchical superiors in Paris could decide but lack the necessary information, control over which enables the field services to preserve a measure of autonomy. The result is a dysfunctional recourse to centralization to protect the administration from its clientele, coupled with comprehensive regulation. Bureaucratic power is exerted by making general standardized rules and having the discretion to ignore or adapt them in particular cases, such discretion being generally reserved to the senior officials at the centre. French administration is characterized by being rule-bound in principle but swamped by exceptions in practice. This is because rule enforcement becomes a bargaining counter when applied in particular cases. Four-fifths of the French public feel both that they are treated by civil servants as anonymous cases, without personal consideration, and that everyone is not treated equally. Some are singled out for favouritism. Taxation provides an excellent example of the accuracy of this public sense of official unfairness. The Rueff Committee asserted in 1958 that 'French finance is honeycombed with special exceptions and exemptions. The burgeoning of exemptions results from the surrender of public authorities to pressures from private interests, always in the guise of the public interest.'[26] More recently, the general legal prohibition of sea pollution was qualified by numerous prefectoral exemptions in particular instances. To secure conformity from those of the administered who can resist the rules, officials may be prepared to make an exception because the prime aim of a bureaucratic system is the avoidance of conflict.

When the equilibrium is disturbed and conflicts generate irresistible pressures to change, decisions are transferred up the hierarchy to those who alone have the necessary authority to make the adjustments in an excessively rigid system. When

made, changes must apply everywhere because of the centralized nature of the bureaucratic system. The crisis brings into
play the agents of change who are the indispensable mediators
between the administered and the administrators in a situation
where the old rules are no longer effective. The agents of change
*par excellence* are those senior civil servants who belong to the
mobile, meritocratic élites known as the *grands corps*. Their 'old
boy network' re-establishes face-to-face dealings, at the highest
level, as a corrective to the compartmentalized character of
French administration. It is at this level that the indispensable
interdepartmental co-ordination takes place. Disturbing the
sluggishness verging on paralysis into which a highly bureau-
cratized system all too easily subsides is the special task of these
mandarins. They are expected to restore internal communications so that the various parts of the administration can be
united and the public service given impetus as well as cohesion.
Their *esprit de corps* is dedicated to the attainment of what they
conceive to be the public interest. Imparting substance to this
protean concept is regarded as their particular if not their
exclusive prerogative; a propensity that the Fifth Republic's
transfer of power from legislature to executive and from law to
regulation has exacerbated.

Much more important than the civil service classification into
four general grades is the 'vertical' division into some 1,200
corps, which usually correspond to functions within particular
ministries rather than the acquisition of specialist qualifications.
At the summit of this vertical hierarchy and superimposed on
the horizontal classes are the *grands corps*. Their main channels
of recruitment are by competitive examination. The *Ecole Nationale d'Aministration* (ENA) has a legal, diplomatic and economic
emphasis. The engineers are trained at the *Ecole Polytechnique*
(known familiarly as 'x') and its two principal extensions, the *Ecole
Nationale des Mines* and the *Ecole Nationale des Ponts et Chaussées*.
Established as recently as 1945, the ENA was consciously
modelled on the eighteenth-century, specialist élite school
tradition of the mining and road engineers schools (established
in 1747) and the *Polytechnique* (established after the Revolution
in 1794, although Napoleon subsequently put its students into
uniform, like his own creation the prefects). It represented a
triumph for those who wanted to extend to the whole senior

civil service the prestige and independence of the *grands corps* by making the ENA an élite school excluded from the relatively egalitarian university system. Warnings against the establishment of a techno-bureaucratic caste – 'a corps of senior civil servants who would decide public business in an almost sovereign fashion, sheltered from initiatives by the people'[27] – were discounted.

France has for centuries been convinced that the state should train its own servants outside the ordinary university system, regarded as too theoretical in its educational emphasis. Governments have preferred to rely on specialist post-entry training, stressing practical experience applied to the tasks of the public service, provided under their control. This unique tradition of technocratic training was extended from the engineering schools to the recruitment and training of the other *grands corps* through the ENA. Together, the ENA and the engineering schools are the source of administrative leaders, the graduates of the former being infused with some of the technocratic characteristics of the latter. Both provide a general as well as a specialist training, although there is a more 'generalist' economic and legal emphasis at the ENA. This valuable combination of administrative and technical expertise, in conjunction with highly selective post-entry training, increases *esprit de corps*, a source both of cohesion and of rivalry. The ENA has an annual output of approximately one hundred and forty, *Ponts et Chaussées* of about sixty. The close ties developed in the years at these élite institutions prove invaluable, not merely in advancing the career of the individual senior civil servant but in overcoming the rigid compartmentalism of French administration. Neither the American partisan colonization of the top echelons of the civil service through the nineteenth-century 'spoils system' and the twentieth-century transplants from business (Republicans) and universities (Democrats), nor the British reliance upon unassertive and non-partisan amateurs selected from among the academically successful, would appear to have proved a match for their French counterparts. However, distrust of the school-made technocrat has been fostered by the fact that 'expertise' provides no immunity from error. Rather, it may increase both the self-assurance of the decision-maker and the magnitude of the miscalculations. Each period has its equivalent of the French Panama Canal fiasco and associated political scandals, which may have prompted the remark of a famous banker, a French Rothschild: 'There are three ways to ruin: gambling, women and engineers. The first two are more agreeable, but the last is more certain.'

The nursery from which the ENA has hitherto recruited the overwhelming majority of the future administrative élite is the Paris *Institut d'Etudes Politiques* (known familiarly as '*Sciences Po*' after its forerunner). The founder of the *Ecole libre des Sciences Politiques* wrote in 1871 that it was vital to reinforce the bureaucratic bulwark against the pressures of democracy which he foresaw: '... democracy cannot be halted. The higher classes ... can only maintain their political dominance by invoking the right of the most capable.'[28] A century later we can see that the validity of Boutmy's warning that the old élite of birth and wealth should be bolstered by merit has been recognized and implemented. Although recruitment has extended to the lower-middle class, the successful ENA candidates (like those of the other *grandes écoles*) come predominantly from children of the upper-middle class, notably the senior civil servants, senior private sector executives and the liberal professions. The élitist link between the *grandes écoles* and the *grands corps* is only an extreme case of France's unequal educational opportunity being reflected in the Parisian upper class origins of the senior civil service. Despite the rhetoric about 'democratizing' recruitment, little progress had been made prior to the 1983 attempt to extend the intake from among experienced local councillors, trade unionists and organizers of voluntary associations. This is perhaps because it was never seriously intended by the privileged 'caste' who are the beneficiaries of the system, content to co-opt to a self-perpetuating meritocracy. Such co-option is facilitated by the large part played in ENA training by senior civil servants.

Another aim of the 1945 reform establishing the ENA was to unify recruitment to the senior civil service and increase mobility within it. Not merely was the ENA to replace the separate recruitment to the non-engineering *grands corps*, but a new interdepartmental corps of civil administrators, attached to the prime minister's office, was intended to contain the pretensions of the traditional *grands corps* to occupy the top posts throughout the civil service. However, in allowing the successful ENA candidates to choose which corps they would join according to their examination rank, the custom developed that the fourteen best candidates went to the high-prestige *grands corps*, thereby fortifying the traditional divisions within the civil service and preventing the emergence of a unified administrative class. A 'pecking order' prevails, the attractive corps being those of the inspectorate of finance,* linked with the ministry of finance, the administrative lawyers of the *Conseil d'Etat*, the public accountants of the *Cour des Comptes*, the diplomatic corps associated with the ministry of foreign affairs and the prefectoral corps attached to the ministry of the interior. The civil administrators corps (which absorbs two-thirds of the ENA output as well as most recruits from within the civil service) is the source from which senior posts in the high prestige ministries (finance, foreign affairs, interior) are first filled, with those at the bottom of the examination results list going to the 'less eligible' ministries such as labour and health. They also staff the less elevated posts in the more attractive ministries, attraction being measured partly by the disparity in earnings between similar posts in different ministries. Out of an optimum total of 1,048 civil administrators, the target allocation between ministries gives the lion's share to the ministry of economic affairs and finance (450), with the ministries of the interior and industry being the only others entitled to over a hundred civil administrators. Despite attempts at reform, certain ministries were notoriously 'under-administered', in the sense that they had been shunned by the best ENA graduates.

Civil administrators generally remain immobilized for most of their career in a single ministry. Members of the *grands corps*, prior to moving out of the civil service into senior managerial posts in a public or private corporation through the practice known as *pantouflage*, or directly into politics, occupy many of the top posts in the key central departments, notably in the prime minister's office and the ministry of finance. The dominance of Paris and of the ministry of finance was reflected in the fact that in 1968, out of some 1,500 ENA graduates in the public service, 1,300 were Paris-based and 700 were attached to the ministry of finance, an administrative bastion of the one and

* See below, p. 179.

indivisible republic, together with the ministry of the interior. A staging post for a finance inspector or councillor of state to a top post in a ministry will be membership of a *cabinet ministériel*, the personal staff attached to each minister. This staff, situated at the point where administration and politics are at their most inextricable, provides a vital link between the political and administrative executive.

French ministries are compartmentalized aggregations of divisions which are themselves confederations of autonomous *bureaux*. The lack of co-ordination between and within the various divisions is due to the jealous regard for their independence both of each senior civil servant, and of the minister. The interposition of a secretary-general, an official head of each ministry on the pattern of the British permanent secretary, has therefore been avoided (except at the ministry of foreign affairs), ministers preferring the head of each division to be directly responsible to them. The minister can thereby more effectively retain political control over the choice of priorities, the director of his *cabinet* becoming the *de facto* source of administrative co-ordination within the ministry. Usually, there are weekly meetings between the heads of all the ministry's divisions and the minister, either accompanied by all his staff or simply by the director. The director is at the focal point of the ministerial communications system. He receives all documents to be signed by his minister, selecting those he will refer to the minister because of their political importance and dealing with the remainder himself. Instructions to officials from the director are deemed to come from the minister himself. As well as co-ordination within the ministry, the director of the minister's personal staff is also responsible for preparatory co-ordination between ministries at the highest level. When the minister cannot attend an interministerial meeting, he is usually replaced by the director of his *cabinet*. On each Tuesday, preceding the Cabinet meeting on Wednesday, the directors of the personal staffs of all ministers meet at Matignon to prepare the ground.

The overwhelming majority of the official members* of ministers' personal staffs are recruited from the senior civil service. This is indicative of the fact that they are more a parallel hierarchy to the heads of the ministry's divisions than substitutes

* This is exclusive of the numberless 'unofficial' and 'clandestine' members.

for the parliamentary secretaries and parliamentary private secretaries which abound in the British system. It no doubt reflects an acknowledgement of the greater need in France to ensure bureaucratic accountability to ministers than ministerial accountability to parliament. Another advantage of recruiting civil servants is that they can continue to draw their pay although on leave from their previous posts. However, this salary will be supplemented, perhaps out of secret 'special funds' provided by the prime minister. About three-quarters of the most important posts of director and specialist adviser are usually recruited from among the *grands corps*, notably the administrative lawyers of the Council of State and the economic experts of the Finance Inspectorate. Members of the prefectoral corps generally occupy half the posts of *chefs de cabinet* (not to be confused with the *directeurs de cabinet*), who are primarily responsible for supervising relations between the minister and his ex (and future) constituents, parliament and the press, political work in which they are well experienced. Parliamentary attachés keep the minister informed about the state of parliamentary business and when his presence is required. They also keep an eye on the activities of relevant standing committees and during the parliamentary recesses they share in the task of answering the voluminous correspondence from deputies and senators.

The 1981 Mauroy Government recruited a much larger number of official members of ministers' personal staffs than did the outgoing Barre Government: 360 as against 234. It was also characterized by broader recruitment, less dependence upon the *grands corps* and a greater inclination to recruit from outside the senior civil service. Even though they were 50 per cent more numerous, the Socialist-led Government was served by ninety-four graduates of ENA compared with a hundred and three for the Barre Government, and by twenty-five *polytechniciens* against thirty-two. The Mauroy ministers were served by thirty-seven civil servants who did not belong to a *grand corps* or have ENA training, whereas this category numbered only eleven under Barre. As one would expect from the dominance of a party that owes so much to the teaching profession, their number rose from thirteen in the Barre period to fifty under Mauroy. Other non-élitist categories whose recruitment increased were women (seventy-one as against twenty), full-time party officials (twelve compared to none) and trade union officials (eleven as against two).

The bulk of the personal staff consist of specialist advisers and *chargés de mission* who have been given responsibility for special areas of the ministry's work. They discharge four main functions. First, they prepare memoranda for the minister on matters to be considered in Cabinet, their role ranging from almost pure research to actual decision-making as far as the ministry's policy is concerned. Second, they co-ordinate the work of the ministry in their field and conduct its relations with other ministries, involving numerous meetings with the members of other ministers' staffs. They deal with the interest groups who seek to influence the ministry or whose support the ministry wishes to mobilize on behalf of its policy. They also play an important part in dealing with the hundreds of thousands of requests, from those of ministerial colleagues down to those of local notables seeking special favours, which often amount to no more than speeding up a decision. Third, they draft outlines of the minister's speeeches and interviews. Fourth, they supervise the implementation of the ministry's policies, necessitating close and frequent contact with the senior officials who are their opposite numbers in the ministry. The role of the minister's personal staff varies between ministries, tending to be especially great in those that are either relatively new (culture) or excessively routine-bound (agriculture) and so badly need the administrative leadership that a *cabinet* can provide. It tends to be relatively more circumscribed in its role in the ministry of foreign affairs, which possesses a secretary-general supported by powerful divisions capable of resisting any propensity to invade their spheres of action.

Although they are drawn mainly from the ministries themselves, these specialist staff members are often in role conflict with their 'line' colleagues who run the ministry's divisions and who have frequently themselves been ministerial staff members, often in the same ministry. Their respective roles, with different political and administrative priorities meeting at the crucial point at which they must be either reconciled or subordinated one to another, bring the bureaucratic desire for autonomy into conflict with the need for change. It is as members of the minister's personal staff, rather than as heads of the ministry's 'line' hierarchy, that senior civil servants are most effective as agents of change. It is in this role that they can win, at an early age, accelerated promotion to the hierarchical posts within the minister's discretion (although heads of divisions are appointed by the Cabinet, and the president or prime minister may have his say). In their 'line' posts, they will become more concerned to administer according to the rules rather than to make exceptions for reasons of political expediency or imaginative innovation. However, the system enables the appointment of the staff member who prepared a reform to the 'line' post in which he can ensure that it is faithfully implemented. The government can also make discretionary appointments to the *grands corps* (notably as prefects and councillors of state) of those who have given it loyal political-cum-administrative service, so the link between these corps and service on a ministerial staff is further strengthened by appointment to the corps afterwards. Should differences develop between a minister and the head of a division within the ministry, this will normally be settled by promotion or at least transfer to an equivalent post elsewhere.

Much has been made of the contrast between administrative stability and political instability in France, at least until the advent of the Fifth Republic. While this is valid, its significance should not be exaggerated, because members of ministerial staffs, like ministers, often survived Cabinet crises under the Fourth Republic. On the other hand, the tenure of office by the heads of divisions may be under three years, as was the case with the ministry of foreign affairs during the Fourth Republic (average of 2·7 years) compared with ministers of foreign affairs who served an average of 1·6 years. Overall, however, while ministers averaged 1·1 years in office under the Fourth Republic, division heads held their posts for an average of 4·1 years. The gap narrowed under the Fifth Republic to an average tenure of 2·9 years for ministers and 3·4 years for division heads between 1958–66. Significantly, in the light of the subsequent May 1968 crisis, the most unstable ministry was that of education, whose ministers held office for an average of 1·2 years and whose division heads survived for 2·3 years.[29]

A political career is especially tempting to public employees in France because they need not give up their public service career when embarking on hazardous electoral ventures.

Whereas in Britain civil servants must resign their posts to *fight* an election, in France, win or lose, one can progress up the scale during one's extended leave of absence, which involves a much more tolerant view of the requirements of civil service neutrality. The first three presidents of the Fifth Republic were all public servants, as were the first eight prime ministers, though one must bear in mind that in France teachers are public servants. The election of Mitterrand as president in 1981 marked a return to the Fourth Republic, whose two presidents had both been lawyers, as were six of the thirteen prime ministers. His choice as prime minister was a former teacher. However, for the first time under the Fifth Republic, neither the president nor the prime minister had graduated from a *grande école*!

This should also be placed in the context of a comparison of the occupational background of ministers under the Fourth and Fifth Republics (up to 1976 in the latter instance). In both cases, public servants (including teachers) predominated, though the number increased from 33 per cent to 55 per cent. The number of lawyers, by contrast, fell from 26 per cent to 10 per cent and of businessmen less dramatically from 16 to 11 per cent. Among public servants, there was a spectacular shift from a predominance of teachers among the public servants under the Fourth Republic (41 against 25 senior civil servants) to a predominance of senior civil servants under the Fifth Republic (116 against 29 teachers).[30] However, the electoral victory of the left in 1981 marked a resurgence of the *République des professeurs* against the *République des hauts fonctionnaires*, especially in the National Assembly but also in the Government, administering a rebuff to what had appeared to be the irresistible encroachment of the bureaucracy. Despite criticisms that they were indulging in a 'spoils system' and creating a 'Socialist Party state' to replace the 'Giscard state' they had condemned, the 1981 Government – with certain exceptions such as television, the cultural sector and the rectoral* services of the education ministry, where sweeping changes were made – allowed the bureaucracy to play its role of ensuring the continuity of government. The penetration into politics of the administrative élites has not yet involved an equivalent politicization of French administration.[31]

* See below, chapter 7, p. 216.

# 5 Public Order and Civil Liberties

*Public power and public service: the tradition of French legalism*

As we saw in chapter 1, state sovereignty was a sixteenth-century revival of a Roman Law conception of the ruler's unlimited power. The government used its police power for the maintenance of public order and security. The leading French seventeenth-century jurists who formulated the 'apology' for absolute monarchy on the Louis XIV model used the elastic concept of the public interest to justify what Domat called 'the universal policing of society'. Together with Le Bret, whose *Traité de la Souveraineté du Roi* was 'inspired' by Richelieu, Domat developed a theory of comprehensive police power which reflected the post-medieval state's aspiration to unlimited hegemony and expressed the unbounded capacity for state intervention that has been such a feature of French political and administrative life. The ruler alone could judge what was in the supreme interest of the state and *raison d'état* substituted the authority of the ruler for the justification of any government action through the judicial process.

This traditional state idealist French public philosophy, which survived the transition from the royalist 'police state' to the republican 'legal state', was recalled by President Pompidou in an April 1970 speech to his ex-colleagues of the *Conseil d'Etat*: 'All our law stemmed from the conception of a strong state, stronger perhaps for limiting its intervention to the most characteristic functions of public power: justice, defence, order. In these spheres, the state alone expressed the general interest and alone took the decisions to ensure that it prevailed.' (Pompidou's emphasis upon the limited range of state intervention was a revealing combination of his traditionalist views about the past and his personal preferences for the future.) He went on to justify this monopoly of coercive decision-making: 'Only the state ... can have a complete and disinterested vision of the general interest.... For more than a thousand years, France has owed its existence to the state, a state to bring it together, organize it, extend it and defend it not only against foreign threats but equally against group egotisms and rivalries.' This paternalistic conception of a state prerogative police power, conceived as the general regulation of French society for the public good, is indivisibly concerned with domestic and foreign threats to national security, with ominous implications for civil liberties.

Until the end of the Second Empire, the traditional principle that the sovereign state was not responsible for its actions reigned unchallenged, except by liberal advocates like Tocqueville of the rule of law on the Common Law pattern. The isolation rather than separation of powers, achieved by the Revolution and reinforced by Napoleon, strengthened the autonomy of executive power, the instrument of popular sovereignty, which was made independent of the ordinary courts in 1790. However, although the thrust of the French tradition has been to subordinate the judiciary to the administration, there was a liberal counter-attack, especially under the Third Republic, against the autonomous administration being a judge in its own cause. The Council of State, initially the most elevated of Napoleon's authoritarian instruments of executive domination, reintroduced an element of liberalism. It counterbalanced the requirements of administrative action by the protection of the rights of the administered, establishing that the responsibility of the executive and its agents was the rule and immunity was exceptional. The dangers involved in making the executive independent of the judiciary were partially corrected by the Council's emergence from the 1970s as an independent administrative legal authority through the functional separation of those parts of the government machine concerned with legal work from those doing administrative work. The Council demonstrated its independence by drastically curtailing the *raison d'état* principle that any governmental act was immune from judicial review if it was politically inspired. The only overt survivals of the doctrine of state prerogative power are strictly enumerated (including notably the use of emergency powers under Article 16, the conduct of diplomacy and of war). However, we shall see that the legacy from regal, revolutionary and imperial absolutism is much more pervasive than this would suggest.

The early years of the Third Republic were also marked by an attempt to replace 'public power' as the basis of administrative law by 'public service', corresponding to a shift from an authoritarian to a liberal democratic polity. Although the public service criterion was adumbrated in 1873, it was only in the first decade of the twentieth century that its implications were fully worked out. Public service was loosely defined in terms of the satisfaction of a public need as conceived by the state's agents, guided by the general interest norm. The main advocate of the new view, the constitutional lawyer, Léon Duguit, emphasized the changing character of state activity, shifting from the sovereign assertions of power in the fields of police and war to the provision of economic and social services. Wishful thinking supplementing observation, he went so far as to claim that 'in place of the regal, Jacobin and Napoleonic conception of the state as power is substituted a fundamentally economic conception of the state, which becomes the co-operation between public services functioning under the control of the government.'[1] This reassuring view, so appropriate to a replacement of the warfare state by the welfare state, which seemed plausible just prior to the First World War, never held the field unchallenged. Duguit's main rival among French jurists, Maurice Hauriou, argued that public service had not replaced public power as the synthetic norm underlying administrative law; they were its dual supports and of the two, public power was the more important, qualitatively if not quantitatively.[2] The public service norm has since been partially abandoned as imprecise in definition and inoperative as a criterion of the sphere of administrative law (public services such as social security and public corporations being the responsibility of the ordinary courts). However, the commitment to the principles of equal access to public services, equality of treatment of the administered, and neutrality, are of immense value in an administrative system addicted to the discretionary adaptation of the rules to suit the political convenience of governments. The survival of the public service criterion in competition with the norm of public power reflects a reluctance to subordinate the purpose of executive action to those in control of the executive, the service of the public to the public's 'servants'.

## *The citizen's rights in principle and in practice*

Whilst the French Revolution bears part of the responsibility for strengthening the executive as against the judiciary, it sought to protect the citizens from government by proclaiming in the Declaration of the Rights of Man (Article 2) that the fundamental purpose of political organization was to preserve man's natural rights, including the right to resist oppression. Freedom of the person from arbitrary detention, freedom of thought and expression, and freedom to own property, were the rights that seemed most important in 1789, together with the presumption of innocence until guilt was established and the accountability of government to the people. However, Articles 3 and 6 confer sovereignty on the nation and declare that 'law is the expression of the general will'. Consequently, although these and other rights were later enshrined in preambles to successive constitutions, there was no provision for judicial appeal against violation of these rights, the citizen being left at the mercy of a sovereign legislature which represented popular sovereignty. The Third Republic did nevertheless extend public liberties substantially; notably by guaranteeing the right of assembly and press freedom in 1881, the right to form trade unions in 1884, the right to set up associations without prior government approval in 1901, and religious freedom in 1905. This period also witnessed the birth of the League of Human Rights (during the trial of Emile Zola in 1898, arising out of the Dreyfus Affair) which has given institutional expression to the defence of civil liberties in France, although each 'affair' has stimulated an *ad hoc* response, particularly by intellectuals. A measure of the 1981 Mauroy Government's commitment to civil liberties was that sixteen of its members belonged to the League (Minister of Justice Badinter being on leave from its central committee), Mauroy in 1982 being the first premier to attend its congress since Blum at the time of the Popular Front in 1937.

In 1946, the Preamble to the Constitution of the Fourth

Republic added equal rights for women, the right to employment, to collective bargaining and to strike, protection of the sick and the aged, and equality of access to education and culture. However, many of these are patently aspirations rather than enforceable rights, although the reaffirmation of the Declaration of 1789 and of the 1946 Preamble in the 1958 Constitution became the basis in 1971 for an important decision of the Constitutional Council concerning the right of association, to which we shall return. The aspirational character of the 1946 Preamble, reflecting the libertarian socialist tradition within the Resistance, is also of importance because it inspired the early reforms of the Mitterrand presidency. In addition to the reaffirmation of the Revolutionary right of asylum for the politically persecuted, the 1946 Preamble succinctly stipulated some principles of economic democracy and public ownership that have been reflected in the reforms of 1982. The assertion that 'Any property and undertaking, which possesses or acquires the character of a public service or of a monopoly, must come under collective ownership', was considered by anti-nationalizers on the Right as restricting the right to nationalize, but the Constitutional Council in 1982 agreed with those who argued that it did not preclude extending public ownership beyond those firms that qualified under the terms of the Preamble. The 1982 extension of workers' rights, generally as well as in public enterprises, can be linked with the 1946 affirmation: 'Each worker participates, through his delegates, in the collective settlement of working conditions as well as in the management of enterprises.' One should note in passing the deliberate exclusion of 'freedom of education' (discussed in chapter 7) although a decision of the Constitutional Council in 1977 ruled state aid to church schools constitutional. Whilst there is a general consensus on religious freedom, the conflict over the 1905 separation of church and state has made public subsidies to private schools a persistent bone of political contention.

Any assessment of the extent to which the homeland of Voltaire has lived up in practice to the principles of human rights that have been asserted with such resounding rhetoric is bound to be somewhat selective and subjective. Past history – notably the Vichy regime coinciding with Nazi German occupation, colonial wars in Vietnam and Algeria, the 'May events' of 1968, the economic insecurity of persisting recession – has left unsavoury legacies which Mitterrand made it a priority to abrogate or attenuate. Quite apart from the respect for the right to life reflected in the abolition of capital punishment (a right not respected by the Revolutionaries of the 1790s or their successors up to the 1970s) and which President Giscard had not been prepared to carry out, partly because public opinion, previously favourable to abolition, had swung in support of the guillotine, past timidity has been overcome in numerous ways. For example, while France took a step forward by ratifying the European Human Rights Convention in 1974, it denied its citizens the right of individual recourse to the European Human Rights Commission when a right guaranteed by the Convention was violated. While Giscard never followed up his initial enthusiasm for a code of fundamental individual liberties, the first half of his presidency was marked by a number of extensions of personal liberty. The abolition of film censorship (censorship in general had been abolished in 1789 but was quickly reborn) in 1974; the liberalization of abortion and divorce by mutual consent in 1975; the protection of citizens from the consequences of the multiplication of computerized data banks and the reduction of official secrecy by allowing the 'administered' access to official documents in 1978; all these, whatever their limitations in terms of practical application, indicated a will to secure a genuine extension of personal liberty.

Whereas it was the liberal element in Giscard's liberal-conservatism that predominated from 1974–8, from 1978–81 he showed the more repressive side of his double-faced ideology. The Bill to institute a French equivalent of *habeas corpus* and give practical expression to the 1958 Constitution's Article 66 assertion: 'No one may be arbitrarily detained', was withdrawn in 1979. Taken in conjunction with the slowness with which cases come to trial, the result is that large numbers of people in gaol – nearly 40 per cent of the prison population – consist of individuals who are presumed innocent, awaiting trial, often for years on end, some of whom commit suicide before their case is reached.[3] Responding – some would say over-reacting – to a popular wave of fear, motivated more by an increasing number of petty rather than serious crimes, though spectacular examples of international terrorism undoubtedly heightened the collective psychosis, the Government cracked down in repressive fashion in its 'security and liberty' legislation which was abrogated by the Mauroy Government. This legislation was characterized by suspicion of general judicial laxity in law enforcement, coupled with a trust in police that involved encouraging indulgence to the point of outright permissiveness by the judiciary when the police overstepped the legal bounds. Latent xenophobia – exacerbated by the large immigrant population, attracted during the years of rapid economic expansion and labour shortage, which redoubled at a time of inexorably increasing unemployment – resulted in arbitrary expulsion as a matter of spurious urgency denying the victims the customary legal guarantees, and which offered scope for pre-electoral exploitation.

The ambivalence of Frenchmen, who simultaneously look to the state to protect them from disorder yet resent its tendency to infringe their freedom, is coupled with a tendency of those of right-wing views to emphasize the threat of disorder, while the left are inclined to stress the danger to personal liberty.[4] In the process, the independence of the judiciary – never a strong point of successive French regimes, though indispensable to the protection of civil rights – came under increasing pressure prior to 1981, since when the balance has been redressed somewhat.

### The role of the judiciary and its auxiliaries

The establishment of a Constitutional Council in 1958 was part of the attempt by the authors of the new Constitution, notably Debré, to preserve its innovations from subsequent counter-attack. The champions of the traditional doctrine that the legislature was the repository of national sovereignty had to be prevented from eroding the constitutional constraints imposed on parliament. This involved another departure from traditional French practice, the Constitutional Council being entrusted with the power to decide that laws passed by parliament were unconstitutional. The behaviour of the executive was not subject to judicial review by the Constitutional Council, being the preserve of the Council of State. The Constitutional Council's main function and early activities marked it down as a watchdog on behalf of executive supremacy. Although the presidents of the two chambers of the French parliament choose six out of the nine members, the remaining three – including the president – are chosen by the president of the republic. However, because the presidents of the republic and Assembly have so far shared the same political views, there has been a majority of six to three in favour of the Gaullist interpretation of the Constitution which may become a Socialist majority in 1986. Furthermore, there has been a tendency to appoint men who have been active politicians and there have been cases of movement from the Council into active politics, notably by Pompidou when he became prime minister in 1962. Former President Giscard chose not to take his *ex-officio* seat on the Council in 1981, an indication that he intended to remain too actively engaged in politics to sit comfortably in the Council. While the examples of supreme constitutional courts in the United States, Federal Germany and Italy indicate that political influence over the membership of a body called upon to decide politically controversial matters has been unavoidable, the degree of politicization attained in France is particularly great.

The existence of a Constitutional Council to which the three men who appoint its members – the presidents of the republic, Assembly and Senate – together with the prime minister were until 1974 alone capable of referring issues of constitutionality, has not merely restricted the powers of the legislature *vis-à-vis* the executive. It has made the citizen's constitutional rights, as set out in the 1789 Declaration of Human Rights and in the Preambles to the 1946 and 1958 Constitutions, judicially enforceable as they have not been hitherto. In 1950 the Council of State had already invoked the Preamble as embodying 'the fundamental principles that should inspire legislative action as well as that of government and administration'. However, because civil liberties had never been precisely defined and because of the difficulty in getting an issue raised before the Constitutional Council, it was not until 1971 that the Council moved from regulatory to normative action.[5]

Faced by mounting unrest amongst its own parliamentary and extra-parliamentary supporters at the violent challenge to authority and order from the extreme left, the Government and

139

especially the minister of the interior, Marcellin, decided in the words of St Just to deny freedom to the enemies of freedom. The minister instructed the prefect of police in June 1970 to refuse the 'friends of the *Cause du Peuple*' – a periodical whose editors were sent to gaol until Jean-Paul Sartre assumed the editorial role – registration under the 1901 Act, essential if it was to have a legal existence. However, the Paris Administrative Tribunal quashed the refusal to register the association, which it declared should be automatic. Even if the government regarded an association as subversive (the *Cause du Peuple* had been the organ of the *Gauche Prolétarienne*, dissolved in May 1970) it could not be outlawed in advance. Dismayed at this judgment, the minister of the interior had a Bill prepared and adopted by the Cabinet at a meeting on 9 June 1971, amending the 1901 Act guaranteeing freedom of association.

The main purpose of this Bill was to give prefects the power to refuse registration to any association which they thought would engage in illicit activities, subject to a subsequent decision of the courts. The government would thus be in a position to decide in advance whether an association should be presumed to be illicit and, even in the event of a contrary decision by the courts, delay the association acquiring legal personality meanwhile.* Having initially intended to proceed by decree, the minister of the interior accepted the Council of State's advice that a bill would be necessary and secured parliamentary permission to discuss his Bill as a matter of urgency. It was rushed through the Assembly between 2 am and 4.30 am on 24 June 1971, being carried against left-wing opposition by 373 votes to 97. On 28 June 1971, however, the Senate rejected the Bill as unconstitutional (by 129 votes to 104) and Alain Poher, its president (Pompidou's former opponent at the 1969 presidential election), was pressed to refer the Bill to the Constitutional Council should the Assembly persist. The two chambers having failed to reach agreement (the Assembly confirming its support for the Bill by 357 votes to 100), the president of the Senate referred the Bill to the Council, which gave its verdict two weeks later. It transpired, despite the secrecy of the vote, that a majority of six to three in the Council ruled that by virtue of the

* Because of the backlog of work in the courts, instead of an association enjoying the benefits of the delay, the government would be the beneficiary.

Preamble to the Constitution, the right to form an association 'cannot be subject to advance authorization by either the administrative or even the judicial authorities'. The Council, by this decision, emerged as a guardian of civil liberty capable of imposing respect for constitutional rights even on the president and his ministers.

However, there is a lively debate between French constitutional lawyers on the extended role of the Council, some regarding it as a usurpation of parliamentary sovereignty, whilst others consider that it has at last made France a state in which law is supreme, even over the will of parliament. By 'a subtle combination of prudence and boldness' – prudence predominating in the pre-1971 period, during which Gaullist loyalism ensured that the Constitutional Council did not strike down the referenda of 1961-2 even though it advised the president unofficially that they were unconstitutional – and boldness particularly thereafter, the Council claimed that it could, without appeal, identify and assert the primacy of the fundamental principles of the French constitution.[6] It has continued to steer a middle way, some say zigzag, between a quietist acknowledgement that the will of the people's representatives should prevail and the activist temptation of government by judges, who lay down the law to politicians prone to put short-term expediency before the protection of basic rights.

The tendency of politicians to allow ends to determine their view of the means is clear from the frequent and effective use to which the left-wing members of parliament put the 1974 reform that allowed sixty deputies or senators to refer a bill to the Council, despite the criticism of it that they had made and continued to make, headed by future President Mitterrand.[7] The Socialists in particular placed the defence of liberty at the forefront of their referrals, which accounted for fourteen out of twenty-four initiated in the period 1974-9. A notable victory was the 1977 decision by the Council striking down an Act authorizing the police to search cars on the highway without a warrant. However, when they acquired a parliamentary majority in 1981, the Socialist deputies were inclined to revert to earlier criticisms of the composition of the Council, intended to deny it the right to challenge the popular will. Whether or not it was intimidated, the Constitutional Council – which had, in confirming the constitutionality of the Abortion Act of 1975, repudiated any claim to judge the desirability of legislation – did not overrule any major piece of the Mauroy Government's legislation. It merely held up the Nationalization Act so that the compensation provided could be substantially increased.

While the extension to sixty deputies or senators of the right to refer legislation to the Council – a reference which must be made immediately the law is passed and before it is formally promulgated – has substantially increased its workload, the bulk of its decisions are concerned with electoral appeals. Between 1958–78, its 484 decisions resulted in the invalidation of twenty-five deputies, nine from the Opposition and sixteen from the majority parties. This reflects a marked change from the Fourth Republic, when parliamentary validation resulted in the Opposition being victimized by partisan decisions.[8] The substitution of a judicial for a political process has meant greater fairness, even though invalidation continues to remain a controversial matter.

The Constitutional Council and the Council of State have more in common than their proximity in the Palais Royal. They use similar judicial procedures, related to the fact that the Constitutional Council's early membership, including its first president and first two secretaries-general, were members of the Council of State. The latter's direct influence as a source of personnel for those parts of executive decision-making where politics and administration are most intermingled, as well as its expanded advisory function owing to the extension in the executive's activities, have somewhat overshadowed its traditional judicial function of protecting the administered. Nevertheless, the Council of State deliberately sought to increase judicial control commensurately with the extension of executive power, in contrast with its policy under earlier republics of strengthening a weak executive. This intention emerged most clearly in its use of the general principles of law contained in the Preamble to the Constitution to restrain claims by the executive power that the necessities of government or *raison d'état* should prevail over judicial scruples. There is some rivalry between the venerable Council of State and the relatively new Constitutional Council, decisions of the latter having priority in cases of conflict.

While individual citizens cannot have recourse to the Constitutional Council, no such restriction applies in the case of the Council of State. Although the plaintiff has to prove his case against a minister or official, the inquisitorial nature of the French judge in this instance works in the citizen's favour as the Council will require the production of relevant official files and the justification for the regulation or decision made. This procedure ensures the enforcement of the personal accountability for administrative acts that in Britain is evaded through the fiction of ministerial responsibility. The Council's main achievements as a champion of individual rights through the enforcement of administrative law have been through annulment on five grounds of acts by which the administration has exceeded its powers. The narrowest and earliest ground is *ultra vires*, action beyond the powers attributed to the administrative authority. Secondly, the formal or procedural irregularity of an administrative act may lead the Council to quash a decision or regulation. Thirdly, the abuse or misuse of power for a purpose other than that for which it was granted involves the administrative judge in an examination of the intentions of the public agent. On this ground an administrative act may be quashed because discretionary power has been used improperly, being inspired, for example, by personal enmity, corruption or political favouritism. Fourthly, there may be no legal justification for the action or it may be held that the alleged motives do not exist. Finally, the purpose of the act may be illegal.

Nevertheless, the constraints upon the judicial control exercised by the Council of State are important. First, the Council has refused on grounds of political discretion to interfere in certain matters, treated as unchallengeable acts of government. Secondly, governments have frequently resorted to *ex post facto* legislative validation of acts of dubious legality, thereby removing them from the Council's jurisdiction either before or whilst the Council is examining them.[9] Thirdly, since 1959 parliament has annually given *ex post facto* validation in the Finance Act to regulations and individual decisions quashed by the Council. Fourthly, until 1980 – when the administrative courts were empowered to enforce their judgements – the executive frequently refused to implement the Council's judgements, varying in degree from procrastination to inertia and even manifest bad faith, combined occasionally with explicit criticism of the verdict. Such non-implementation could be partial or total or the delay could be such as to render the judgement ineffective. It was estimated that about *a third of the council's decisions were so nullified in practice*, with the ministry of finance being particularly adept at circumventing the Council's judgements in taxation matters.

French administrative justice is both extremely inexpensive and extremely slow. Because of its backlog of work, the Council is itself to blame for rendering many of its decisions ineffective. Thus the 'law's delay' fortified 'the insolence of office' and in 1973 a French version of the British adaptation of the Scandinavian ombudsman was instituted. The 'mediator', as he is called, has become a more influential and active institution than the British parliamentary commissioner for administration because of his wider terms of reference and a more 'political' conception of his function. Thus, despite his title, the British ombudsman is a former senior civil servant while the French ombudsman is a former politician. Whereas the Council of State and the administrative courts continue to be relied upon to enforce the legality of decisions and procedures, the mediator concentrates on ensuring that public officials behave in a reasonable and equitable manner when complaints are made that they have not acted in accordance with their 'public service mission' (Article 1 of the 1973 Act of Parliament). This principle means that the mediator and his staff may not only investigate complaints involving central ministries; they can also deal with complaints against local authorities and those public enterprises that enjoy a monopoly (essentially the transport and energy public utilities). He has access to all departmental documents and files other than those concerning national security. Individuals cannot complain directly to the mediator but must go through a member of either house of parliament. Rather than establish local ombudsmen as in Britain, the mediator has since 1978 had a local representative in each *département*. Despite having a much heavier workload than his British counterpart, the French mediator has a much smaller staff in Paris, relying instead upon the services of the various ministerial inspectorates.[10]

The mediator is required to produce an annual report to the

president and to parliament. In 1977, 6,900 cases were dealt with, of which about 90 per cent were within the mediator's terms of reference. Even when a grievance cannot be investigated by the mediator, it is usually passed on to a specially designated person or liaison unit in the ministry concerned or to the relevant user committee attached to each ministry, which is presided over by a member of parliament. The ministries most subject to complaints are finance (tax matters) and solidarity (social security payments). Of much greater significance are the many suggestions for changes in administrative procedures, departmental regulations and legislation that arise from the complaints made. Of the twenty-one specific recommendations made in 1977, ten were accepted and eight were still under discussion in mid-1978. An earlier report, in 1975, had recommended a right of public access for 'the administered' to government documents concerning their own cases which was enacted in 1978 but its implementation has met predictable resistance from the ministries.

The combination of governmental appointment of prominent former politicians to the office of mediator with independence and impartiality in the holder's behaviour raises especially acute problems in the case of the Paris mediator. The first incumbent of this office was a councillor belonging to the majority party and an assistant mayor, albeit a former prefect with more than twenty years' experience in the prefectoral corps. He consequently cannot be 'an external critic of the municipal administration' of which he is a part.[11] Far from seeking to publicize embarrassing cases of maladministration, the Paris mediator, established by Jacques Chirac in May 1977, acts as an 'intercessor', attempting to secure speedy redress behind the scenes, thereby dampening down sources of public discontent with local government. Local citizens have direct access to the Paris mediator, but as is the case with the national mediator complaints must be made in writing and will only be countenanced if an initial attempt to secure redress has been unsuccessful. As an insider of senior status, the Paris mediator has no restriction upon his ability to consult all records and files or to question any municipal officials. He receives in excess of a thousand complaints annually, over a quarter being accounted for by housing (with fairness in allocation being more at issue than procedural faults), followed by requests to review discretionary welfare benefit decisions. Many complaints are lodged about central government (mainly postal and tax) services, as well as public corporations and social security agencies but relatively few against the police (5·7 per cent of all cases in the first two years of the Paris mediator's existence) and these concern the protection of public safety, not matters of public violence or the rights of those in police custody.

While citizens have secured increased protection in such day to day matters, their freedom to protest has been less circumscribed by *raison d'état*. The State Security Court, offspring of the early 1960s terrorism and subversion from the extreme right seeking to defend the indivisibility of Algeria and France, was used from 1968 until 1981 primarily against the extreme left and autonomists from the overseas departments. Until its abolition in 1981, the State Security Court was kept busy despite attempts by the Senate in 1963 to prevent its establishment and again in 1970 to secure its abolition, and despite the repeated attacks by Mitterrand against this manifestation of the Fifth Republic's 'permanent *coup d'état*'. It was abolished early in the Mitterrand presidency, bringing to an unlamented end a court that had rendered services rather than judgements.

The ordinary judicial hierarchy, headed by the minister of justice, bears the indelible mark of Napoleonic authoritarianism with its requirement that the judiciary should be a docile extension of executive power. The public prosecutors, who represent the government and form a quarter of all judges, are most directly under government control but the osmosis between the judges who sit on the bench and the prosecutors enables the government, through its control over promotion, to favour the pliable members of the judiciary. So, though the non-prosecutors are irremovable, they are in practice no less dependent upon government, in contrast with members of the Council of State where promotion is by seniority rather than at ministerial discretion. The virtual subordination of the bench to the prosecutors in turn leads to the dominance of the police, whose minister of the interior is much more powerful than the minister of justice. Forced to remain content with less than 1 per cent of the national budget, the ministry of justice devotes its energies to the organization of the courts, codes, prisons, probation and pardons. The crisis in recruitment to the judiciary is in part a consequence of the decline of 'judicial power' in France both as a function and as an institution.

The public standing of the courts in France is low. The number of those who consider that the judicial system works badly has consistently exceeded by a wide margin those who believe that it works well. Thus in 1977, 71 per cent of the French public thought the judicial system worked badly, 56 per cent describing it as remote, 58 per cent intimidating, 68 per cent slow and 86 per cent complicated and expensive. Furthermore, a majority thought that judicial decisions were influenced by political pressure (a view held by 78 per cent of Communist supporters, 64 per cent of Socialist supporters but also 46 per cent of Republican supporters and 41 per cent of RPR supporters).[12] If the public have a low opinion of the courts, the courts return the compliment. The judicial system gives the representatives of the public, the jury, a rather modest role in the assize criminal courts. Since 1941 (a legacy of the Vichy regime) the nine jurymen and three judges decide their verdict together, which, despite the requirement of a majority of eight votes, allows the president of the court to exercise a decisive influence on the verdict.

The judge as an instrument for the investigation of crime on behalf of public power adopted the church's inquisitorial procedure, legalized by Colbert in 1670 which assumed its modern form with Napoleon in the shape of the examining magistrate. Together with the provision for remand in custody for twenty-four hours (increased to forty-eight with the semi-automatic approval of the public prosecutor), this has effectively neutralized Article 9 of the Declaration of the Rights of Man which asserted the presumption of innocence until guilt is proved. When a trial begins, defence and prosecution are formally on an equal footing but it is preceded by a protracted phase during which a prima-facie case is prepared by the police and the examining magistrate. French procedure is directed at securing a confession of guilt. Generally, the examining magistrate is not concerned at how the confession has been obtained by the police, even though the person brought before him shows obvious signs of having been beaten up. The police know that the examining magistrate will not inquire into their actions because he is in practice subordinate to the ministry of justice's public prosecutors, who will not allow the minister of interior's police to be censured by the judiciary. Such police immunity, coupled with the examining magistrate's dependence on the police for his information and the knowledge that his promotion prospects depend on his pliability, converts him in practice into the auxiliary of the police commissioner. The examining magistrate may himself be under police surveillance if his loyalty to the government is in doubt. In cases which are politically sensitive he may receive very explicit threats of the career consequences of independent action.[13] This means that when the police, and counter-espionage services, are themselves implicated in a political crime, as allegedly in the murder of the Moroccan exile Ben Barka, the minister of justice can prevent proceedings leading in dangerous directions. The indivisibility of the judiciary from the police is a day-to-day demonstration of the unitary nature of the one and indivisible state in 'the classic land of political scandal'.[14]

Two more recent cases of political intervention in judiciary processes both involved the increasing problem of extradition related to international terrorism, both occurred in 1977 and both involved Federal Germany. In the case of Abu Daoud, a leading member of the Palestine Liberation Organization, political intervention resulted in extradition being expeditiously refused and Daoud hurried out of France a free man, while in the case of lawyer Klaus Croissant, with Baader-Meinhof terrorist links, political expediency dictated that instant extradition should preclude the possibility of an appeal. The Giscardian presidency contained numerous instances of alleged manipulation of judicial procedures by ministers of the interior and of justice, the president himself being the leading actor in the attempt to prevent Roger Delpey, an associate of the former emperor of Central Africa, Bokassa, from making embarrassing disclosures about gifts of diamonds to Giscard.

The appointment of France's most eloquent criminal lawyer, Robert Badinter, as minister of justice, betokened a new era in the Mitterrand presidency, reflected in the numerous legal reforms rapidly enacted, as well as by an attempt by a former interior minister to discredit him. In words that implicitly reproached his predecessors, Badinter proclaimed that it was not the function of the minister of justice 'to render justice and it is especially not for him to suggest to the judges what their decision should be. As long as I am minister, I shall never seek to influence judges. A large part of my legislative effort will in fact be to reduce the prerogatives of the minister of justice.' Despite attempts to suggest the contrary, this libertarian poacher turned libertarian gamekeeper categorically insisted: 'There will be no left-wing justice to follow right-wing justice.'[15] His reassertion of the claims of law against the requirements of order, reflected in a spectacular conflict in 1982 with Minister of the Interior Defferre (a fellow member of the League of Human Rights) over police power to make identity checks, demonstrated that judicial subordination could no longer be counted upon in the close collaboration required between the 'forces of law' and the 'forces of order' exemplified in the notion of 'judicial police'.

## *The police*

'A judge without a policeman is nothing. A policeman without a judge is everything.'[16] Whilst the first part of this assertion by a group of French judges is generally true, the second part is misleading in its exaggeration. Still, it is a salutary corrective to the formalistic treatment which this subject often receives in France. Its truth derives from the fact that France has not, in this as in other spheres, broken the grip of that statesman-policeman, Napoleon. Ironically, he is remembered for his legal codes, which were really a legacy from the Revolution, rather than the surreptitious police state which he built with the help of a master policeman–statesman, Fouché, like him brought to power by Sieyès as part of the 1799 Brumaire *coup d'état*. A ministry of police had been established in 1795 by the counter-revolutionary directory in the hope that all plots would in future be foreseen and forestalled. Fouché's achievement, as Napoleon's instrument, was to put the police above the law. The requirements of public order, whose guardians were the police, had priority over the protection of the citizens' freedom. The refusal to recognize a legitimate opposition loyal to the regime has meant that the police must be entrusted with the elimination of all opposition and the surveillance and repression of all domestic enemies. In such a situation, 'every branch of the administration has a part which subordinates it to the police'.[17] The French failure to institutionalize opposition has resulted in a semi-permanent cold civil war, which led successive ministers of the interior to continue to see in the *gauchistes* the threat to state security which they had been in 1968.

Because of the extensive prerogative police power that exists in France and the latitude accorded to the police forces in exercising these powers, of all the liberal democratic countries, the French police system would most effortlessly fit into a total-itarian form of government which the fear of revolution and civil war might bring about. The ministry of the interior, which absorbed the ministry of police in 1818, having lost in the nine-teenth century the wide range of welfare functions that it used to discharge, relies largely upon the prefects and the police to impose its conception of public order. The prefects are con-trolled through a political affairs division, for which they pro-vide a political intelligence service on behalf of the government, which is useful for electoral as well as police purposes. This division is also responsible for dissolving local councils and removing mayors – who have police powers in communes with a population of under ten thousand people – although there is a local authorities division which deals with most of their acti-vities.

The ministry's four police divisions come under a secretary-general of police but he does not control the whole of France's police forces, of which there are several, pluralism being re-garded as a safeguard against excessive police power. The min-istry of the interior controls some 120,000 police, 70 per cent of whom belong to FASP, a trade union that has a left-inclined leadership but is not affiliated to any confederation. Since 1941, the urban provincial police or *Sûreté Nationale* operate in the communes with a population of more than ten thousand. Pri-mary responsibility for maintaining order falls on the CRS, a mobile reserve force of 15,000 men who combine military dis-cipline and organization with civilian control and functions. In addition, the ministry of defence controls some 85,000 *gen-darmes*, recruited from among servicemen, who act as military police to the three armed services but are also the police in the communes with less than ten thousand inhabitants. This is the role of the 'white' departmental *gendarmerie* (45,000 men). The squadrons of 'red' mobile *gendarmerie* (17,300 men) are organized regionally and they are equipped with tanks and helicopters. They are reserved for use in times of crisis. Finally, there are a number of specialist units of the *gendarmerie* (9,500 men), such as the republican guard (2,730 men) which is for use in Paris, notably on ceremonial occasions. The *gendarmerie* also play a part in collecting information for use not only in combating crime but which also can be passed on to the political police. A 1971 instruction (abrogated but replaced by the Mauroy Government in 1981) from the head of the *gendarmerie* laid down that all new residents should systematically be identified and information about them collected, from sources ranging from the town hall to the *concierge*. It has been estimated that some 200 million index cards exist thanks to this saturation method of collecting information, which is being computerized and will be available within seconds thanks to an electronic transmission system called *Saphir*.[18] All Frenchmen are potential suspects.

This brings us to the two most mysterious police divisions: the general intelligence service and counter-espionage. The former constitutes the French political police. The *Renseignements Généraux*, created in 1907 by Premier Georges Clemenceau, who rejoiced in the title '*le premier des flics*', is staffed by 3,000 full-time policemen assisted by numberless informers paid out of interior ministry secret funds. It has the task of collecting information – from published documents and its own confidential opinion polls through to opening mail and telephone tapping – in each *département* under the control of departmental and regional commissioners of the republic, who forward the information to its Paris headquarters. In 1973 there were nine sections, the range of whose functions is revealing. The first section, special political affairs, had two units responsible respectively for the Communist Party and PSU on the one hand and revolutionary movements on the other. The second section, general political affairs, also had two units, dealing with other left-wing and centre parties and with right-wing parties. The third section handled industrial and trade union affairs, split between the public and private sectors. The fourth section dealt with economic and financial matters, while the fifth section's two units handled foreign and overseas French affairs. Section six was concerned with the press, radio and television; section seven handled links with other French police services and certain foreign political police services; while section eight dealt with inquiries and opinion polls. Section nine was responsible for collating and synthesizing all the information reported and preparing a daily bulletin and a weekly summary for the eyes of the minister of the interior, the prime minister and the president of the republic, with a monthly bulletin receiving somewhat wider circulation.[19]

Telephone tapping is a technique widely used by governments both in crime detection and to obtain political information for use against the domestic political enemies of the government and not just for counter-espionage. Despite periodic claims that telephone tapping for political purposes has ceased, it is clear that it persists. Investigation by a 1973 Senate committee of inquiry made little headway as did the Senate's rejection of the budget secret funds allocation for telephone tapping in the same year. 1973 was also marked by the discovery by the editor of the satirical weekly, *Le Canard enchaîné*, of an attempt to install 'bugs' in its new premises. This scandal was compounded by the judicial cover up of the refusal of the police to testify before the examining magistrate, the case being buried without those responsible for ordering or carrying out this illegal escapade ever being brought to justice. It was reported in 1973 that the many people whose telephones were being tapped at the time included François Mitterrand and Michel Rocard among opposition politicians, Giscard d'Estaing and Michel Poniatowski (Giscard's first minister of the interior from 1974–7) among pro-government politicians. Several political parties' headquarters telephones were tapped, some departmental offices of the Communist Party, CGT and CFDT received the same attentions, while not even the *bien pensant* FNSEA escaped. Both left- and right-wing extremist movements had their telephones tapped, as did some universities and three weeklies: *Le Canard enchaîné* (to discover the source of its many well-informed official leaks), the extreme right *Minute* and the left-wing *Nouvel Observateur*.[20]

On resigning as minister of the interior, Poniatowski claimed that over the three years he was in office, only 400 to 500 telephone taps had been authorized (note this word), over half concerning counter-espionage and the remainder involving especially serious criminal inquiries such as drug trafficking.[21] Few would give credence to this claim, if only because in many instances the prime minister's authorization was dispensed with. This doubtless occurred in the 'bugging' of the *pavillon* at the bottom of the garden of the prime minister's residence, the Hôtel Matignon, when his relations with the president became strained in the mid-1970s, Chirac being suspected of plotting against Giscard there. This transpired when the former head of the intelligence agency SDECE, replaced by Mauroy in 1981, told him to beware of talking freely in the summer-house, which on investigation was found to contain microphones installed by SDECE agents.[22] French public opinion in 1977 seemed to be divided mainly between those who thought that the telephones of selected politicians, journalists and senior officials were tapped (42 per cent) and those who did not know (44 per cent), the highest percentage of affirmative answers (68 per cent) coming from the best informed upper-middle class professions. It is too early to form a considered judgement about whether the Mauroy Government has been able to resist the temptation of telephone tapping for partisan purposes to which its predecessors have succumbed, but given President Mitterrand's repeated condemnation of this practice and his forbidding it when minister of the interior in 1954, there are cautious grounds for sceptical optimism.[23]

There is an overlap between the *Direction des Renseignements Généraux* and counter-espionage or *Direction de la Surveillance du Territoire* (known as DST) the activities of whose 1,000 agents used to include spying on communists, who were regarded as foreign agents. Whilst the general intelligence service was born in the struggle against Boulangism in the late 1880s, counter-espionage was brought under the ministry of the interior as a result of the Dreyfus Affair, and the distrust of the war ministry's *Deuxième Bureau* which it aroused. There is also a substantial overlap with the work of the SDECE, the euphemistically entitled external documentation and counter-espionage section, nominally responsible only for activities outside France threatening national security. It was directly under the prime minister until 1966 when, following the Ben Barka affair, it was transferred to the ministry of defence so that discipline could be restored. Its staff of over 2,000, financed partly out of secret funds, includes some 'analysis service' agents engaged in telephone tapping. Since 1970, the appointment of a civilian rather than a general to run the SDECE, coupled with a reorientation of its work towards industrial and scientific espionage, is part of an attempt to reduce the traditional interservice rivalry with the DST. It was reorganized in 1982 and renamed the External Security Division (*Direction Général de la Sécurité Extérieure or* DGSE for short).

The brutality of French police methods is notorious and is related to the fact that police efficiency is judged by the number of arrests and convictions achieved. The habitual use of force to extract confessions has sometimes led to the death of the detainee. Any act of self-defence against the police is treated as 'rebellion', and as we have seen, the judiciary almost invariably sides with the police. Far from being punished, those responsible have frequently been promoted and apart from isolated protests, notably from the League of Human Rights, which helps police victims with legal advice, the French public seems to accept such police behaviour fatalistically. Although at a time of crisis, such as June 1968, the majority of French vote for 'order', they detest the police who are responsible for enforcing it. During the period of police persecution of the *gauchistes* that followed, under the aegis of the minister of the interior, Marcellin, far from the public considering that the police were acting with undue severity, there was public support for greater rigour. Such support was weakest among young men, the better educated, those living in Paris, and those of left-wing political views. In such a context, some policemen are likely not merely to use force but even their firearms indiscriminately and with impunity. Many a minor criminal is shot 'whilst attempting to flee'.[24]

Reluctance to take disciplinary action is due to the feeling of dependence that French governments have upon the police, as well as the conviction that 'spying, brutality, arbitrary use of power and preparedness to take the law into their own hands is an integral part of the nature of any police system'.[25] A police strike in 1958 helped undermine the Fourth Republic and an attempt by Pompidou to placate rampaging students by implying that the police were to blame came close, in mid-May 1968, to provoking a police strike which might have destroyed the Fifth Republic. Only generous wage concessions enabled the police unions to prevent a spontaneous strike, and since then the minister of the interior has deliberately assumed the role of the '*premier des flics*', delivering frequent eulogies of the police, guardians of the state and the government. Nevertheless, police morale has remained low because they feel that they are not being sufficiently rewarded for doing the government's dirty work. Even the Socialist minister of the interior, Gaston Defferre, who sought to reassert ministerial control, accepting the resignation of the head of the Paris judicial police with the words 'the cemeteries are full of irreplaceable people', nevertheless had to make concessions to the public anxiety at the increase in crime. In 1980, a crime or an offence was being committed somewhere in France every twelve seconds. The daily rate was five murders, thirteen armed robberies, twenty-four drug cases, eighty-three violent robberies, 586 car robberies, 734 burglaries, and 1,183 thefts from vehicles. Out of a total of 2·6 million crimes and offences (of which one million were solved) 87 per cent were aimed at monetary gain and one-third were located in the Paris region.[26] As a result of the public obsession with security, some of the more radical suggestions of the 1981 Belorgey Report aimed at securing judicial control over the police were not acted upon by Defferre and the increased scope for identity checks instituted by Alain Peyrefitte was perpetuated. With the rising crime statistics and increasing sense of insecurity, President Mitterrand's determination to confine the police within strict legal limits, being more intolerant of injustice than of disorder, is bound to come under persistent strain.

## The domestic role of the military*

As the French police are also armed, it would be a misnomer to refer to the military, as one does in Britain, as the 'armed forces'. The *gendarmes* are a permanent link between the police and the military. Furthermore, the military have, notably during the Algerian war, waged 'police actions', for which they are not trained, in which the temptation to torture is not resisted and its utilization by the ordinary police is encouraged. The services have their own parallel political police, or military security, which makes routine inquiries into the political opinions of every young conscript, and to which the ordinary police are required to furnish information.[27] This is because the army does not see

* Defence policy will be discussed in chapter 8.

its role simply as that of protecting the country's territorial integrity against foreign enemies. The regular army is associated through a joint military-commissioner of the republic staff with the CRS and *gendarmerie* in the *Défense opérationelle du territoire* which, according to a 1962 decree, seeks to 'deal with enemy forces over the whole country, whether they are "implanted", parachuted, landed or infiltrated', in the context of nuclear or subversive war. Thus the military also protects the regime against revolution by internal enemies, but in 1958 the army itself played a major part in overthrowing the Fourth Republic in a forlorn attempt to preserve the indivisible union of Algeria with France. However, in retrospect, the period between the defeats of 1940 and 1962, in which de Gaulle at the start set an example of military indiscipline and then at the end quelled his would-be imitators, was an interlude in the traditional military obedience to civil authority.

The post-Revolutionary French solution to the problem of military–civil government relations was to give the army autonomy, allowing the military to regulate itself within a closed and united apolitical community. The Third Republic went so far as to deprive military personnel of the right to vote and stand at elections or belong to political parties. In return, the post of minister of war was usually held by a general on active service until the anti-militarist reaction following the Dreyfus Affair.[28] One of the most important achievements of the Fifth Republic, after an era of delegations of civil power to the military, has been to curtail military autonomy drastically.

Regular army officers have their own professional grievances which may become sources of disaffection. The twentieth-century decline in the social and meritocratic élitism of the pre-First World War army has been reflected in its 'proletarianization' by promotion from the ranks, whilst fewer and fewer direct-entry aristocrats and graduates of the *grandes écoles* choose a military career. A good example of this is the waning attraction of the military academy of St Cyr (founded by Napoleon) and the refusal of most graduates of the *Ecole Polytechnique* (which Napoleon militarized) to pursue a military career. The early nineteenth-century Saint-Simonian vision of the 'industrial army' of the future, led by *polytechniciens*, has been achieved, thanks to a broadening of what the notion of service to the state implies for a state-created élite. While increasingly colonizing top positions in French public and private sector business (foreign firms clearly not fitting into the notion of service of the state), the *polytechniciens* retain an important role in the most dynamic side of the military machine: the strategic nuclear programme. The nuclear deterrent forces now absorb an increasing share of the budget, while the bulk of the army seem demoralized, having lost any function with the end of colonial wars. As Alfred de Vigny wrote of the *Servitude et grandeur militaires* after the heroic Napoleonic era: 'Today, as the conquering spirit withers, the only greatness which a noble character can bring into the military profession appears to me to be less in the glory of fighting than in the honour of suffering in silence and of accomplishing with steadfastness duties which are often odious.'[29] As a corollary, ex-servicemen's organizations (of which the largest, UFAC, has three million members) are far less influential than they were under the Fourth Republic and the ministry of ex-servicemen has dwindled into insignificance.

Under the Fifth Republic there has been a marked evolution in the Revolutionary legacy of compulsory military service. Conscription was broadened into national service in 1959 to include non-military defence service, and a 1970 Act reduced military service to one year. In the interim, a 1965 Act had provided a third type of national service through technical assistance in French overseas departments and territories or technical co-operation with foreign countries, particularly ex-French colonies in Africa. The reduction in the size of the French services has meant that only about half are conscripts, though they form a majority of the army. Conscription remains popular and a combination of military opposition and high unemployment has meant that the Mauroy Government decided against reducing the length of service to six months. In 1982, however, special military courts, which had existed in France since the fourteenth century and were more recently identified with the two trials of Dreyfus at the turn of the twentieth century, were abolished. However, the Mauroy Government shows no greater tolerance than did its predecessors towards 'soldiers' committees', which developed in France between 1973-5, the minister of defence (Charles Hernu) having opposed the idea of trade unions for soldiers at the time.[30]

The enduring mystique of compulsory universal military service is reflected in the difficulty and belatedness with which provision for conscientious objection was made in France and the extent to which it is still not accepted by public opinion. Between 1952 and 1961, 470 conscripts were imprisoned because, on conscientious grounds, they 'refused to obey' orders to join the services, many of them being Jehovah's Witnesses. In 1962 the end of the Algerian war and an ardent one-man campaign by a veteran anarchist Louis Lecoin, culminating in a twenty-two day hunger strike, led de Gaulle to press a reluctant government and parliament to enact legislation, which they did in 1963 only after tortuous manoeuvres. The Act grants conscientious objectors a hearing before a board consisting of a judge, three officers and three government nominees, with an appeal to the Council of State. If their objection is sustained, they are discharged and must compete double the length of the normal period of national service in a noncombatant branch of the forces or in civilian work.

In contrast with countries like the Netherlands (18 per cent) or Federal Germany (17 per cent) only 0·5 per cent of French conscripts apply for exemption from military service on conscientious grounds. This is because propaganda (including disseminating information about the legal provisions) encouraging conscientious objection is severely punished as 'undermining

*Table 15*
*Applications for exemption from military service by conscientious objectors, 1964–78*

| Year | No. of applications Made | No. of applications Accepted | Accepted (%) |
|---|---|---|---|
| 1964 | 348 | 274 | 79 |
| 1966 | 59 | 42 | 71 |
| 1968 | 101 | 64 | 63 |
| 1970 | 261 | 175 | 67 |
| 1972 | 789 | 539 | 68 |
| 1974 | 596 | 458 | 76 |
| 1976 | 766 | 554 | 72 |
| 1978 | 1,208 | 938 | 77 |
| 1964–78 | 7,251 | 5,655 | 78 |

Source: adapted from J.-F. Théry in *Conseil d'Etat. Etudes et documents*, No. 32, 1980–81, p. 124.

the morale of the army'; because civil forms of national service in developing countries are available; and because 25 per cent of those called up are exempted on medical or other grounds anyway. However, Table 15 shows that there has been an increase in the number of applications in the 1970s and that nearly four out of five are accepted. The type of service has been broadened, especially after 1977, since when most conscientious objectors work for the National Forestry Service or for approved private welfare agencies. However, about half never take up these posts, in which, like soldiers they have no right to participate in political or trade union activity or the right to strike, and the penalties are not of a strongly deterrent nature.[31] Despite this *de facto* tolerance, the myth of the 'nation in arms' continues to inhibit attempts to fully liberalize the status of conscientious objectors in France.

*The mass media and political control over information*

The major contrast between the mass media channels of communication is that whereas the government has a monopoly of television and a semi-monopoly of radio, the press is not owned by the state. This does not mean that it is free from government control but it is more difficult to exercise this control without openly challenging the freedom of the press. To prevent the source from which newspapers draw much of their information being poisoned, the Fourth Republic in 1957 effectively secured the independence of *Agence France Presse* from government control. Unlike Reuters, which is jointly owned by its British, Australian and New Zealand newspaper-customers, or *Tass* which is owned by the Soviet state, the French press agency is controlled by a board, on which a majority of the fifteen members (eight) are chosen by the daily newspaper associations. There are, in addition, two representatives of the *Agence France Presse* (AFP) staff, two representatives of the state radio–television service and three ministerial nominees (of the prime minister, finance minister and external relations minister). The director-general is chosen by the board and can only be removed by a council whose function is to safeguard the AFP's objectivity. The AFP's largest client is the state, which accounts for the equivalent of 180,000 subscriptions.[32] There is substantial direct and indirect state financial aid to the press, amounting in 1979 to 71·5 million and to 2·5 billion francs respectively. Much the largest element is accounted for by preferential postal rates, while exemption from Value Added Tax is another privilege. Direct subsidies have been given to what might be regarded as that part of the quality press which is in financial difficulties because of a combination of low income from advertising and low circulation. The main beneficiaries in recent years have been two left-wing dailies, the communist *L'Humanité* (which sold well under 100,000 copies by early 1982), the dilutedly leftist *Libération*, the Catholic *La Croix* and the trenchant *Le Quotidien de Paris* (which has replaced *Le Figaro* as the most effective right-wing daily, frequently indulges in 'verbal terrorism' and enjoys the financial support of the pharmaceutical industry).

The government does not wish to restore Napoleon's total subordination of the press to state control as an adjunct of the police state, with official papers exclusively disseminating official information. However, its more authoritarian members have, in the past, bitterly resented press criticism of the institutions 'that make for the strength and solidity of our country; the police, the army and the authorities'.[33] It is at times of stress that the freedom of the press comes under governmental pressure, even in liberal democratic regimes; authority regarding freedom of the press as being sacrosanct in principle but expendable in crisis. In France the gap between principle and practice has varied between Republics. The Third Republic was amazingly tolerant towards the extreme right-wing press, which did not merely advocate the overthrow of the regime in the most violent language but incited its readers to assassinate political opponents. This is in contrast with the Fifth Republic's treatment of the extreme left press. As was the case during the Algerian war, selected fringe newspapers were repeatedly seized (not merely the statutory four copies to provide evidence for a subsequent indictment but the whole issue) without any intention of bringing the matter to court but simply to drive them out of existence.

French governments bring pressure upon the press in three ways. Firstly, they can exert legal pressure, not merely by seizure but by frequent prosecutions, to discredit a newspaper at least and to drive it into bankruptcy at worst. This technique has been unsuccessful against *Le Canard enchaîné* (a more effective opposition to government than all the left-wing parties put together in the period 1958–81) which has been able to ridicule those who take it to court so mercilessly that this has deterred prosecutions. In 1980 the minister of justice (Alain Peyrefitte), irritated beyond endurance by the increasingly critical yet damagingly authoritative *Le Monde* and seeking to avenge President Giscard for the attacks occasioned by the attempt to stifle the 'diamonds affair', under the implausible pretext of 'protecting justice' prosecuted it. *Le Monde* is widely regarded both in France and abroad as a model of journalistic rectitude, so prosecution served further to discredit its initiator rather than its intended victim. Conversely, the prolonged failure to proceed with the case against press baron Robert Hersant, who in 1977 was charged by a journalists' trade union with infringing on a grand scale the 1944 ordinance restricting press ownership to a single newspaper whereas he owned a dozen, also demonstrated the capacity of government to ensure selective impunity from the law. The failure to apply the press ordinance has not only benefited the Hersant press empire but this complex is an extreme example of the systematic evasion of its provisions. Thus Hersant, a former deputy, starting with a large stake in provincial newspapers and periodicals, acquired in the 1970s *L'Aurore*, *Le Figaro* (effectively merging them) and *France-Soir*, not merely without the law intervening but with the assistance of government.[34] By early 1983 the Hersant case had still not come to court.

This takes us to the second way in which governments exert pressure upon the press: finance. Not merely do governments have the power to vary the aid already mentioned and to discriminate in the way official advertising is allocated. Many newspaper groups, and notably Hersant, have relied upon state banks to finance their takeover bids or help them through periods of financial difficulty, which is an important source of occult influence. (*Le Monde* is one of the few newspapers to publish its balance sheet.) Lastly, governments can exert influence by developing preferential links with particular proprietors, editors or journalists, denying accreditation for briefings to some and selectively 'leaking' scoops for others. The cumulative result of such official pressures is to spread a subtle but debilitating form of journalistic self-censorship, with most mass-circulation French dailies being depoliticized in the sense of not being party newspapers.

Table 16 shows the estimated readership (not the sales) of the nine most popular newspapers, the absence of the figures for the three Hersant-owned papers being due to the proprietor's refusal to authorize their publication. (Note that these three all had declining circulations and have since continued to decline.) While *Le Monde* retains its pre-eminent place in terms of quantity as well as quality (although it seems to have reached a ceiling of about 1·5 million readers) the most spectacular rise has been that of *Le Matin* which, like *Le Monde*, has offered general support to the Socialist Party and has benefited from the increase in public support for it and its conquest of political power. By contrast, *L'Humanité* has suffered severely from the public disaffection with the Communist Party. On the right, the success story has been *Le Quotidien de Paris*, which has capitalized on increasing resentment against the left-wing government since the Mitterrand presidency with consistently 'no holds barred' polemics, displacing *Le Figaro*, demoralized by the loss of most of its best journalists after the Hersant takeover.

About three-quarters of French homes take a daily newspaper but they are read mainly for relaxation rather than to acquire political information. Despite the substantial growth in the French population since the Second World War, newspaper circulation has only increased modestly and the number of

*Table 16*
*Estimated readership of the nine leading national newspapers, 1979–81* (000's)

|  | 1979 | 1980 | 1981 |
| --- | --- | --- | --- |
| Le Monde | 1,518 | 1,465 | 1,481 |
| Le Matin de Paris | 521 | 582 | 1,032 |
| France-Soir | 1,112 | 935 | N/A |
| Le Parisien libéré | 1,070 | 916 | 1,009 |
| L'Equipe | 819 | 842 | 770 |
| Le Figaro | 862 | 778 | N/A |
| L'Humanité | 608 | 438 | 434 |
| L'Aurore | 493 | 348 | N/A |
| La Croix | 243 | 298 | 300 |

Source: *Centre d'étude des supports de publicité*, reported in *Le Monde*, 18 July 1980 and 12 July 1981.

papers has fallen drastically. As a result of the disruption of the distribution of Paris newspapers during the German Occupation, and the increased interest in local news, the provincial press out-stripped the Paris press in total circulation after the War and has increased its substantial lead. The relative importance of this provincial press is a corrective to the highly centralized character of French political and administrative institutions, particularly if one bears in mind that the number of separate local editions of each paper may exceed sixty. The largest provincial papers tend to be 'apolitical', which means that criticism of the government is rare and muffled. As in local politics, so with the local press, the emphasis is on what unites rather than on what divides. Newspapers with a recognized partisan slant include *Le Provençal*, Defferre's Marseille Socialist daily.

Apart from isolated cases like *Le Canard enchaîné*, which refuses to take any advertising to preserve its independence from business interests and keeps alive the old crusading tradition of French journalism, the bulk of the daily and weekly press are content prudently to make a profit at the price of being politically innocuous. In 1981, the best selling weekly was *Paris-Match* with 5 million readers, followed a long way behind by the more political *L'Express* and *Le Nouvel Observateur*, averaging about 2·75 million readers, with *Le Point* averaging 2·25 million readers. *L'Express* has moved a long way to the right, first under Jean-Jacques Servan-Schreiber and then under Sir James Goldsmith, though it has retained some intellectual respectability thanks to Raymond Aron, who fled from the Hersant-controlled *Figaro*. The *Nouvel Observateur* has taken over something of the role of *L'Express* in the 1950s and 1960s. Although it has not had occasion to emulate the latter's Algerian-war heroism, it serves the same function of regularly providing off-the-peg, 'ready-to-think' ideas for the left-wing intelligentsia.

Since the Second World War, and especially since the advent of the Fifth Republic, the radio and television services have been increasingly subordinated to the state, being converted into the government's docile propaganda instrument. The traditional view that monopoly control of a public service is an essential attribute of state sovereignty is widely held among the French political élite, though not by the general public. The

reluctance to accept opposition as legitimate has meant in practice that French governments have used radio and television to
expound official views to the exclusion of those of the Opposition. Prior to the outbreak of the Second World War radio had
been controlled by an official of the ministry of postal services,
but under the Fourth Republic it was usually controlled either
by the prime minister or the minister of information. The latter
ministry was created during the Second World War and from
1958–69 the minister of information combined the functions of
government spokesman and tutelage over the state radio and
television service. By 1969 it was recognized that for one minister
to discharge these two distinct roles meant the subordination of
radio and television to the government and the ministry of
information was abolished.

The Mitterrand presidency having been marked by yet one
more attempt to reform French radio and television, it is worth
recording his personal role when minister of information during
the cold war period of the Fourth Republic. Determined to
purge the radio staff of Communists who had infiltrated it,
Mitterrand exercised close control of the news through his *chef
de cabinet* who daily met the head of news broadcasting, together
with members of the private staffs of the ministers of interior
and of industry. Speaking in a National Assembly debate in
1949, Mitterrand categorically asserted the primacy of government control in words his Fifth Republic successors would not
repudiate.

Broadcasting is daily involved in politics, the national politics of
defending France's interest ... The government logically considers
that it is the legitimate representative of the French Nation, since it
has the confidence of a majority of the National Assembly and it is its
duty to express the will of the nation ... Among those who are
authorized to speak to the country and the world, are not those who
represent our democratic institutions entitled to pride of place?[35]

This statement corresponds closely with the normative tradition
later expounded by de Gaulle and by Pompidou, the latter
declaring in 1970 that the broadcasting services were the 'voice
of France' and broadcasters should not claim the freedom
accorded to other journalists. So, it caused no outcry when a
head of radio and TV news proclaimed in 1961: 'A journalist
should be French first, objective second.'[36]

While making all due allowance for the cold civil war of the late 1940s, accompanied and followed by the Vietnam and Algerian colonial wars – the latter coinciding with the extension of political control to the expanding TV medium – political interference was only fully systematized after the end of the Algerian war, during Alain Peyrefitte's period as information minister (1962–66). He subsequently recalled his predecessor showing him how to use the battery of buttons on his desk to contact the heads of the various broadcasting services. ' "Everyday at five o'clock you will summon them to arrange the guidelines for the evening news on radio and TV. You can also, whenever you wish, give them orders by internal telephone." ' Peyrefitte, who went on to declare: 'French television was the State in the dining room' and regret that its viewers were treated as *administrés*, relegated his own special invention, the SLII, which institutionalized governmental interference, to a hypocritical footnote.[37]

In July 1968, following the 'events' of that year, the *Service de Liaison Interministérielle pour l'Information* (SLII) was abolished. This secret committee of about ten officials from the major ministries met daily at eleven o'clock from 1963 to 1968, under the chairmanship of an official of the ministry of the interior, to co-ordinate information for the benefit of the ministry of information and the prefects. It also decided which politicians would appear on television and the subject-matter of broadcasts. The assistant director of Television News always attended to receive instructions on the matters to be emphasized or played down, until May 1968 when as part of the revolt of ORTF staff against government manipulation, he ceased to do so. (He was subsequently one of seventy-two who were discharged as a reprisal in August 1968.) The SLII was replaced in December 1968 by an interministerial committee for information, similarly composed, which claimed to confine itself to providing information without actually seeking to interfere in radio and television programmes.

The abolition of the SLII in 1968 and of the ministry of information in 1969, did not make ORTF politically unbiased. It was the ingrained practice of self-censorship, deriving from dependence upon the government, that resulted in the perversion of radio and television. Successive reforms have changed the letter of the law whilst the spirit has remained the same. The 1964 Act, which claimed to make the ORTF independent of government to ensure the impartiality of political information, signally failed in this respect owing to the inability of the governing board to carry out its functions. How could it guarantee the ORTF's independence when this board was constituted so as to ensure a permanent majority of government nominees, half of whom were civil servants representing the major ministries? (In 1968, two were members of the personal staff of the prime minister and one the head of the minister of information's personal staff!) The director-general was in effective control and he exercised it according to government directives. The frequency with which directors-general have come and gone since 1958 suggests that even complete pliability has not guaranteed security of tenure. Part of the reason may be that they have been under pressure not merely from ministers but from ministerial staffs, senior civil servants, prefects, pro-government deputies and influential mayors. The result was that the 1964 Act safeguard, which at the instance of the Council of State required the government to make clear when it was using radio and television for ministerial purposes, was circumvented.

Competition from the 'peripheral' commercial radio stations (so called because they are nominally situated beyond France's borders in Luxembourg, the Saarland, Monte Carlo and Andorra) means that the French listener has some freedom of choice. However, the independence of these stations should not be exaggerated as the French government is a shareholder in all of them either through Havas, in the case of Radio Luxembourg, or through SOFIRAD (*Société Financière de Radiodiffusion*) in the case of Europe 1, Radio Monte Carlo and Sud-Radio.* The two larger commercial stations, covering northern France, Radio Luxembourg and Europe 1 (in which it does not have a majority shareholding) are furthermore dependent on the French Post Office for permission to link their studios in Paris with their transmitters abroad. So, although they express themselves more freely on political matters and have generally been

* The French government owns 17 per cent of Radio Luxembourg; 34 per cent (but 46 per cent of voting shares) of Europe 1; 83 per cent of Radio Monte Carlo and 99 per cent of Sud-Radio. See *Rapport de la commission d'étude du statut de l'ORTF* (known as the *Rapport Paye*), 1970, pp. 50–53.

rather more generous to the opposition parties, they have to be careful not to provoke suppression. In the spring of 1982 the listener ratings were as follows: Radio Luxembourg, 25 per cent; Europe 1, 24 per cent; France-Inter, 16 per cent; Monte Carlo, 8 per cent. This reflects a continuing decline in the popularity of state radio compared with commercial radio.

Although the use of television for propagandist purposes was even more uninhibited than in the case of radio, especially by the twenty-three regional television stations set up by Peyrefitte in 1965 (with regional prefects daily suggesting what to comment upon and whom to interview) there is little evidence that it helped the Governments of the Fifth Republic. The frequency with which ministers appeared and the total exclusion of the opposition leaders in fact proved very counter-productive at the 1965 presidential election. The opposition candidates achieved great impact when each received a total of two hours on television and two hours on radio to expound their programmes. Since then, homeopathic doses of opposition politicians were administered to the French public throughout the periods between elections to counteract the attractions of novelty. The relative fairness shown during elections was more than compensated for by the bias between elections, both in general political reporting and more specifically in the selective transmission of debates in the National Assembly and from party congresses.

Opposition resentment at such discrimination came to the boil in April 1968 when a censure motion attacked the Government for 'confiscating the ORTF for its personal propaganda' to the exclusion of the Opposition and those such as Giscard d'Estaing, who was at the time giving the Government only critical support and was punished by being banned by ORTF. Although this motion was defeated, the May 'events' quickly embroiled the mass media in political controversy as the commercial radio stations were accused by the Government of helping to provoke and spread the student riots by their incendiary reporting. Forced to act as a fire brigade rather than an accurate news service, the cream of the ORTF journalists unprecedentedly criticized their organization for failing to report properly and pilloried the television news in particular for 'failing to resist government pressure'. They followed this by joining the general strike, demanding an end to government interference in ORTF, and held out until mid-July, long after the manual workers had ended their strike. Not only did they lose their fight for an impartial and independent ORTF. On the pretext of reducing staff, the Government chose the beginning of August (when most of France is on holiday) to dismiss the ringleaders of the strike, administering a lesson on the dangers of seeking to restore dignity and independence to the profession of ORTF journalism.[38]

Despite a brave attempt by Prime Minister Chaban-Delmas in the early years (1969-72) of the Pompidou presidency and the 1974 reform at the start of Giscard's presidency, no real progress towards the autonomy of broadcasting occurred. While direct ministerial censorship declined, this was seldom necessary thanks to a partisan policy of the president hand picking the people that held all the important posts, especially the directors of news. A striking example of the 'covert and internal' control over the news that followed the Giscardian purge was the 1974 demotion and 1977 promotion of Jean-Pierre Elkabbach, who was subsequently frequently used by Giscard as an interviewer.[39] Not surprisingly, Elkabbach was dismissed, the only one formally dismissed by the end of 1981 under the Mitterrand regime, and though much opposition play was made with the more or less voluntary ejection of most of the partisan Giscardian appointments, nothing remotely on the scale of the 1974 sacking of 1,641 staff (including 210 journalists) was instituted. There have been less reassuring aspects of the new regime, however. Whilst the appointment of Communist journalists would seem to be a desirable break with previous proscription, an agreement between the Socialist and Communist Parties that only those Communist broadcasters should be selected whose names appeared on an approved PCF list smacked of a left-wing version of covert control by partisan appointment.

A more tolerant, pluralistic side of the Giscardian legacy was that political parties and trade unions were permitted to present their own short programmes on the third channel's *tribune libre* and each major party in parliament was entitled annually to make four fifteen-minute party political broadcasts on the two TV channels which reached a much wider audience. It had been promised that the right to make such broadcasts would be extended to the trade unions but this was not done until the Mauroy Government took office. Access to TV is important between as well as just before elections because it is the most influential of the various sources of public information. A 1980 poll, allowing more than one source to be mentioned, rated TV at 46 per cent, with radio at 37 per cent, daily newspapers at 39 per cent, periodicals at 16 per cent and opinion polls themselves at 19 per cent.[40] French television devotes about a third of its programmes to news and current affairs, so any bias can have a significant impact. This can be negative as well as positive, too much propaganda having a boomerang effect, especially because the public primarily wants to be entertained.

The new master of French broadcasting was, until 1982, not the minister of communication but Mitterrand's *directeur de cabinet*, André Rousselet, who demonstrated a significant measure of continuity with the past in terms of attitude when he declared: 'The legitimacy of universal suffrage comes before the journalist's legitimacy.'[41] However, it was the minister of communication who prepared and presented the 1982 Act on Audiovisual Communication. Among the general principles set out, the most significant innovation is the institution of a 'right of reply' to those impugned (though not in a money-making context) analogous to that which individuals have had in relation to the press since 1881. To make the rules that would 'guarantee the independence of public service broadcasting' and ensure a balanced pluralism, a 'High Authority' was established on the model of the Constitutional Council. Its specific functions, in addition to implementing the general right of reply, include the regulation of the right of reply to government communications, electoral campaign and party political broadcasting, and the protection of children and adolescents. Of the nine-member Authority, six members were chosen in 1982 by the Socialist presidents of the republic and of the National Assembly and three members were chosen by the Oppositionist president of the Senate. Ironically, the Authority's composition has been attacked by the Opposition – which had previously defended the composition of the Constitutional Council against left-wing criticism – while the majority parties have rallied to its defence. Clearly, partisan appointment does not *necessarily* entail inability to act effectively in defence of 'independence' and 'balanced pluralism' but Prime Minister Mauroy's spirited defence of the failure to cut the umbilical cord between the representatives of 'national sovereignty' and the Audiovisual Authority does not augur well for the future if the past is any guide.[42]

The left's capacity to reform will also be judged by the way it handles the sensitive issue of local radio, which cumulates the objective of decentralization with that of ending the state monopoly of broadcasting. By a repressive 1978 Act, the Giscard presidency had sought to stem a surge of pirate stations promoted from 1977 by 'radio hams, commercial enterprise, local council and political fringe groups such as homosexuals, feminists, immigrant workers and ecologists'; followed in 1979 by the more formidable CGT station *Lorraine Coeur d'Acier* (defending the survival of the recession-ridden steel town of Longwy) and the Socialist Party's *Radio-Riposte* (started in protest against government interference in broadcasting).[43] The Government responded by setting up three local radio stations but also, in defence of the state monopoly, ordered a break into the Socialist Party's headquarters and prosecuted, amongst others, its first secretary, François Mitterrand. The case had not been concluded by the time of the 1981 presidential election and was later tactfully withdrawn.

The Socialists were confronted, after taking office, with an even more formidable upsurge of pirate radio stations (1,080 were counted in early 1982) and quickly decided to legalize them by an Act of November 1981, establishing a commission to undertake the highly controversial task of allocating scarce radio frequencies for a maximum period of three years. Faced with what has been described as 'Italian style anarchy', it is required to exclude stations that propose to finance their programmes by advertising. A left-wing government has had the embarrassing task of resuming Giscardian jamming, but preserving public control has become virtually impossible thanks to the proliferation of portable radio transmitters. The advent of satellite and cable television will in turn force French governments to face up to the problem posed by an incredulous André Malraux, celebrated novelist and de Gaulle's minister of culture from 1959–69: 'How can one govern a country where the government does not have a television monopoly?' The perennial battle between the norm of indivisible authority and an obstinately plural reality continues, even though the location of the battlefield shifts and the combatants change. The hysteria engendered by the fear that the left will dominate the mass media is all the more curious because the most perceptive liberal conservative analyses of the pre-1981 years identified them as an era of left cultural hegemony, albeit confronted by the countervailing power of the right's political hegemony.[44] Since 1981, there is a danger of political and cultural hegemony coinciding, except that there had been a tendency for cultural dominance to swing to the right in the 1970s as Marxism beat a retreat.

### A cautionary conclusion

Despite all that has been said in this chapter about the weaknesses in the protection of civil rights in France, and despite certain superficial resemblances to the Soviet police state, individual Frenchmen stand an incomparably better chance than would the Soviet citizen of surviving relatively unscathed in their encounters with authority. France is, despite all its authoritarian features, fundamentally a liberal democracy in which personal rights are not automatically sacrificed to *raison d'état*. She has a stubborn libertarian tradition of popular resistance to authority. There is a great deal of truth in the quip that, whereas in Britain everything is permitted except what is forbidden, in the Soviet Union everything is forbidden including what is permitted, whilst in France everything is permitted including what is forbidden. This is especially true since the advent of the Mitterrand presidency, during which the claims of civil rights have received greater weight compared to the requirements of public order or the convenience of public power. Despite demagogic exploitation by some right-wing politicians of public fears of insecurity, Minister of Justice Robert Badinter tenaciously defended against unscrupulous vilification the view that the rule of law must not expediently yield to periodic bouts of public panic. Ironically, this reassertion of a cardinal liberal principle has come, not from its nominal champions but from the Socialist left, despite the electoral price that must be paid for resisting popular prejudice in a democracy.

# 6 Economic Policy: By Whom and How It Is Made

Owing in part to the belated nature of her industrialization and exposure to international competition, official France, unlike Britain or the United States, had only occasionally, during the Second Empire and Third Republic, even paid lip service to market values until the late 1960s. French governments had for centuries alternated between policies of passive protection and active promotion – state-sponsored capitalism and state capitalism – based upon close collusion between the private sector and its public senior partner. The legendary timidity of the mass of French family firms meant that it was public rather than private enterprise that innovated and took risks. Despite the dramatic industrial revolution through which France has been going in the last three decades, and is still undergoing, the weight of this long-standing *dirigiste* tradition still makes itself felt in the sense of dependence upon government, which French businessmen more or less explicitly acknowledge. In November 1968 the president of the CNPF asserted that far from the growth in foreign competition requiring a withdrawal of the national government's protective and supporting intervention, it was a further justification of such assistance. 'The salient feature of this new phase of our economic development is the decisive role that states will be called upon to play. International competition will involve the whole nation. Left to themselves, firms cannot face this competition alone.'[1] This view is shared not merely by a majority of businessmen but by the French public in general. The propensity to support 'strong' state intervention cuts across all categories and provides a cultural underpinning to the political behaviour, especially of those in authority, that we shall discuss below.

*The political co-ordination of state economic intervention*

Overall economic co-ordination is carried out in France through an elaborate network of mainly informal and *ad hoc* interdepartmental committees and interministerial committees and councils rather than by the Cabinet. The most important of these is the Economic Interministerial Committee, which usually meets weekly under the chairmanship of the prime minister, its only other permanent member being the finance minister. Ministers and senior civil servants attend when invited (notably the budget minister, the president's economic adviser, the planning commissioner, the head of regional and spatial planning, or the governor of the Bank of France) but its main function is to resolve conflicts between the prime minister, the minister of finance and the spending ministers, prior to endorsement by the Cabinet. These conflicts will arise when the prime minister supports expenditure demands that have been rejected by the minister of finance. Particularly in the latter half of June each year, the prime minister spends a lot of time settling disputes that have arisen between the spending ministries and the finance ministry in the preparation of the budget. The disputed matters are reported to the government's general secretariat, where they are examined by its economic adviser and by the economic and budgetary advisers on the prime minister's personal staff. Issues which cannot be settled amongst officials are then dealt with by the prime minister, the minister of finance and the minister concerned, the finance minister winning about 90 per cent of such conflicts. The prime minister's decision is final unless either the spending minister or the finance minister chooses to appeal to the president of the republic; or the president, informed by his economic adviser, who is present at such interministerial meetings, elects to make his own decision through an interministerial council at the Elysée. To avoid an open clash, the spending minister appeals to the president through his staff, the president intervening before the prime minister takes his decision. The decision not to devalue the franc in 1968 was very much the personal decision of President de Gaulle; the decisions to devalue in 1969 and not to revalue in 1971 were taken by President Pompidou. At a press conference on 22 December 1971, President Pompidou made his intimate involvement in economic policy clear when he declared: 'You can be certain that the prime minister, the minister of economic affairs and finance and I myself are attentively following the situation day by day and that, if necessary, we would take the measures required to maintain the level of employment and expansion at a satisfactory rate.'

Apportioning influence over economic policy decisions among the triumvirate of president, prime minister and finance minister in general terms can only be done in an approximate way. By contrast with the Fourth Republic, when the finance minister was in a dominant position, especially in budgetary matters, under the Fifth Republic the president and prime minister have played a much more active role. The finance minister has been forced on to the defensive, compelled to provide the resources to meet commitments of which the president or prime minister approve. President Pompidou intervened much more extensively than did President de Gaulle, while the creation by President Giscard (finance minister from 1962-6 and 1969-74) of a Central Planning Council which met monthly had much more to do with extending and institutionalizing presidential control than with planning. The low water mark of the finance minister's influence under the Fifth Republic occurred between January 1960 and January 1962, when the former governor of the Bank of France, Wilfrid Baumgartner, was frequently short-circuited by the prime minister* and when the National Plan was being given great emphasis by president and prime minster. A spectacular but untypical example of occult influence by a presidential economic adviser is afforded by the case of Jean-Maxime Levêque, who held this office from 1960-4. From 1962, he warned President de Gaulle of the increasingly serious inflationary tendencies that neither Prime Minister Pompidou nor Finance Minister Giscard d'Estaing treated seriously, resulting in the imposition upon them of the 1963 Stabilization Plan,[2] for which Giscard was subsequently made the scapegoat. Despite subsequent ups and downs, the endemic economic recession has strengthened the hands of finance ministers and although Prime Minister Barre subordinated the finance minister to his authority, there has since been a partial restoration of the traditional financial veto over the expenditure

* He replaced M. Pinay, in circumstances described briefly in chapter 4, p. 107.

proposals of all other ministries, which are treated as irresponsible advocates for their sectional clienteles. The consequence has been a partial usurpation of the co-ordinating role of the prime minister by the finance minister with the president intervening as ultimate arbiter.

An important element in the restoration of the traditional power of the finance ministry was the revival of the pre-Keynesian principle of the balanced budget. This aim was inspired by Jacques Rueff, an economist who had the ear of President de Gaulle. In addition to influencing de Gaulle's views on international monetary policy, Rueff's liberal conservatism encouraged the Government in 1963 to adopt a commitment already long standing in Federal Germany: that public expenditure should not increase at a faster rate than the national product. This was the prelude to the 1964 application of the aim of a balanced budget in the preparation of the 1965 Budget, utilized by Giscard d'Estaing as part of the public relations facade for the Stabilization Plan curb on public expenditure. Balanced budgets have owned much to the artifice of selective inclusion and exclusion of items. The fundamental purpose of this fictional balance was not merely to impress the conservative electorate with the housekeeping rectitude of the finance minister; it was to disengage the Treasury from its previous task of substantial short-term borrowing from the public, and to channel these funds into long-term investment in public and private corporations, a role transferred notably to the *Caisse des Dépôts*.* It was the prelude to a neo-liberal attempt to free these corporations from the detailed control of the finance ministry over their investment policy and to reduce the tendency of the French public to affix political blame upon the government for economic mishaps. However, the deflationary policy followed by Giscard, inspired in part by the Rueff-de Gaulle desire to compel the United States to conform to the discipline of the gold standard, contributed to de Gaulle's poor showing in the first ballot of the December 1965 presidential election and to Giscard's dismissal from office in January 1966.

To whom does the French public attribute the power to take economic decisions? Table 17 indicates the public's assessment in 1971 of the way in which responsibility should be apportioned

* See below pp. 183–5.

Table 17
Who should take the blame when things go badly? (%)

| Responsible | Sphere of public policy | | | |
| | Order | Education | Prices | Taxation |
|---|---|---|---|---|
| President of the republic | 36 | 26 | 16 | 14 |
| Prime minister | 36 | 28 | 20 | 11 |
| Minister of finance | 1 | 2 | 38 | 54 |
| Assembly deputies | 5 | 14 | 5 | 6 |
| No reply | 22 | 30 | 21 | 15 |

Source: IFOP poll, 21 September 1971, published in *L'Express*, 27 September 1971, p. 13.

between the president, prime minister, finance minister and
Assembly deputies on four major issues of public policy. There
was a marked difference in allocation between the two economic
issues (prices and taxation) and the two non-economic issues
(order and education). Whereas most blame was attributed
almost equally to the president of the republic and the prime
minister on the non-economic issues, when it came to economic
matters the position was more complex. Here, the finance minister was singled out as the main culprit, with the president and
prime minister nevertheless sharing some of the blame. The
Assembly deputies were rightly exonerated from responsibility
except in the matter of education, where the unanimous vote in
favour of the Faure Act of 1968 was held against them. (The
large number of abstentions on this question might be due to
public inability to express the view that the real culprits were
either the ministry of education, the students or the teachers.*)
As to the main beneficiaries of the influence exercised, the same
poll indicated that 59 per cent (79 per cent of the Government's
opponents and 35 per cent of its supporters) regarded President
Pompidou's policy as primarily favouring big business. The
public impression of presidential bias is significant when it is
linked with the fact that the finance inspectors, who form the
élite of the finance ministry, as well as occupying other top posts
in the civil service and public corporations, frequently move
while still in their prime into private business. This facilitates

* See below, chapter 7. Considering the importance sometimes attributed in the
problems encountered to inadequate financial provision for education, the negligible
blame attached to the finance minister is interesting.

administrative as well as political concerted action in the management of the public and private sectors.

## The ministry of economy and finance

In France, as in Britain, there have been several unsuccessful attempts to avoid the tendency of overall economic policy to be subordinated to a ministry with a financial emphasis. In both countries, two major attempts were made by left-wing Governments (in France during the Popular Front Government of 1936–7 and when Mendès France was minister of the national economy in 1944–5). The aim was to plan the economy in a medium-term perspective and not simply to steer the economy through unpredictable squalls with the aid of the annual budget. In all four cases, the failure to check the power of the ministry responsible for the nation's finances restored the priority accorded to short-term budgetary and balance-of-payments considerations over the planned growth of the national economy, free from lurches between 'stop' and 'go'. However, before Britain embarked on the first of its post-war failures, in France the birth of the Planning Commissariat in 1946, which was to acquire a modest but respected and independent position *vis-à-vis* the finance ministry, ensured that medium-term planners would be tolerated and then accepted into the exclusive club of economic decision-makers. In 1963 the creation of the office of regional and spatial planning delegate general represented an extension of medium-term planning from a purely sectoral phenomenon – dealing with particular industries or public services – into an assessment of the implication of national economic decisions for particular regions considered as intermediate structures between the central government and local authorities. However, the absorption of the rival ministry of the national economy into a ministry of finance and economic affairs and then into the current ministry of the economy and finance did not represent the centralization in an overall coordinating ministry of the power to make economic policy. The staffs of the planning commissioner, and until 1972 of the regional planning delegate general, were answerable to the prime minister. This enabled him to challenge any attempt at economic omnipotence or omnicompetence by his rival for overall control under the president. Nor have these changes meant that the re-entitled ministry has ceased to be primarily a ministry of finance, which is the name that is still currently used.

There are problems of identity in terms of the ministerial hierarchy within the department and its administrative unity. These difficulties have been marked by periodic reorganizations. Thus, whereas it had been customary in the Fifth Republic for the finance minister to have a junior minister under him primarily concerned with budgetary matters, conflicts between Finance Minister Fourcade and Prime Minister Chirac in the period 1974-6 led Chirac's successor, the economist Raymond Barre, to assume direct responsibility for economic affairs, albeit with a subordinate minister to whom he delegated day to day responsibilities. However, by 1978, the expedient of dividing the ministry between separate ministers for the economy and for the budget was tried as another way of allowing the prime minister or the president to step in and settle matters of economic policy. With the advent of the Mitterrand presidency, yet another rearrangement was made. In the Mauroy Government, a single ministry of the economy and finance was reconstituted, with Jacques Delors at its head. While there was a separate minister responsible for the budget, Laurent Fabius was subordinate to Delors, though with ministerial rank, somewhat analogous to the position of the Chief Secretary of the Treasury relative to the Chancellor of the Exchequer in Britain. Furthermore, Fabius had under his direct control not merely the powerful budget division but also the taxation, customs and public accounts divisions. His close political relationship to Mitterrand within the Socialist Party meant that he was able to go directly to the president when he disagreed with Finance Minister Delors. Part of the confusion in 1981-2 about government economic policy among the press and public arose from the markedly different emphasis placed upon the need for austerity voiced by the two ministers with economic responsibilities, exacerbated by the prime minister's attempts at clarification and not wholly clarified by the presidential gloss on the issues. It may also be relevant that in contrast to the economically well-qualified tandem of Giscard and Barre, neither Mitterrand nor Mauroy gave much evidence of having mastered even the less arcane mysteries of economics (for whatever these are worth).

The superiority complex of senior finance ministry officials is based upon the fact that the ministry is in a stronger strategic decision-making position to all other ministries, who come as supplicants for financial favours. Corresponding to this relationship, the finance ministry's divisions and bureaux contain officials whose function is to supervise or short-circuit the activities of every other ministry. Thus the sub-divisions of the Budget and Treasury Divisions concerned with the nationalized industries may in practice take over the tutelage role assigned to other ministries. We have seen that finance usually gets its way in the interdepartmental committees which meet to resolve disputes. Furthermore, its senior officials represent the best of ENA. They colonize other parts of the machinery of economic authority. Thus, of the seventy finance inspectors who left their *corps* during the first decade of the Fifth Republic (apart from the nineteen who took over divisions or sub-divisions of the ministry of finance), twelve went to senior administrative posts in other ministries; twelve joined the personal staff of a minister (six joining the staff of the minister of finance or his minister for the budget); seventeen became managers of public corporations (eight in banks); and six took posts abroad (three in the EEC).[3] If to the inspectors are added the many finance civil administrators who move to prominent positions in other ministries or public agencies, a very powerful network of influence over economic decisions enables those in command at the finance ministry to count confidently upon securing acquiescence to their wishes.

However, the ministry of finance is too large and complex to be the cohesive and monolithic organization frequently depicted. The finance ministry would be more appropriately described as a federation of divisions, each of which is itself subdivided into autonomous bureaux which the minister's personal staff make valiant attempts to co-ordinate. The finance minister's *cabinet* is headed by a director who is not only the co-ordinator of the work of the ministry's divisions but the person whom other ministers initially contact, the director being almost permanently in his office whilst the minister of finance is frequently away. To keep the minister informed of the main economic issues and provide liaison with the most important divisions, about ten specialists are assigned particular duties within

Governing France

the *cabinet*. Treasury, budgetary, tax, industrial policy and planning, prices and incomes, internal trade, foreign economic relations and agricultural policy are regular candidates for such special treatment, indicative of the importance attached to them. Those selected are usually drawn from the ministry's divisions as men marked out for promotion and have the approval of the directors of the main divisions. Consequently, there is little likelihood of conflict between the staff and line decision-makers in the finance ministry.

The Finance Inspectorate audits the finances of most state institutions (except nationalized industries) and concerns itself with the efficiency as well as the legality of public expenditure. After five years' service they are free to leave and they often go off to positions of power inside and outside the finance ministry. They have, for example, enjoyed a semi-monopoly of the top posts in the treasury, budget, foreign economic relations and taxation divisions since the Second World War. The finance inspectors supervise the very extensive field services of the finance ministry, notably those concerned with taxation and public accounts. At this stage of their career, these Napoleonic creations are concerned with the rigorous enforcement of the central rules, and as such they deprive the ministry's local financial services of any initiative, all deviations from the rules having to be referred back to Paris. On leaving the inspectorate they are generally used as agents of change necessary to overcome the inflexibility of the centralized regulations they previously enforced but their old boy network provides enduring cohesion between the command posts of the financial directorate.

The finance ministry's two main centres of power are the Treasury and the Budget Divisions. Considering the volume of its work, the Budget Division has a small, high-powered staff consisting almost exclusively of civil administrators. They are responsible for preparing the main budgetary estimates and the framework of assumptions which the finance minister will use in the budget discussions; for advising on parliamentary questions and amendment during budget debates; and finally for supervising the implementation of the budget to ensure that expenditure accords with appropriations. In this latter task, the financial controllers play a major part, being attached to the

180

major administrative departments to carry out checks on expenditure by the ministry concerned before the expenditure is made and to maintain a running audit. Janus-like, they also act as financial advisers to the ministry to which they are attached, a duality of role resembling that of the prefect. The controllers are used by the Budget Division to secure information about the weak points in the expenditure estimates of 'their' ministry, and by the spending ministry which consults them on the preparation of estimates and seeks advice on how to deal with the budget division. It has been claimed that this results in co-management of the ministry's activities by the financial controller and the minister.[4] We shall return to the Budget Division when we examine the budgetary process, but the political advice to the minister on the consequences of alternative decisions by the director of the Budget Division as well as his role in implementing the decisions taken, make him a key figure in the financial techno-bureaucracy.

Francois Bloch-Laîné, a key figure in post-war French public financial administration, played a crucial part in 'transforming the treasury from being the budget's banker into the economy's banker'.[5] Despite the attempts at state disengagement and alignment with the Anglo-American-style money markets – in conformity with the acceptance of what were seen by the neo-liberals as the concomitants of international capitalism, whose logic had been adopted in the 1950s and which reflected the Giscardian revulsion from Bloch-Laîné's creative use of public intervention in the service of national planning – from the mid-1970s a stringent form of credit control was instituted. Committed until 1981 above all else to defence of the French franc, credit control – which is determined by the Treasury, in conjunction with the Bank of France after the finance ministry's Forecasting Division projection of money supply is received – takes the form of quantitative loan targets for all providers of credit backed by severe sanctions if these targets are not strictly adhered to. However, unlike the Anglo-American monetarist ascendancy, there has been no disposition to subordinate macro-economic policy to monetary targets aimed at reducing inflation at almost any cost. On the contrary, the monetary targets are fixed in the light of political judgements about the size of a tolerable budget deficit and level of interest rates, arrived at after advice from the Treasury Division and the Bank of France, in the service of macro-economic policy. So, although during the Mitterrand presidency the size of the budget deficit was allowed to increase, this did not represent a reversal of a continuing practice of putting policy ends before monetary means. The type of credit control used not only allowed the government to pursue, within the constraints of operating in an international economy, macro-economic objectives; it also enabled it to steer the flow of credit to particular parts of the economy to support its micro-economic objectives.[6] However, international pressure imposed a third devaluation within the first two years of the Mitterrand presidency, brutally enforcing the market limits upon state action.

The Treasury Division, in conjunction with the Bank of France and the *Caisse des Dépôts*, is responsible for France's national and international monetary policy, the management of all public receipts and payments, public borrowing and the loan of public funds for public and private investment. The most authoritative sources refer to the finance ministry and the Bank of France as exercising a 'condominium', resulting in a 'somewhat equivocal sharing of functions between two powers. The governor of the Bank of France and the minister of finance are sometimes compared to the pope and the emperor.'[7] Despite the fact that Treasury control over the Bank of France was increased by the Popular Front legislation of 1936 and by its nationalization in 1945, French governments have remained faithful to the intention of the bank's creator, Napoleon, who commented to his treasury minister: 'I want the bank to be sufficiently in the hands of the government, but not too much. ...'[8] It has been felt, as with the Bank of England, that complete government control would place 'monetary power' at the disposal of the short-term political interests of ministers, while autonomy would enable the traditional guardians of monetary orthodoxy to protect the longer-term national interest and increase the confidence of foreign monetary circles.

The 'condominium' (with the Treasury as the senior partner) is exercised through four committees: the National Credit Council, the Banks Control Commission, the Stock Exchange Commission and the Franc Area Monetary Committee. Of these, all presided over by the governor of the Bank of France, by far the most important is the National Credit Council, which advises the government on all aspects of its monetary and credit policy. Its forty-five members include the planning commissioner, officials of the finance ministry, the major economic ministries, the public credit institutions and representatives of industry, trade and agriculture. However, owing to overlapping membership, 'the council is virtually a supplementary board of directors of the Bank of France'.[9] Although nominally merely an executant of policy, the Bank of France's general directorate of credit plays a decisive part in the formation and implementation of monetary policy, with the governor of the Bank being in a particularly powerful position at times of crisis, such as in 1968 or 1982 when the Government needed to borrow substantial sums. The likelihood that the Bank and the finance ministry will see eye to eye is increased by the governor usually being an inspector of finance, Baumgartner (1949–60) and Jacques Brunet (1960–69) both being former finance ministry officials. Their long periods in office also explain the influential role played by the governor of the Bank of France. However, he does not possess the autonomous power that enabled the German Bundesbank president, with the approval of the Cabinet at a meeting in which he participated, to topple a prestigious federal economics minister in 1972.

The *Caisse des Dépôts et Consignations*, which manages funds equivalent to the state's budget, is another Napoleonic creation, although it did not acquire its present name until 1816. Since the Second World War, thanks to the decline in the burden of financing the long-term national debt (owing to inflation) and the rapid increase in the funds of savings banks which form 80 per cent of its deposits, it has become the most important treasury agency in the selective financing of public and private investment. It has concentrated on its traditional role, the long-term financing of local authority public works programmes at low rates of interest; but low-cost housing has now overhauled the provision of other types of public investment. (This building society function is discharged through a subsidiary called scic.) All these loans are undertaken within the framework of the investment priorities fixed by the National Plan and the Economic and Social Development Fund (FDES), the *Caisse* only lending money to institutions other than the

183

central government if they are in receipt of a public subsidy accorded by the finance ministry's economic intervention subdivision. In part, the *Caisse* is thus the Plan's investment bank, with the finance ministry possessing a veto power. Nevertheless, the *Caisse* encourages ministries and local authorities, with the collusion of the ministry of the interior, to over-invest relative to the limits imposed by the finance ministry and the Plan because it will usually supply the funds to make up the difference between what is authorized and what is spent.

The *Caisse* has created a number of subsidiaries, notably the *Société Central pour l'Equipement du Territoire* (SCET). Launched in 1955 at the instance of the finance ministry, it provides the financial logistical support for urban development joint public-private enterprises, in which the public sector never owns less than 50 per cent or more than 65 per cent of the shares. Local authorities are the majority shareholders in the 130 joint enterprises in which SCET is the minority shareholder. They have played a major part in equipping an increasingly urbanized and industrialized France with housing and industrial estates which are beyond the capacity of individual local authorities. In the process, the *Caisse* (through SCET) has been able to exercise a co-ordinating influence over housing policy that rivals that of the responsible ministry and has become the largest landowner and by far the largest property developer in France. It has pioneered the development of tenants councils, an important part of the modern user-consumer movement.[10] SCET's creator was the then director-general of the *Caisse*, François Bloch-Laîné, precursor of the new-style interventionism of the finance official, whose career illustrates the pivotal role in a planned economy of the finance ministry. An inspector of finance who rose to be director of the Treasury Division (1947–52), he then served for fifteen years (1953–67) at the head of the *Caisse*, becoming the leading advocate of the notion of a concerted economy. He headed the most important nationalized deposit bank, the *Crédit Lyonnais*, from 1967–74, when he was unceremoniously sacked by President Giscard, who resented his independence of mind in the service of public causes.

Bloch-Laîné has written of the *Caisse* that it is 'close to the treasury but not identified with it' and recalls the quip: 'The *Caisse des Dépôts* does nothing of which the government disapproves, but it does not do all that it requests.'[11] However, refusal to comply is rare and is most likely to occur in the buying of shares on the stock exchange, where the government may suggest that it help sustain a flagging market or save a French firm from a foreign takeover bid. Its holdings usually did not exceed 5 per cent and almost never exceed 10 per cent. It deliberately acts as a discreet sleeping partner, not exerting a power that would allow it to dominate the French stock exchange, and thereby decisively shift the boundary between public and private economic power. Had the Mauroy Government not sought 100 per cent public ownership, the *Caisse*, in conjunction with the public insurance companies, could have given it control over many of the firms it nationalized at great cost. Thus in 1981 it owned 5·5 per cent of the *Compagnie Générale d'Electricité*, 6 per cent of *Saint-Gobain-Pont-à-Mousson*, 5·6 per cent of *Pechiney Ugine Kuhlmann*, 7·2 per cent of *Thomson–Brandt*, 5·2 per cent of *Rhône–Poulenc*, 28·2 per cent of *Usinor*, 33·2 per cent of *Sacilor*, 4·1 per cent of *Paribas* and 5·7 per cent of *Compagnie Financière de Suez* amongst others.*

Bloch-Laîné made full use of the relative autonomy of the *Caisse* – symbolized by being accountable to parliament through a supervisory committee, not to the government – to make it into a powerful instrument in the development of social welfare at a time when this was not a prominent concern of most of the nation's political or administrative leaders. As he put it with mock modesty, the *Caisse* 'can undertake what the government does not ask it to do, provided that the government is not hostile'.[12] Bloch-Laîné's successor Maurice Pérouse likewise lasted fifteen years from 1967–82, also coming straight from being director of the Treasury Division. His 1982 successor Robert Lion, however, had previously been the director of Prime Minister Pierre Mauroy's *cabinet*, reflecting the importance that the Socialists attach to securing effective control over the levers of financial power through key appointments.

Although, under government pressure, the *Caisse* shifted in the 1970s towards helping productive investment, it did this – except in the case of some public enterprises – indirectly, by providing medium and long-term loan funds for other specialist banks better qualified to deal with industrial and service sector

* On the 1982 nationalizations, see below p. 237.

credit. The most important of these are the *Crédit National* (which concentrates upon large firms but has diversified its clientele to include smaller firms) and the *Crédit d'Equipement des Petites et Moyennes Enterprises* (which mainly helps the smaller firms). They have allowed the Treasury Division and the *Caisse* to deconcentrate some of the work of selective micro-intervention, but it is important to appreciate that the Treasury remains behind the scenes in a supervisory and interventionist capacity. What was involved was a change in the instruments of public intervention rather than a reduction in such intervention. Furthermore, although the *Caisse*, the *Crédit National* and other public banks, such as IDI (the Institute for Industrial Development) are used in the implementation of policies of industrial rescue, restructuring and promotion of strategic industries, the policy decisions are in the hands of interdepartmental committees operated under the aegis of the Treasury's economic intervention sub-division's officials. The most important of these crisis–response committees are the Guidelines Committee for the Development of Strategic Industries (CODIS), the Interministerial Committee for Industrial Restructuring (CIRI) and the Interministerial Committee for Assistance to the Localization of Firms (CIALA), the latter being particularly prompted by the need to deal with the impact of steel industry closures in Lorraine and the Nord. CIALA has the minister of planning as its chairman and includes the regional and spatial planning delegate, the planning commissioner, the directors of the Treasury and Budget Divisions of the finance ministry, the directors general of Strategic Industries and of Competition from the industry ministry and the delegate for Employment. So, despite doctrinal propensities to disengage the state from *dirigiste* practices during the Giscard presidency and especially during the Barre premiership, the institutional devices for discretionary intervention were, under the inexorable pressure of international economic recession, reinforced even prior to Mitterrand's accession to power.

The Treasury Division is responsible, through an office in its economic intervention sub-division, for all state shareholdings, though the *Caisse* may act as a holding company on its behalf and always collects dividends due to the state. The Treasury instructs the state representatives – civil servants who are appointed by the minister of finance – on the policy to adopt at board meetings, but they generally act as sleeping partners. The economic intervention sub-division plays a vital role in determining both industrial and regional policy by virtue of its influence over industrial investment. It thereby reduces the ministry of research and industry and the regional and spatial planning delegacy to the humble role of sorting out the more valid requests for investment funds, saving it the trouble of dealing with private industrialists directly. Furthermore, it acts as banker *vis-à-vis* the investment projects that will be supported in connection with the National Plan through the FDES for which it provides the secretariat, refusing to transfer this very important source of financial power from the finance ministry to the Planning Commissariat which has a less piecemeal approach.

It would be difficult to exaggerate the co-ordinating role of the FDES, another Bloch-Laîné brainchild, in the field of economic policy. This is reflected in its composition. Its management council meets twice yearly under the chairmanship of the finance minister. It includes as regular members the ministers of planning, public works, housing, industry, agriculture and labour (with other ministers attending when directly involved); the planning commissioner, the regional and spatial planning delegate, the directors of four finance divisions (treasury, budget, forecasting and prices); the governor of the Bank of France, the president director-generals of the *Caisse* and of three other public banks. The council discusses the most important national investment decisions, with the director of the Treasury Division introducing each item on the agenda and the finance minister summing up the discussion. Although it is only an advisory body, the fact that all the important people concerned are present gives it decision-making significance in practice. However, there is evidence that the FDES sometimes rubber stamps decisions taken at the highest political level.[13]

Most of the detailed work is transacted in fifteen specialist committees which deal separately with the long-term financing of sectors dominated by nationalized firms; aid to private firms; the capital investment programmes of ministries; agriculture; housing; the cinema industry; and foreign aid. On these committees, finance representatives play a less dominant role, the

Planning Commissariat providing either the chairman (in the case of the committee on loans to the private sector) or secretariat for most of them, the relevant ministry introducing the matters for discussion.[14] Although there was, until 1981, a deliberate reduction in the proportion of total investment financed through the FDES, it still provides the finance minister (who authorizes the allocation of funds that will be advanced either through the special treasury accounts or by a public bank) with a stranglehold on the volume and distribution of investment. The FDES council supervises the implementation of investment programmes assisted by public funds and publishes a detailed annual report of the extent to which they conform with the Plan's objectives.

## The Planning Commissariat and DATAR

The complementary nature of the processes of industrialization and urbanization, and the need to concert them in a medium and long-term perspective at the national and regional levels, involves going beyond the triangle of ministry of finance, FDES and *Caisse des Dépôts* to include the Planning Commissariat and the Regional and Spatial Planning Delegacy. The Monnet Plan, which just managed to catch the ebb tide of Resistance innovation in January 1946, succeeded where the attempts at a ministry of national economy had failed, because it did not challenge the authority of the finance ministry or other administrative agencies and concentrated upon medium-term industrial modernization through planned investment programmes. The First French Plan was initially insulated from the finance ministry's anti-inflationary attentions by the fact that the funds for investment were derived from the American Marshall Plan and that Monnet, the planning commissioner, enjoyed excellent relations with the American government.[15] As well as avoiding a challenge to the finance ministry's monopoly of short-term economic policy, the Planning Commissariat at first concentrated upon relatively non-controversial issues. It mobilized a business and trade union consensus in support of the Plan's targets, although the CGT withdrew from this when the Communists were excluded from the government in 1947. By dint of its modesty and prudence it reduced its administrative and political enemies to a minimum. This helped to ensure that whereas the loss of power by the Labour Party in Britain sealed the fate of a planning experiment that had already lost most of its impetus, the swing to the right in France did not result in the abandonment of national economic planning.

Despite the changes that have subsequently occurred, French planners have never forgotten that their survival and success within the process of economic policy-making has owed more to their skills in political negotiation than to economic expertise. With the Fifth Republic tendency of the president and prime minister to take a much more active interest in planning; the elevation of the Plan's achievements into a prominent place within government propaganda; the appointment of close collaborators of the prime minister to the key post of planning commissioner; the movement of both a planning commissioner and a regional and spatial planning delegate into ministerial office in 1967; the overt politicization of planning became incontrovertible whereas it had previously been played down. The coincidence between the final stages of the preparation and parliamentary approval of the Fifth Plan and the presidential election campaign of 1965 ensured that the politically oriented policy directives of the government would be given controversial prominence. The planning commissioner, whose politically neutral prestige had hitherto been used by the government to secure public identification between its proposals and the public interest, emerged as the instrument of political will rather than the conciliator and arbitrator between official policy and group interests. He was the committed champion of the government's preferences rather than the detached advocate of the dictates of economic rationality.

The independence of the Planning Commissariat from close political control should, therefore, not be exaggerated. While it has never been straightforwardly subordinated either to the prime minister (between 1946-54 and from 1962-81) or to the finance minister (1954-62), the Commissariat's freedom of action is limited. Co-ordination with short-term economic policy was facilitated when it was linked with the ministry of finance, whilst overall co-ordination is promoted by its ability to invoke the authority of the prime minister. The Commissariat is represented on the many bodies through which public economic policy decisions are taken. The commissioner may be summoned to Cabinet meetings and has regular discussions with the president, prime minister and finance minister. He sits on the government bench in the Assembly and Senate when the Plan is being debated and will advise and prompt his political masters. In the Economic and Social Council he is likely to bear the brunt of the debate on the government's behalf. In all three chambers he and his senior staff are closely questioned by the relevant committees prior to the floor debate. Because the Planning Commissariat's work is essentially concerned with formulating problems and influencing decisions at the preparatory stage, as well as co-ordinating and supervising decisions whose implementation will be undertaken by others, it has been able to retain its modest size. The spending ministries regard the planners with favour to the extent that they can gain their support in battles with the finance ministry. Without such support they would expect to be defeated, but when the dispute can be elevated to the point at which the prime minister is involved, the support of 'the Plan' may prove decisive.

Given the Planning Commissariat's success as a type of '"missionary" rather than "managerial" administration',* it was natural in the early 1960s, when it was considered necessary to strengthen central politico-administrative co-ordination of the regional planning without upsetting existing decision-makers, that the Commissariat should serve as a model. There is in the Regional and Spatial Planning Delegacy – the *Délégation à l'Aménagement du Territoire et à l'Action Régionale* (DATAR) – the same small size, informality of style and diversity of recruitment, though in the case of DATAR the fifty or so *chargés de mission* come mainly from the spending ministries and the prefectoral corps. Its greater tendency to recruit members of the *grands corps* facilitates political and administrative co-ordination by providing high level contacts with ministerial *cabinets*, central ministries and regional commissioners of the republic.

Younger and still less institutionalized than the Commissariat, DATAR has been more obviously political from the start.[16] A Fifth Republic creation, it was headed from 1963 to 1967 by a prominent Gaullist grey eminence, Olivier Guichard, who had been a close collaborator of de Gaulle before becoming one of

* See above, p. 46.

Pompidou's closest aides and ministers. The nature of DATAR's activities also involves it more directly and practically in political controversy. It is called upon to deal with sensitive local employment problems and has at its disposal a pump-priming regional intervention fund – *Fonds d'Intervention pour l'Aménagement du Territoire* (FIAT) – for promoting industrial decentralization which it was accused in 1967, with some justification, of using for the '*aménagement électoral du territoire*'. As a result of this great politico-administrative involvement, the regional and spatial planning delegate, like the planning commissioner, although formally a civil servant has sometimes been more influential on major public policy matters than are many ministers.

In the mid-1950s, when planning regions were designated and official action commenced, the finance ministry and the Planning Commissariat played the most active role, but when the inflexible centralist Debré was replaced by Pompidou as prime minister in 1962, the need for a co-ordinated implementation of regional planning was finally recognized. The regionalization of the budget since 1963 not merely strengthened links with the finance ministry and the spending ministries in Paris but improved DATAR's ability to control the overall co-ordination of regional planning where it counts – on the ground.

## *The budgetary process*

Because the budget is the detailed annual presentation in financial terms of present government activity and what it hopes to undertake in the coming year, it has traditionally occupied a pivotal place in public economic decision-making. From its figures, the government's economic policy can be inferred. It is also an excellent vantage point from which to observe how government works and who exercises decisive influence, both in the routine administration of agreed policies and in the initiation of controversial ones. As financial control over taxation and public expenditure was the principal instrument by which parliaments enforced the accountability of governments, the Fifth Republic's drastic modification of the power relationship between executive and legislature has transferred the emphasis in the budgetary process from the autumn parliamentary scrutiny to the winter–summer administrative and political executive preparations and decisions. Although the Assembly finance committee had never been as potent an influence on the budget, even in the heyday of parliamentary sovereignty, as the Budget Division of the finance ministry, the tendency to make the annual budget the 'handmaiden' of the quinquennial Plan (Debré *dixit*), over which parliament has almost no control, effectively concentrates public economic power in the hands of a political and administrative élite. While the 1959 reform of financial procedure installed an executive-dominated budgetary process which subordinated the defence of particular interests to the government's public expenditure priorities, it did not include in the budget the substantial areas of local authority, nationalized industry and social security finance. Without these items – separately controlled by the finance ministry – the budget ceases to ensure financial co-ordination, and overall parliamentary control through the Finance Bill is frustrated. Furthermore, the government has reduced the budget from its traditional function as the centrepiece of government accountability to parliament into a formal accounting framework in which governments annually report their predetermined taxation and expenditure proposals to the legislature.

Budget preliminaries commence a year before the budget comes into force. The finance ministry's Budget Division asks the ministries to send details of their last budget, the basis for calculating the funds that will be necessary to provide the same services at current prices. These *services votés* (continuing commitments already approved by parliament) are voted *en bloc*. Although the bulk of the budget made up of continuing commitments can be subsequently altered, bygones tend to be bygones and politico-administrative scrutiny concentrates on proposed changes. There was an important reform in French budgetary procedure in 1975 aimed at increasing the role of the president at the expense of the finance minister and the prime minister as well as the Budget Division, and allowing the parliamentary finance committees more time before the budget debates.[17] During the first phase from February to April, spending ministries submit their updated estimates for verification to the Budget Division, prior to a political decision, ratified by the Cabinet, fixing the expenditure ceilings and the government's policy priorities. Only after this is done do the ministries prepare detailed estimates within the framework laid down, followed by the customary meetings with officials of the Budget Division. This work is left to civil servants, only surfacing politically when major disputes occur. Each ministry's budgetary strategy is usually in the hands of the budget bureau (habitually called *Service du Budget et des Affaires Financières*) and the minister's *cabinet*, but all the central and field services are involved in the exercise. As it has no authority over the divisions, the budget bureau's role is confined to evaluating the cost of proposed policies. The resolution of conflicts for scarce resources is left to the minister, his *directeur de cabinet* and budget aide. A draft budget is submitted to the minister with an evaluation of the relative advantages of each choice and an estimate of the likely attitude of the finance ministry. The minister's verdicts result in a new draft, setting out the general aims, the anticipated cost and justification of each specific expenditure proposal, which is sent to the finance ministry's Budget Division. In May the head of each ministry's budget bureau and the relevant official in the Budget Division discuss the draft, setting aside any issues on which they cannot agree, and report to their ministers. The minister for the budget will meet each spending minister, the latter significantly visiting the former in his office. Any outstanding proposed expenditures are either settled by the finance minister or referred to the prime minister's *cabinet*, who advise him on his decision, where the matter ends unless the spending minister appeals to the president.

The detailed allocation of each ministry's estimates leads to tough negotiations with the finance ministry's Budget Division. The precaution of referring the budget beforehand to the financial controller* for his comments helps to reduce the conflict with his parent ministry, but the Budget Division's strategy is to place the spending ministry on the defensive by attacking many of its estimates and questioning the timeliness of its projects and the adequacy of the information supplied. The substantial cuts suggested at the start are intended to make the spending ministry concentrate on defending the efficiency with which they discharge their existing activities and allow the Budget Division to appear generous when it eventually concedes some new

* See above, pp. 180-1.

expenditures. The humiliation of spending ministers is reflected in complaints that: 'It is not right that the minister of education should in fact be the subordinate of financial officials who have no political responsibilities'; while a former minister of agriculture attacks that ministry's unbearable subordination to the finance officials, 'involving in addition a daily subjection over frequent decisions on products, prices, credit and markets'.[18]

The spending ministry's strategy has four salient features. It seeks to prevent the reduction of its past programmes, even when funds voted were not spent. When unable to secure priority, it tries to get an average share of increased public expenditure. It uses the Plan and the Commissariat against the Budget Division where possible. Finally, foreign comparisons cannot fail to be relevant: either France is behind and must make up its leeway or France is ahead and must preserve its lead. By July the final readjustments are made and by early September each ministry's draft estimates are distributed to the parliamentary committees. The Cabinet having approved the Finance Bill, the finance minister commends it to the public through a press conference.

The budget must be submitted to parliament before the beginning of October, the Assembly having a maximum of forty days and the Senate fifteen days to debate it on first reading. Article 47 of the Constitution goes on to provide that if parliament has not reached a decision on the budget within seventy days, it can be enforced by ordinance, the procedural presumption in its favour protecting the government from the use of delaying tactics against it in parliament. The executive seems mainly concerned that the budget should pass quickly and unscathed through parliament (by the end of December, the French financial year beginning in January). The government does not seek legislative help in improving financial control. Provided it is willing to set aside about 0·05 per cent of the budget to make a number of minor but politically popular concessions to its own parliamentary supporters, the government can secure the legitimation of its budget by parliament. Finance ministers deliberately make provision for such concessions that allow deputies to boast of their victories at his expense. Insofar as parliament continues to have an influence, it is largely exerted through the Assembly and Senate finance committees. In the Assembly the budget is carefully examined by a *rapporteur général* and over forty assistant *rapporteurs*. Its finance committees hold about fifty meetings a year, including hearings before the budget. Amendments made in parliament are generally insignificant, provoking exasperation by deputies at a ritualistic budgetary process reduced to 'litanies, liturgies and lethargies', in which the government only talks to its supporters, an exchange limited to small talk at that.[19] Ambitious parliamentary intervention, such as the 1971 attempt to end the scandal of massive evasion of death duties (facilitated by the 1952 Pinay Loan) is overcome with minimal concessions, thanks to the support of a reliable parliamentary majority.

Although forbidden by Article 40 of the Constitution to propose increases in expenditure or reductions in taxation, deputies still seek to please their electoral clientele. They are encouraged in this attitude by the government, which accepts some of these amendments in sharing out the tiny fraction of the budget which, as has been seen, it is prepared to yield to parliamentary initiative. Failure to exert parliamentary control over estimates has not led to an attempt to exert *ex post facto* checks along the lines of the House of Commons public accounts committee. French parliamentarians regard such work as of no political or electoral significance. Yet it is estimated that owing to the greater ease with which the government can alter its expenditure after the budget has been voted, 40–50 per cent of the sums involved are modified by regulation.[20] Another result is that budgets voted in overall balance are nevertheless in deficit at the end of the financial year. The government, therefore, remains in undisputed control over all aspects of the budgetary process, the major disputes occurring within the executive.

*The economic planning process*

The main links between the annual budget and the quinquennial Plan, between the finance ministry and the Planning Commissariat, are provided by the Forcasting Division and the National Statistical and Economic Studies Institute (INSEE). The latter assembles the general statistical data necessary for

national and regional planning, as well as undertaking forecasting work based upon past economic performance.[21] The
finance ministry's Forecasting Division, hived off in 1965 from
the Treasury Division, was an attempt to establish a high-powered challenge to the Planning Commissariat. The Forecasting
Division prepared the 'economic budget', which represents the
short-term assumptions on which the budget for the coming
year is planned. Each autumn, and again each spring, the
Forecasting Division prepares an economic and financial report
(the latter aspect being mainly the work of the Treasury and
Budget Divisions). It indicates the current year's performance
and next year's growth perspectives for production, consumption, investment and foreign trade that underlie the Finance
Act to which it is appended. This 'economic budget' should
provide the vital link between short- and medium-term economic forecasting and the economic policy pursued, without
which the objectives of economic planning are unlikely to be
achieved.

Until the 1982 reform of the planning process, the forecasting
framework, which embodied at a very early stage the government's political choice between the alternative possibilities
available, sought to confine all subsequent discussion within a
statistical straitjacket, the government's preferences being
treated as the only economically rational ones. The popularity
of the term 'indicative planning' tended to place a misleading
emphasis upon the 'generalized market research' and 'reduction-
of-uncertainty' aspect of concerted forecasting, rather than the
Plan as an instrument for working out and monitoring the
carrying out of the government's social and economic policy in
the medium term. French national and regional planning goes
beyond the rational calculation of what is collectively possible
or probable, as revealed by projections and forecasts, to a
government attempt to reconcile them with the politically pre-
ferable. This is done by a strategic use of all the instruments of
economic and social policy in conjunction with extra-govern-
mental organizations, who have the capacity to facilitate or
frustrate public action, to secure the achievement of more or less
explicit quantitative and/or qualitative objectives. The politically explosive nature of some objectives, such as the willingness
to tolerate a higher rate of unemployment or to accept a rapid

rate of exodus from agriculture to industry and services, means that some of the government's targets will not be stated clearly. However, while seeking to bamboozle its opponents, the government must not mislead itself. So, like a systematic tax evader, it must keep more than one account of its activities. Nor is the planning process comprehensive, several substantial but politically sensitive categories of public expenditure, such as defence, social security, foreign aid and farm income supports, having so far evaded the Plan's grasp. Nevertheless, although the National Plan is partly a public relations exercise, it provides a relatively accurate guide to the ideological and practical orientation of French economic policy, as is clear by contrasting the periods before and after 1981.

During the presidencies of Pompidou and Giscard (covering the Sixth to the stillborn Eighth Plan), as economic policy-making was concentrated increasingly in the hands of the president and his staff, it was harder to disguise the fact that the Plan was that of the government rather than of the nation, and as circumstances or the government's priorities changed, the commitments ceased to be much more than expressions of provisional intentions. So, paradoxically, increased political control was combined with decreased political commitment. The planning commissioner's membership of the Central Planning Council, instituted by President Giscard in 1974, provided regular monthly occasions for the concerns of the Planning Commissariat to be ventilated at the highest level, but it seems that the planning commissioner tended to be informed rather than fully share in decision-making. The *ad hoc* and short-term preoccupation of the president, his ministers and their *cabinets* meant that the planners increasingly had to concern themselves at best with piecemeal programming rather than achieving an overall strategy. While the day to day influence of members of the Planning Commissariat was not necessarily reduced substantially in the interministerial committees, the decline in the significance of the medium-term, macro-economic framework within which particular decisions had their place, meant that the Plan had to adapt itself to fit the immediate requirements that it had been unable to anticipate or bend to its purpose. This was most obvious in the lack of commitment of ministers and their senior officials to planning, taking their cue from

President Giscard who regarded his task as day to day improvisation, 'managing the unforeseeable'. Whereas de Gaulle had regarded the Plan as the instrument for implementing a comprehensive and grandiose policy and Pompidou had sceptically been content with using planning in support of the 'industrial imperative', the late 1970s witnessed general disillusionment with Plans to which the president was clearly not committed. Despite the attempt in the Seventh Plan (1976–80) to protect a hard core of twenty-five priority action programmes from the vagaries of short-term pressures by giving them budgetary guarantees, the Budget Division officials steadfastly refused to regard themselves as required to carry out even this part of the Plan.[22] They were confirmed in this view by the fact that few of the spending ministry officials with whom they dealt bothered to refer to the Plan or even to keep copies of either the Plan or the priority action programmes concerning their ministry in the room in which they worked.

The increased political control of planning meant that although the planners themselves retained some esteem as possessing a measure of independence of judgement from the government, the Plans themselves were regarded as wholly subordinated to government policy. By the late 1970s, the Monnet myth of modernization by concertation between the interested parties represented in the planning commissions had evaporated, as had the belief fostered by Pierre Massé (planning commissioner during the high water mark of planning in the early 1960s) that planning could reduce market uncertainties. Jean Ripert, planning commissioner during the preparation of the last pre-Socialist Plan to be implemented, the Seventh Plan, actually had to be reluctantly drafted into office because he was unwilling to keep up appearances when planning was increasingly discredited. His successor, Michel Albert, who had been a former collaborator of Prime Minister Raymond Barre, protested in a confidential letter to the prime minister (subsequently leaked to *Le Canard enchaîné*) that statements had been inserted into the text of the Eighth Plan which were intended to persuade the public of the success of the government's economic policy in the run-up to the 1981 presidential election. His damaging admission that the Eighth Plan evaded the problem of rising unemployment – presenting 'as a risk what is a certainty'

– and proposal of a level of public investment that was inconsistent with the 1981 budget decisions, confirmed the general view that planning had been cynically subordinated to the needs of tactical political convenience.[23] Although the trade unions, led by the CFDT, persuaded the Planning Commissariat to compare the effects of work sharing by a massive reduction in the working week to $35\frac{1}{2}$ hours with either giving preference to protecting the balance of payments or increasing the rate of investment, thereby returning to the promotion of full employment as the main goal of national economic planning, the government was intransigently committed to policies treating employment as a residual factor. Though the CFDT and CGT did not boycott the final phase of the preparation of the Eighth Plan, as they did in the case of the Sixth and Seventh Plans, they categorically disassociated themselves from its governmentalized analysis and policies.[24] It was not much of an exaggeration for critics of the Eighth Plan to claim that the only figures it contained were the page numbers.

The left that came to power in 1981 had long been committed to a much more ambitious conception of planning, predicated upon the belief that the scope for social and economic change and the margin of political choice was much greater than anything even de Gaulle had attempted. Pierre Mendès France had sketched out twenty years earlier the democratic and decentralized yet rigorous national and regional planning institutions that were intended to become the centrepiece of political life, focusing political debate upon the alternative policy choices and simultaneously planning from above and from below.[25] Similar ideas had been developed by the CFDT, notably in the 1959 report on democratic planning,[26] so that both on the political and industrial wings of the non-communist labour movement, the ground had been prepared for a drastic change in the direction of French planning, both in its methods and in its objectives. The immediate effect of the Mitterrand victory was to render the Eighth Plan, intended to cover the period 1981–5, stillborn. In fact, 1981 was the first year since 1947 when no National Plan was in operation in France. The minister responsible for national and regional planning, Michel Rocard, who was very much in sympathy with the ideas formulated by Mendès France and the CFDT, concentrated initially upon preparing a two-year Interim Plan (1982-3) which had a dual purpose. It was intended to allow a reversal of policies that it was hoped would enable the French economy to resume its expansion, as well as to reform the planning process so that the Ninth Plan would coincide with the last five years (1984-8) of President Mitterrand's term of office. Such a synchronization of the planning and political timetable had been an important element in the Mendès France proposals, and it would now be possible to see if the hazards of political and economic circumstance could be confined within the sedate limits of a quinquennial calendar.

Who were the new actors that were to carry out a not-so-new strategy? As we shall see, there are a mass of new actors or old actors playing new roles in the regional part of the new planning process but at the centre the picture is simpler. Given the familiar problem of reconciling the Plan with the budget, it was an ingenious move to put a former finance ministry Forecasting Division official and inspector of finance (Michel Rocard) in charge of planning, and a former planner and CFDT trade union official in charge of finance (Jacques Delors). However, Rocard suffered the severe handicap of being Mitterrand's unsuccessful rival as Socialist presidential candidate in 1981, for which he had not been forgiven. Furthermore, he was regarded as a personal as well as politico-administrative rival by Delors, with the further complication that the budget was more especially the responsibility of the ambitious Fabius. Another potentially helpful personal link between planning and finance was the appointment of Hubert Prévot as planning commissioner after briefly working on Rocard's staff. After serving in the finance ministry's Forecasting Division from 1961-74 and following Rocard out of the PSU into the Socialist Party, he had been seconded to the CFDT as confederal secretary responsible for economic affairs from 1974-81, so he provided a link between the traditions of enlightened techno-bureaucracy and democratic planning. Prévot's assistant planning commissioner was Yves Ullmo, who represented the pre-Giscardian commissariat, where he had worked from 1963-73, latterly as head of its economic section, before moving to INSEE and then the OECD, a safe refuge when the French climate became hostile to planners. The appointment in 1981 as head of regional planning of

Bernard Attali, twin brother of Jacques Attali, an influential member of President Mitterrand's personal staff, helped to strengthen links between the planning agencies and the policy makers. The links between the Commissariat and the top political decision-making centres were strengthened by the fact that two planners joined the private office of the president and four were recruited to the prime minister's private office. So, there was a nucleus of people committed to making new-style planning work at the centre of affairs.

Indicative of the desire to link planning with parliamentary democracy – rather than the previous emphasis upon techno-bureaucracy with a corporatist camouflage, parliament playing a formal, negligible role[27] – a committee was established in January 1982 to re-examine the techniques and methods of planning and was placed under the chairmanship of the National Assembly's finance committee chairman, Christian Goux. Its March 1982 report formed the basis of the 1982 Act on the reform of planning. Starting from an analysis of the decline in planning that had occurred from its early 1960s Gaullist apotheosis as an 'ardent obligation', planning's fourfold functions – conceived as forecasting; concerting interests with a view to making their demands more realistic; offering an attractive vision of the kind of society being developed; or achieving administrative co-ordination – had all regressed.[28] Even the priority action programmes experiment, aimed in part at overcoming administrative inertia, had succumbed to the Budget Division's hostility, so that the programmes scheduled for the Eighth Plan were shorn of all medium-term financial commitment. Returning to Monnet's view that planning should be based upon national consensus and not merely the will of the government, which had itself failed in recent years, the Goux Committee stressed the need to create the conditions for a 'dynamic social compromise' based upon 'a widely shared diagnosis of the crisis'. Until its composition was changed, the Economic and Social Council (with its anti-left majority) was not regarded as the body best fitted to achieve such a consensus, so the creation of a National Planning Committee was suggested, made up of people actively involved rather than 'organization' men. The Plan's implementation depended above all on establishing firm links between the five-year Plan and the annual budgets, themselves based upon programme budgets in each ministry. To ensure that the Plan's priorities were honoured in practice, programme laws would be necessary to give them legislative force, and officials of the Planning Commissariat would need to take part in the annual spending ministry–Budget Division meetings. Ensuring the government's financial commitment to the Plan was not sufficient. Contracts would have to be signed with public and private enterprises to ensure that the Plan's objectives would be implemented by firms. As we shall see, similar planning contracts were also to be signed with regional councils and local authorities.[29]

The new planning process prescribed by the 1982 Act laid down that for each future Plan there would be two planning laws. These would not, as hitherto, distinguish between the guidelines and the Plan proper but between the strategic choices and objectives phase, voted upon by parliament in the spring session of the year preceding the implementation of the Plan, and the application phase, voted upon in the autumn session along with the budget for the first year of the Plan. In this second phase, the legal, financial and administrative measures necessary to carry out the approved strategy are described, as well as the agreements made with the government's 'social and economic partners' to secure joint implementation of the Plan. This second Act would set out the five-year priority implementation programmes (successors to the Seventh Plan's priority action programmes) as well as how resources would be redeployed from non-priority areas of expenditure. Each Finance Bill would be accompanied by three-year projections of public expenditure, which would take into account the financial commitments represented by the priority programmes. In addition to the consultative National Planning Committee, which would represent a wide variety of economic, social and cultural interests, with the minister for planning as its chairman and the planning commissioner and the head of regional planning as its *rapporteurs*, a parliamentary amendment provided that there should be a joint parliamentary planning body consisting of ten deputies and six senators to keep an eye on the preparation and implementation of each National Plan. The National Planning Committee took over the preparatory work of devising the Plan which had hitherto been the government's responsibility, although at the start of the Committee's work the government would present a statement of its intentions and guideline policy proposals. This was intended to ensure greater freedom for the planning process from executive control, thereby making a reality of the claim that it was the nation's and not just the government's Plan. Each spring, Parliament receives a report from the National Planning Committee on how the Plan is being carried out, and each autumn, during the 'budgetary session', it receives a joint report from the planning and budget ministers on the implementation of the Plan's priorities in the Finance Bill.

A striking innovative feature of the new planning process is its emphasis upon decentralized regional planning as well as planning from the centre. While this is consistent with the political decentralization discussed earlier,* there are un-doubted problems of simultaneously planning from above and from below, by function and territorially. These difficulties were encountered during the Seventh Plan experiment with region-ally and locally initiated priority action programmes.[30] It would appear that the reliance has been placed principally upon the exchange of information between the centre and the regions (notably through regional council answers to a questionnaire), upon increased regionalization of the budget and through the signature of contracts between particular regions and the government. The latter need to be approved at least three months before the second Planning Act if they involve expendi-ture commitments. Although the regional councils are supposed to submit their priorities to the centre sixteen months before the commencement of the five year planning period, irreconcilable conflicts will occur between national and regional priorities, especially in regions where the Opposition is in political control. The scope for all sorts of difficulties, in what is a well intentioned but very cumbersome procedure, is vast.

None of the French Plans have to date been implemented without a major hitch. The First Plan's targets were achieved a year late; the Second Plan, thanks to Edgar Faure's 'eighteen-month plan' of 1953–4, exceeded its targets; the Third Plan was scaled down by an Interim Plan covering 1960–1, only for the results to be nearer the original targets; the Fourth Plan was

* See chapter 2.

modified by the 1963 'Stabilization Plan'; while the Fifth Plan was going badly until it was unexpectedly rectified by the May–June 1968 crisis and devaluation in 1969. Both the Sixth and Seventh Plans were drastically revised while the Eighth Plan hardly got started before it was scrapped. The Court of Public Accounts in a 1966 Report stated that from one-quarter to one-third of the funds annually allocated to ministries were not spent until up to four years later, the ministry of education being especially prone to sluggishness. The delay either held back currently budgeted investment schemes or led to the abandonment of the previous programmes. The delay also exacerbated the effects of inaccurate cost estimation, with the result that less could be achieved with the funds allocated. Finally, new projects were given priority without foreseeing the effects on existing projects.[31] Improvements have been made in getting public investment programmes and budget authorizations into step, but serious divergences between Plan and performance, measured by annual expenditure, continue to occur. When one adds to such problems of political chance and bureaucratic inertia the domestic and international economic pressures, one cannot but be sceptical about the ability of any government, however secure in office and committed to 'democratic planning', to carry so ambitious a revolution in economic policy-making through to a successful conclusion. When governments wrestle ineffectually with the task of preventing the remorseless rise of unemployment, what hope is there for overweening attempts at making a reality of economic democracy? What they can do is shift the ministry of finance out of the Louvre to make way for more art treasures and this President Mitterrand, to his credit, had decided will be done. Fortunately for the Ninth Plan's credibility, the 1982–3 runs on the French franc occurred early enough to allow the new 'rigour' in economic policy to replace the heady expansionism of the Interim Plan that was supposed to cover those turbulent years.

# 7 Elusive Autonomy: Education and Public Enterprise

While it is not customary to consider state education in conjunction with the industries and services that are collectively described as public enterprise, in problems of organization and management, in economic and budgetary importance, education raises similar questions to those that occur in the nationalized sector. However, because of the key role that it plays in the processes of political socialization and social stratification, education is a far more central task of government than running the railways or coal mines. This pride of place has been reflected in the close control that successive French governments have exerted over education, conceived either as the matrix of political and social stability or as the instrument of political, economic and social modernization. These functions potentially bring the state educational system into conflict with the family and the Church, which have been rival socializing agents. Furthermore, the development of an industrial society has meant that new demands are made by the economic system, affecting both the scale and content of the education provided. In these circumstances, government's relation to the educational service becomes a matter of pervasive importance.

Governments are reluctant to relinquish centralized control over education as an instrument of public power. However, it is increasingly difficult to insulate education from intervention by parents, Churches, businessmen or local authorities. By the early 1960s, senior ministry of education officials were themselves questioning the traditional combination of close central control and isolation from social pressures and were speculating about the possibility of promoting autonomy relative to government and reducing it relative to society. Insofar as the main proponents of nationalized industry in France were inspired by a desire to socialize without bureaucratizing, to increase the public service role of the nation rather than the power of the state, there has been a comparable search for a type of public institution which is responsive to public demands without being subordinate to the government. However, the attainment of autonomy has proved elusive, both in education and in public enterprise.

### Dualism and division in French education

Even before the French Revolution, voices were being raised to defend the claims of the nation-state against the Church in matters of education. In a prophetic 1763 'Essay on National Education', La Chalotais, the attorney general of the Brittany *parlement*, asserted: 'I claim for the Nation an education that depends upon nothing but the State, because it belongs to it in essence; because the Nation has an inalienable and imprescriptible right to educate its members; because in the end the children of the State must be brought up by the members of the State' and went on to declare that education should be 'of the State, by the State, for the State'.[1] This opening shot in a battle that continues to sway back and forth, even under the Fifth Republic, has the virtue of brutality. The claim for a state monopoly over education, in place of a virtual Church monopoly, sets one of the normative limits within which the argument has since been conducted.

While the state attained a dominant position over education by the end of the nineteenth century, the whole of pre-Revolutionary education was dominated by the Church, with its emphasis on protecting the young against corruption by society rather than upon preparation for a productive role within it. Although secularized, education's traditional function of preserving and transmitting the timeless culture, transcending the changing demands of society, economy and polity, survived almost intact. However, the Napoleonic and republican traditions each gave a different twist to the fundamental task of indoctrination inherited from the Church. Over and above the encyclopaedic emphasis of French education, the schools imparted a religious respect for the language and a pride in national identity and in France's cultural achievements. As half of the French population did not speak standard French before the mid-nineteenth century, the primary school teachers were regarded as missionaries of national unification dedicated to the rigorous elimination of regional languages and local dialects. This work of linguistic proselytization and cultural assimilation was facilitated by the Imperial University established by Napoleon in 1806: a hierarchical, centralized state monopoly control of all schools and teachers, 'state Jesuits' whose political function Napoleon clearly formulated. 'My main purpose is to have a means of controlling political and moral opinion . . . As long as people are not taught from childhood whether they should be republican or monarchist, catholic or atheist, the state will not fashion a nation; it will be based on vague and uncertain foundations, constantly exposed to disorder and change.'[2]

The restoration monarchy transferred the educational monopoly to the Church except in higher education. Despite a period of liberalization under the July Monarchy, the 1848 Revolution convinced the conservatives of the need to promote Catholic schools as an anti-revolutionary bulwark. A duopoly was instituted that entrenched the clerical versus anti-clerical conflict thereafter, the notorious Falloux Act of 1850 increasing the number of Catholic primary schools fivefold in the next thirty years. A powerful secularist retort came in the 1880s, establishing a free, secular and compulsory system of publicly provided education for children aged six to thirteen. Ideally, it sought to overcome France's ideological split by seeking to enforce neutrality and equal respect for all beliefs, especially through state control over school textbooks whose use could be forbidden by the minister of education on the ground that they were not neutral. This threatened a colourless uniformity and conformity with official truth, leading to a Catholic demand for 'freedom' now that the Catholic hierarchy no longer controlled public education. However, the bitter anti-clerical struggle that followed the post-1882 replacement of 'moral and religious' by 'moral and civic' instruction in the primary schools meant that civic education was regarded as an opportunity to indoctrinate the young with a secular republican ethic underpinning the new regime.

At this time the primary school teachers were the anti-clerical equivalent of the priesthood, providing – along with the Masonic lodges – the rudimentary organization that the Radical Party, which did not have an organized mass following, needed at the local level. Especially in the rural areas, the primary school teachers wielded great power, acting as the mayors' secretaries and chief assistants in some twenty-five thousand communes at the turn of the century. However, as the fervour went out of the anti-clerical struggle in the first half of the twentieth century, the role of civic education declined into its present bloodless formalism. It consists of dogmatic normative abstractions mixed with legalistic descriptions of the political and administrative organization of France, proceeding from the commune to the national government, with international affairs being reached by the end of secondary education. The limited time and teachers' enthusiasm devoted to civic education, which is sometimes simply replaced by history and geography, is significant in a country whose teachers are likely to be socialists or communists. The relative neutrality of French state education is evidenced by the fact that its products imbibe patriotism rather than any clearcut partisan orientation. Far from civic education being the vehicle for political indoctrination, the universal indifference with which it is regarded indicates conclusively that one must look elsewhere for the pedagogy of political commitment.

What are the dimensions of the strictly educational cleavage between Catholic and state education? Some 15 per cent of those in full-time education frequent private, i.e. generally Catholic, establishments (which account for 93 per cent of private pupils and students). The proportion varies substantially: about 13 per cent of kindergarten and infant pupils; 14 per cent of primary pupils; about 20 per cent of secondary pupils and a mere 3 per cent of the university and *grandes écoles* students. The regional variations in secondary education are very great, ranging from about 10 per cent in Limousin to over 40 per cent in Brittany and 34 per cent in Paris. (The three Alsace–Moselle departments, detached from France between 1871–1918 when Church and state were separated, are a special case, exempted from the anti-clerical legislation of that period.) The 1905 separation of Church and State meant that the clergy were no longer salaried officials, but the cost of this freedom was high and the Vichy regime came to the financial rescue from 1941–5. The financial straits to which the Catholic schools were reduced by the late 1940s led to a vigorous campaign for state aid by the 'free school' lobby. This was organized by a secretariat whose constituent elements were a one and a half million strong National Federation of Ex-Pupils and a 750,000 strong Parents Union. Its main political lever was the Parliamentary Association for Free Education, drawing on the right and centre parties. The resistance to using public funds to subsidize Catholic schools was organized by the National Committee for Secular Action, whose main supporters were the 500,000 state school teachers of the National Education Federation – notably the primary school teachers of sni – the 1,200,000 family strong Federation of Parents of state school children, the Educational League (over half of whose 2,700,000 membership are children), the major trade unions and left-wing political parties.

The battles between these two lobbies culminated in the 1959 Debré Act when the ascendant right legislated in favour of the Catholic school lobby. However, Prime Minister Debré was keen to resolve the dispute once and for all by a non-sectarian compromise which would promote rather than frustrate national unity. The Act provided that Catholic schools which were prepared to offer a public service on a par with state schools should sign contracts with the ministry of education which could be of two types. They could either conclude an 'association agreement', whereby the Catholic school would teach according to the regulations and curricula of state education, in return for public payment of the staff and the expenses of running the school; or they could enter into a 'limited agreement' under which the state paid the teachers salaries, approved their appointment, and inspected them but had no influence over the curriculum. (This latter option was forced on the government by the Catholic school lobby but was intended to be temporary and transitional to the 'association agreement'.) Despite bitter opposition from the secularist lobby and its political allies (who threatened nationalization of all schools that accepted public subsidies when the left returned to power), the 1959 Act was quickly passed by large majorities in both the Assembly and Senate. The agreements were prepared by the prefect in each department, in conjunction with regional and local officials of the ministry of education; the resort to prefects indicated a distrust of the traditionally secularist education ministry and reliance on the prefects' political sensitivity. Although up to 1964 the prefects had rejected some 1,700 applications to sign a 'limited agreement' and nearly a hundred proposed 'association agreements', a large majority of Catholic primary schools signed a 'limited agreement' while secondary schools favoured the 'association agreement'. By 1981, 98 per cent of the 10,000 Catholic schools had entered into agreements, 71 per cent of primary schools having signed 'limited agreements' (perpetuated by Presidents Pompidou and Giscard) and 99 per cent of secondary schools having signed 'association agreements'. Nevertheless, the state's financial support for Catholic schools, which increased from 4 to 13 per cent of the education ministry's budget from 1961–81, did not prevent a steady fall in the percentage of children educated in Catholic schools, the public sector growing twice as fast as the private sector from 1958–76.

The fundamental ambiguity about whether the Debré Act would perpetuate scholastic segregation or facilitate gradual integration of Catholic schools into the state system was not resolved in the 1960s and 1970s. While the right of Catholic schools to exist was challenged by only an irreducible minority of advocates of a state monopoly of education, proposing control without subsidy, their right to subsidy with minimal control was only surreptitiously extended, thanks to the pressure of the Parliamentary Association for Free Education upon sympathetic ministers. The search on the left, meanwhile, was for acceptable alternatives. While the solution of neither subsidy nor state control – reflected in the slogan, 'state funds to state schools' – meant the probable disappearance of most Catholic schools, there remained the possibility of negotiating a generalization of the Debré Act's 'association agreement' to all Catholic primary schools, as a stepping stone to the left's objective: 'a single, secular public service' covering all schools, including those in Alsace–Moselle. This last alternative was Mitterrand's preference, as he made clear as early as 1977.

There are two opposing conceptions. Both are based on traditions, convictions and commitments whose roots lie deep in the French nation's body and soul. ... We, who reject indoctrination and all idea of an official school, believe that the pluralism of ideas, beliefs, cultures and ethnic groups and the right to be different can and should be exercised as part of the public service of education. We fear the conservation of an educational dualism, the institutionalization of two competing systems financed by the state; the private one, leaning increasingly to the right because of the conservative notables who are gradually replacing the priests as headmasters, the public one, hastily and imprudently accused of being left-wing. ...[3]

This circumspect approach, based upon a knowledge that public support for the retention of state subsidies for private schools portended dangerous electoral consequences if a 'school war' broke out, meant that as in the past it was the right that sought to force the issue to the forefront of the 1981 elections.

However, the bogey did not work in 1981, a conspicuous and exemplary electoral victim being Guy Guermeur, the Breton deputy who had been secretary and then chairman of the Parliamentary Association for Free Education in the 1970s. The National Committee for Secular Action believed that the long awaited hour of its revenge had come. However, it was disheartened to see the studied circumspection with which the Socialist minister of education, Alain Savary (selected in preference to the more militant spokesman on education issues, Louis Mexandeau, posted to the ministry of telecommunications) handled the issue, giving priority to preserving 'educational peace'. At a mass rally of nearly a quarter of a million people in May 1982 to celebrate the centenary of the secularist Ferry laws, Savary stressed the need to make secularism the basis of consensus, not dissensus. 'We must always bear in mind that although the republic is one and indivisible, we have become more aware of its diversity. So, because secularism is tolerance and pluralism, one of tomorrow's essential battles will be to ensure that the one and indivisible republic gives each of its citizens the means to be faithful to his own associations.'[4] This undogmatic stress upon unity in diversity was reinforced by Prime Minister Mauroy's emphasis upon the need to secure agreement, confirming Mitterrand's 1977 commitment to persuasion rather than imposition. So, although this rally was the first meeting at which all sections of the political and industrial left were present since celebrating Mitterrand's presidential election victory a year earlier, there was disappointment that rapid and decisive progress was not going to be achieved to create the unified and secular educational service they had been promised.

A major reason why the political leaders of the left did not give way to the precipitate fervour of their activists was that the public opinion polls had for years shown that the secularist lobby was unrepresentative of mass views, even on the left. Thus in 1977, 64 per cent of the public favoured state subsidies to private schools (including 51 per cent of Socialist voters) with 27 per cent against (43 per cent of Socialist voters) and 9 per cent expressing no view.[5] Table 18 shows that whereas right-

*Table 18*
*Public attitudes towards private v. public education in France,*
*February 1982*(%)

|  | *All* | *Right voters* | *Left voters* |
|---|---|---|---|
| Retain present system | 55 | 80 | 36 |
| Present system with reduced subsidies | 12 | 9 | 15 |
| No subsidy but no state monopoly | 9 | 3 | 15 |
| Private schools integrated into a 'single, secular public service' | 18 | 5 | 31 |
| No reply | 6 | 3 | 3 |

Service Indice – Opinion poll in *Le Quotidien de Paris*, 24 March 1982, p. 9. See also Ibid., 25 March 1982 p. 11.

wing voters are strongly in favour of retaining a high level of subsidization of private schools, left-wing voters are divided over the issue. It transpires that the private schools are valued not so much for religious reasons as that they are thought to be a better preparation for future careers, even though they are not so good at training future citizens. Both public and private schools are regarded as not strictly neutral politically but secularism is identified with political and religious toleration rather than neutrality, showing that Savary's approach was one that enjoyed majority support.

The dualism of French education has not been due to religious cleavage alone but to class divisions as well. The place of Latin in the secondary school curriculum illustrates both the religious and the class sources of divisiveness in French education. Latin's symbolic importance should not be underestimated. 'The feeling that the French have always had that they are the true heirs to Roman culture has been reinforced by religion. Latin is the language of Catholicism,'[6] although it has been replaced by the vernacular. Furthermore, Latin has traditionally provided a barrier between the non-vocational education of a leisured middle-class and working-class education for menial tasks of production. That it still has influential supporters is evident from an instruction published in the official bulletin of the ministry of education in 1967 which claimed that Latin constituted the main medium of contemporary thought! Latin was a major obstacle to the development of comprehensive secondary education but, more particularly since the Haby Act of 1975, performance in mathematics has become a more meritocratic selector between those school children who are only considered fit for the less esteemed occupations and those who can compete to enter one of the *grandes écoles* or at least a university.

As some of the bitterness ebbs from the religious obstacle to national unity, social inequality becomes a central issue between left and right, with the left acting as the champion of the one and indivisible republic. The class cleavage in French education was, until the extension of the school leaving age beyond primary education, a clear one between elementary mass education for manual employment and republican citizenship and secondary and higher education to train the economic and political élites. The working classes were taught obedience to their social betters by what H.G. Wells, in the English context, described as education 'of the lower classes, on lower-class lines, with specially trained inferior teachers'. Despite a formal commitment to equality and respect for a classless general culture presupposing the existence of a neutral general interest, French education has reflected, reinforced and legitimized the class divided nature of French society. The meritocratic 'career open to talent' has been almost exclusively of benefit to the middle classes, with 'democratization' of the educational system being mainly due to pressure by the lower-middle class to gain access to the institutions that have hitherto been the preserve of the Church-going upper-middle class. For example, there is a close correlation between religious belief and the class character of the senior civil service, practising Catholics being disproportionately likely to attain such posts, especially in the *grands corps.*[7] Despite all the rhetoric about general culture, the economic, administrative and political élites have maintained a quasi-monopoly of recruitment to prestige professional training in the *grandes écoles* and in the law and medical faculties of the universities, which control access to prestigious economic, administrative and political positions in French society. The discontinuous ladders to social advancement by educational merit ensure that an apparent equality of opportunity can be combined with a maintenance of inequality, the high student failure rates in French university education being a tribute to its social as well as its educational selectivity.

Although the monolithic, one and indivisible University of France, embracing all educational institutions and controlled from Paris, lost its Napoleonic grand master, the attempt at monopoly control over the educational process survived, a prey to the creeping paralysis of bureaucratization from the Third Republic onward. This obsessive preoccupation with universal regulation led the teachers, in self-defence, to convert the rules into a stubborn protection of their vested interests. So, although in the 1960s the ministry of education at times issued on average three circulars a day, securing compliance was quite another matter. It had, for example, failed in 1959 to obtain a reduction in the very long school holidays in France and was to fail again in 1969, on both occasions owing to resistance by the teachers' organizations.

The ministry of education, which in a centralized system was the sole potential source of innovation, was faced on issue after issue with an insoluble problem. Sweeping reform – alone acceptable because it respected sacrosanct national uniformity – proved impossible owing to corporate resistance; while piecemeal reform, which might have avoided a head-on collision with opponents, was ruled out as the source of arbitrariness and diversity such as existed in the decentralized English system. Other Napoleonic legacies were the emphasis upon nation-wide examinations to ensure central control over selection to the élite; the damaging fragmentation between teaching, research and professional education (each entrusted to separate institutions), the central role being accorded to the *grandes écoles* which embodied the Napoleonic ideal of the 'engineer-administrator';[8] and the draining away of all talent to form a hyper-centralized,

Parisian intellectual élite. However, although the Paris-based public service cornered the scarce resource of trained intellectual talent, the ministry of education has not been successful in obtaining its share. One education minister, Olivier Guichard, claimed in 1970 that he had been given an impossible task: 'there is no political or administrative post in France that is as monstrous as that of national education minister. The notion that a politician can supervise 811,000 civil servants and a budget of 27 milliard francs with the help of a skeletal headquarters staff is far-fetched.'

There have been frequent attempts to reorganize the ministry of education as well as the educational programmes, indicative of the difficulty of either perfecting the administrative instrument or attaining the educational objectives.[9] In 1974 higher education was put under a separate minister, which in due course led to such extensive and arbitrary ministerial intervention that it was reunited with the rest of education in 1981. However organized, the ministry of education has usually been prevented by its very centralization from securing more than incremental changes. Until 1981, the Fifth Republic ministers of education had to face an opposition alliance of a minority in parliament but a majority in the teachers and parents associations. Despite the well publicized conflicts between them, the ministry of education enjoyed close, quasi-corporatist ties with the representative primary and secondary school teachers' unions. However, they were prepared in 1977 to oppose the attempt to promote comprehensive education because of their desire to embarrass the government politically.[10] Under the Fourth Republic their power was so great that the ephemeral education minister's name was sometimes confused with that of the general secretary of the primary teachers' (SNI) or secondary teachers' (SNES) unions, which constituted respectively over two-thirds and one-tenth of the National Education Federation's membership. A senior official recalled that 'even the directors were inclined to be more attentive to the behests of the unions than to the minister's orders, as it was very likely that the latter would finally reflect the former'.[11] The strength of the SNI – which organizes 90 per cent of state primary schoolteachers – is based on its local share in educational management but it is as centralized in its organization as the education ministry.

Although of predominantly left-wing political convictions, the teachers were in favour of radical reform or revolution in every sphere other than education, where they submitted to change only when their desperate attempts to defeat it had failed. The largest parents association has been cross-pressured by the fact that it has close ties with the sNI and so has difficulty in championing reforms to which the teachers are opposed. Nevertheless, parents have a significant voice in French schools and this is a sphere in which public participation made significant advances, with government support, in the 1970s.

The ministry's field services are run by twenty-seven rectors, the regional educational prefects who were created by Napoleon in 1808 to represent the central government and guarantee that unity of education which has been both the pride and despair of France. It is only since 1972 that the 'academic regions' have been broadly aligned with the standard regional pattern, which is indispensable to the effective regional planning of educational expenditures. However, the Paris region has been divided into three academic regions, the attempts to control 1,700,000 pupils, 180,000 students and 80,000 teachers having finally been recognized as extravagant. Prior to 1950, almost all decisions were taken by the ministry in Paris. As the volume of work grew with the numbers educated, piecemeal deconcentration developed until in the 1960s a policy of timid but systematic transfer of decisions to the rectors was adopted. Like the prefect, the rector commands the channel of communications (information, advice, decisions) between the field services and the minister.

Although the rector must be qualified to teach in a university, his appointment is at the discretion of the Cabinet. As the central ministry has come to see itself as the echelon that conceives, advises and supervises, delegating detailed management to the field services, the rector has become a decision-maker rather than a mere transmitter of orders from Paris. While the centre fixes the number of posts of each type allocated to the academic regions, the rector and his skeleton staff (about 130 in an average-sized academic region) decide to which institutions the posts are attributed. He supervises and inspects the educational establishments in his region and vets their budgets. However, it is realized that to avoid congestion at the regional level, a further stage in the deconcentration process is imperative; delegation to the end of the command hierarchy, to the academic inspectors who run the education ministry's field services (especially primary education) in the departments. At both the regional and departmental level there is a problem of reconciling the commissioner of the republic's desire to achieve overall co-ordination with the traditional separateness of educational organization. For most matters the academic inspector can escape the commissioner of the republic's attempt to monopolize administrative power. Subordination to him would probably compromise the collaboration between the primary school-teachers union (SNI) and the primary school inspectors in the matter of promotion to coveted posts in the towns. This practice maintains the high level of recruitment to the SNI, but their participation in joint management at the local level undermines their challenge to official authority at the national level.

## Universities and grandes écoles

The late eighteenth-century revolution that replaced birth by competitive examination as the main criterion for selection to fill important posts in France, helped to conserve the dominance of the ascendant bourgeoisie in ways which have provoked a revolt of rising frustrations. The happy few were recruited and trained outside the university system through the *grandes écoles*, the exclusive caste of school-made leaders being preserved from the cultural factory of mass education into which the university system degenerated as a concession to official egalitarian rhetoric. Far from increasing social mobility, early selection through competitive examinations helped maintain the traditional social structure by providing it with an impersonal and respectable justification. In practice, examinations merely confirmed the advantages acquired by birth into a particular social class and sanctified it as merit. The centralized and standardized nature of the educational system was a further obstacle to the sort of innovation that would have spared France the decline in science which she underwent in the nineteenth century, and the cultural and institutional cataclysm that threatened to engulf much more than higher education in 1968. For too long the revolutionary trilogy inscribed on public buildings had proved a hollow mockery. 'An educational system which rests on the ideal of equality but in which failure is the lot of most people, which teaches fraternity but stresses competition, and which celebrates liberty but offers most individuals only limited options, is a source of chronic social tension and hostility.'[12]

There have been many interpretations of the 1968 crisis that commenced at the Nanterre campus of the University of Paris and rapidly developed into a generalized crisis of paternal, educational, industrial and political authority. It culminated in a reassertion of presidential authority and the reaffirmation of the electoral process as the source of legitimacy in a liberal democracy. Conspiracy theorists stressed the role of the ultra-leftist groups, while devotees of the 'generation gap' emphasized youthful revolt. The feeling that the source of discontent was at a deeper level of values was expressed by those who talked about a rejection of the consumer society, the emergence of a cultural revolution or a 'crisis of civilization' (Malraux *dixit*). A more traditional analysis interpreted the 1968 crisis as either a spectacular example of a familiar type of class conflict, exemplified by the general strike, or a political crisis that was resolved by holding a general election to allow the voters to decide who should govern. Although all these interpretations contribute something to an eclectic view of the 1968 May–June crisis, it was no accident that the educational system, and more especially the University of Paris, should be the link in the chain that snapped under strain. It exemplified, in an extreme form, the hyper-centralized and authoritarian character of French institutions, too petrified to cope with new pressures.

The University of Paris was part of a system subjected to escalating demands for access to higher education – particularly from lower-middle class parents – reflected in the rapid increase in the numbers that had achieved the minimum university entrance qualification (the *baccalauréat*) at secondary school. Those who wished to preserve the traditional system proposed to stem the tidal wave by severe selection, pointing out in addition that there would not be enough posts of high status for the numbers of graduates that an unselective entry would disgorge. The threat that selection would be imposed by the Government in 1968 contributed to an atmosphere of panic which initially ensured a sympathetic public response to the eruption of student demonstrations, particularly after student confrontations with the police. When the incidents that sparked off the crisis occurred, the University's lack of autonomy and the absence of an effective student union organization with whom negotiations could take place precipitated a political crisis, involving in turn the education minister, the prime minister, the president of the republic and finally the regime itself. When the regime was finally rescued from collapse, de Gaulle recognized that a fundamental reform of the educational system had become inevitable and called on the astute Edgar Faure to take on the role of education minister with the task of rapidly remedying the university system's combination of apoplexy and paralysis. To avoid the political consequences of a cultural revolution, the most adept exponent of dynamic conservatism was summoned to persuade a reactionary parliamentary majority to accept the minimum changes that the circumstances required, under the guise of re-establishing order as well as undertaking overdue reform.

To grasp the exceptional character of Faure's achievement, one must realize that the normal incubation period for a major educational reform since 1945 has generally been about nine years – the time during which a crisis has persuaded the interest groups and public opinion to accept change and allowed the minister to galvanize his sluggish bureaucratic machine into coping with the problem. However, there have been illustrious predecessors – notably Jules Ferry, the only premier simultaneously to hold the education portfolio – who have presented major items of reform legislation within weeks of taking office. Appointed Minister on 12 July, Faure prepared his University Guidelines Bill in August, secured its acceptance by the Government in September, followed by the parliamentary debates in October and promulgation in early November. Faure was helped in the Bill's preparation by the brilliant team of collaborators who formed his private office although it was he personally who wrote out the first draft of the Bill. Imagination having failed to seize power in the spring of 1968, Faure was determined that the powerful should show themselves capable of imagination in the autumn. For this he needed the support of the president and the prime minister against those, such as the minister of the interior, who saw the problem essentially as the

Governing France

repression of conspiratorial groups, and the arch-centralist
Debré, then finance minister. Faure received remote but decisive
encouragement from the president, and more hesitant backing
from the prime minister (particularly unenthusiastic when it
came to implementing the 1968 Act). This support sufficed to
see him through when allied with a sympathetic press, his own
indefatigable exertions and a mesmerizing eloquence projected
by radio and television, notably during the direct transmission
of the parliamentary debates.

The Bill was the subject of laborious pre-parliamentary discussions and compromises between Faure's closest collaborators
– attacked by the Gaullist right as 'leftists' – and those of the
prime minister and finance minister. Faure had consulted an
unprecedented number of representatives from various educational organizations, many of them anathema to his parliamentary majority. Unable to deliver a frontal attack on the Bill's
principles – the creation of an autonomous, pluralistic, partici-
patory and multidisciplinary university system – because they
had been approved by de Gaulle, the backbenchers focused on
Faure's suspect entourage or on especially sensitive details in his
proposals, notably the postponement of Latin in secondary
schools and the supposed violation of the neutrality of state
education through tolerance of political discussion inside universities. The amendments made before the Bill went to parliament – by the Higher National Education Council, the Council
of State and the Government – left its major guidelines intact,
but the finance ministry and the Council of State, as guardians
of centralist administrative orthodoxy, played a major role in
restricting the universities' financial autonomy and in curbing
the powers of the new National Council of Higher Education
and Research. The National Assembly's cultural affairs committee suggested that the Assembly should adopt further
amendments reducing the much debated 'participation' of students in the running of the new universities. Faure's tactical
ingenuity throughout was calculated to depoliticize the issue as
much as possible, relying upon the sympathy of the left-wing
Opposition and the discipline of the right-wing majority to
create at least a semblance of consensus. Many of the Assembly
amendments passed were prepared with the help of the minister's personal staff and used to reverse concessions reluctantly

made in Cabinet. When the Act was passed after thirty-two hours' debate in the Assembly (by 441 votes to 0) and twenty hours' discussion in the Senate (by 260 votes to 0), Faure appeared to have achieved his desired aim of unanimity, as the Communists, who abstained, were to play the most active part in seeking to make the Act work.[13]

However, it was one thing to persuade parliament to pass the University Guidelines Act unanimously; it was quite another to secure its faithful implementation. As the Assembly's *rapporteur* on the Act, former rector Jean Capelle, had written of the pre-1968 situation, a French university was 'a mere juxtaposition of various subjects, each represented by one professor, isolated in his field'. One cannot understand the bitterness of the attack on the 'mandarins' unless one appreciates the servitudes occasioned by the primordial significance of 'the professorial chair, connoting a domain of knowledge belonging literally to one man who reigns over it as an absolute monarch until he has reached retirement age'.[14] In place of the Napoleonic professor, the new Act introduced councils composed of teachers (including non-professional staff) and students based upon departments (called UER) which would be united into universities of a manageable size. The elected university councils in turn choose a president, a professor on whom devolves the responsibility for effective management of the university and for preventing each department from resuscitating the impervious aversion towards interdisciplinary ventures. However, whilst the 1968 Act proclaimed the autonomy of the universities to be designated (forty-three provincial universities and thirteen Parisian universities), its explanatory memorandum made clear that there would be limits to this autonomy, of a financial, administrative and pedagogical character.

Predictably, these limitations on university autonomy have been applied in a restrictive fashion. The reassertion of the education ministry's power, exercised from Paris and by the rectors, as the guardian of central administrative and pedagogical uniformity, and the finance ministry's role as the authority on financial rectitude, has prevented the decentralization that was a fundamental aim of the Act. The university teachers, traumatized by the speed and scale of the changes, have generally facilitated the reduction of autonomy to a fiction by their pusillanimous preference for passing awkward responsibilities on to the central ministries as a way of minimizing conflicts within the university. However, when it came to electoral participation, the university teachers voted massively whilst students, especially in arts and social sciences, abstained in large numbers, a fact which in part reflected the hostility to the reform of a significant fraction of active students. The main beneficiaries of this indifference were the Communists, who were able to win a large number of the student seats on the departmental and university councils.

The fact that the *grandes écoles* emerged unscathed from the 1968 events exemplifies another crucial aspect of dualism and division in French education: that between the teaching and research conducted in universities and the vocational training conducted (except for law and medicine) in the *grandes écoles*. Because the latter were regarded as indispensable to the stability of society and the efficiency of government, they had to be preserved from infection by the disorders of the universities. The *grandes écoles* had from their birth a vital, practical service role: providing the country with the disciplined leaders, administrative, industrial, technical (and later political) to enable it to function effectively. By contrast, the universities, especially in the non-vocational faculties which stressed the role of the intellectual as a critic rather than as a pillar of the social order, could be allowed to enjoy the irresponsible delights of calling all aspects of society into question.[15] Consequently, the selective élitism of the *grandes écoles* had to be preserved at all costs, while the universities could become a playground for politicization and frivolous experiments in autonomy, participation and multidisciplinarity, although the 1983 Savary reform seeks to push universities towards vocational education. The state-trained élites meanwhile could continue to run the public enterprises and other activities too important to be left to those educated in universities.

## Nationalization as state capitalism

In contrast to Soviet Russia, where public ownership of the means of production is the doctrinaire rule, and the United States where it is the doctrinaire exception, in Britain, Italy and

France a substantial public sector developed in the twentieth-century within a mixed economy that remains predominantly in private ownership. Whereas in Britain the private sector has traditionally enjoyed greater prestige and power than the public sector, in France the situation is reversed, with pervasive consequences for public policy. While the large private firms in Britain are the senior partners in the mixed economy, in France it is public enterprise that sets the pace. Although there has been a recent rehabilitation of the market and of competition in the EEC context, France has never officially adopted the ideology of free competition. The long-standing tradition of state intervention took the form of public enterprise as early as the seventeenth century and the state capitalism that subsequently developed owes more to mercantilism than to socialism. Public enterprise's regal past helps to explain the relatively high degree of public satisfaction with the nationalized industries, the minimum of denationalization backlash when the Right has been in power, and the widespread support for further extensions of public ownership; these attitudes cutting across all parties and classes.

It was the semi-revolutionary fervour of Liberation France of 1944-6 that engendered the mood of pro-nationalization consensus to which the bulk of the public sector owes its existence. Although a left-wing parliamentary majority, active trade union pressure and a widespread desire to punish unpatriotic industrialists played their part, it was under de Gaulle's aegis that France not only extended public ownership but established a comprehensive social security system and started national economic planning. De Gaulle made it clear in his memoirs that his aim was not to end the exploitation of man by man. 'It is to the state that it falls to build the nation's power, which henceforth depends upon the economy. The latter must be directed, all the more so because it is deficient, because it needs to renew itself and because it will not do so unless prevailed upon. Such, in my view, is the principal motive for the measures of nationalization, control and modernization taken by my government.' Most of the legislation setting up the major public enterprises was adopted virtually unopposed by the constituent Assembly in the months after de Gaulle resigned in 1946, while the 1946 Constitution enshrined in its Preamble a commitment to public

ownership.* It was the Socialist Party that was most enthusiastic about extending nationalization in 1945, the Communists
then holding the doctrinaire view that public ownership was
only significant if it was carried through after an anti-capitalist
revolution. The priority accorded to nationalizing the major
deposit banks and insurance companies was due to the left's
interwar experiences, which resulted in the fear that, like the
Popular Front, post-war reform would be halted by the 'wall of
money'. While desire to master money power (also a feature of
the 1982 nationalizations) was the most conspicuous feature of
'popular trustophobia', the nationalization of electricity, gas
and coal swiftly followed.[16] However, the socialist inspiration
was quickly replaced by a reassertion of statist *dirigisme*. This
was supplemented by technocratic control by the managers of
these public enterprises, resulting in a modernizing dynamism
rather than an extension of democratic control over the economy.

It would be wrong to dismiss as of no interest the quarter
century between the post-war nationalizations and the return
of the issue to the political agenda with the signature of the 1972
Common Programme and the enactment of that programme a
decade later, despite the intervening disputes between the
Socialist and Communist Parties. There was a silent but substantial incremental growth of the public enterprise sector, of
which successive right-wing governments were either unaware
or to which they turned a blind eye, through a capitalist-style
diversification and establishment of subsidiaries by the more
entrepreneurial corporations. Edouard Bonnefous, chairman of
the Senate's finance committee, pointed out in 1975 that the
three hundred nationalized firms of 1950 doing 5 per cent of
France's business had increased to eight hundred firms doing
11 per cent of the national turnover a quarter of a century later.
The extensive secondary and tertiary shareholdings by public
enterprises largely escaped both public notice and public control. Subsidiaries are immune from investigation either by the
commission responsible for checking the accounts of public enterprises or by parliamentary finance committees, the Senate
finance committee making a formal protest in July 1972 against
the Government's refusal to allow such inquiries into the use
of public money. The Assembly's finance committee special

* See above, chapter 5, p. 136.

*rapporteur* on public enterprises estimated that in 1971 some six hundred firms involving thirteen different ministries were concerned. These were firms in which the state directly or indirectly owned at least 30 per cent of the shares although the number exceeded a thousand if all holdings were included. It was calculated in 1965 that the electricity, gas and Renault corporations each owned shares in over a hundred firms, though in the case of the last two, 40 per cent of their holdings were of less than 1 per cent of the firm's capital. The number of public enterprise holdings were increasing annually by an average of thirty, so that the public sector incrementally expanded with minimal controversy. Thus, although Presidents Pompidou and Giscard initiated a policy of partial privatization, through selling off minority shareholdings in some public corporations (so that, for example, when the policy was reversed by total renationalization in 1982 the state only owned 91 per cent of the *Crédit Lyonnais* and BNP banks), they only partially compensated for the simultaneous and surreptitious extension of the public sector.

If one considers the pre-1982 public enterprise sector, one cannot identify a criterion that accounts for the peculiar collection of industries which have been nationalized in France. There were both monopolies and competitive firms; heavy and light industries; those vital for national security and others that were not; firms crucial to steering national economic development and others that were not; enterprises dependent on state subsidy (the *Les Invalides* of capitalism) and others that made profits. Nevertheless, two major types of public enterprise could be distinguished: those in the administrative economy sector, which were public service monopolies, and those in the competitive, market economy sector, approximating most closely in their behaviour to private business.

The public service monopolies were constituted principally by the power and transport corporations, which together accounted for some 60 per cent of the value added by nationalized industries and 70 per cent of their manpower and investment. It was this infrastructural, public utility sector that was primarily used by government as an instrument of both long- and short-term public policy. It was also this sector's technological dynamism after the Second World War that helped galvanize both private industry and government into an accept-

225

ance of rapid economic growth as the norm. The main fuel and power corporations were *Charbonnages de France, Electricité de France* and *Gaz de France*; of these by far the most important was and is the electricity corporation, giving rise to the extravagantly polemical epithet '*Etat* – EDF'. In this vein it has been claimed – reformulating Lenin's famous slogan 'communism is the Soviets plus electricity' – that 'For EDF, the French republic is electrification plus universal suffrage.'[17]

A more accurate, if still somewhat excessive, way of putting it is that EDF has been a state within the state, having been the prime author and moving force behind the 'all-electric' energy policy and the inordinantly ambitious French electro-nuclear policy. The modest way to put EDF behaviour is to argue that all large firms seek autonomy through control of their environment, extending their control over supplies and market, over technological innovation and over finance. While energy policy was dominated by cheap and then expensive oil from the 1960s, and although it has been largely determined within France by three clusters of actors: political (president, prime minister, industry minister), financial (Treasury and Budget Divisions of the finance ministry) and operational (the electrical and petroleum public corporations), one thing emerges strongly. The most striking feature of French energy policy, even before the onset of the 1973 crisis, was the switch from imported oil to domestically produced nuclear energy. 'There can be no reasonable doubt that the initiative for almost all aspects of the nuclear programme comes from the EDF ... There is a remarkable similarity between the propositions of EDF in the late 1960s and early 1970s and the basis of the present national energy policy.'[18]

EDF's dominant influence must be credited in part to the tandem of its managing director, Marcel Boiteux, and chairman, Paul Delouvrier (Boiteux succeeding Delouvrier as chairman in 1979, thirty years after joining EDF), but more especially to its control of the advisory body that shaped public policy decisions: the consultative committee for the production of nuclear based electricity, commonly known as the PEON committee. However, to achieve its dominant position, it had first to assert its primacy over the Atomic Energy Commissariat (CEA) and protect itself from the constraints that the finance ministry sought to impose upon its expensive ambitions.

By 1970 EDF appeared to have achieved both these goals. As long as de Gaulle was president, his prime reliance upon nuclear power for France's independent deterrent and his insistence on using French rather than American technology meant that the Atomic Energy Commissariat was in the driving seat.* However, his replacement by Pompidou meant that a political obstacle was removed; the Cabinet in November 1969 took the crucial decisions about the use of American reactors that substituted the primarily commercial preoccupations of EDF for the military and industrial patriotism of the CEA.[19] Thereafter EDF and CEA worked closely together to overcome the finance ministry objections to the demands for massive provision of capital to fund the enormous electro-nuclear investment programme. Following on the 1967 Nora Report recommendation that public enterprise autonomy should be promoted by signing medium term contracts with the government, EDF saw its opportunity to free itself from financial constraint. With Simon Nora the right-hand man of Prime Minister Chaban-Delmas in 1969, a 'programme contract' was signed in 1970 to cover the 1971-5 period despite six months resistance by the finance ministry, which was concerned to keep electricity prices down even if this meant EDF had less profit for investment. However, the programme contract was short-lived because of the rapid rise in EDF indebtedness and the departure of Chaban-Delmas from office in 1972.[20] This allowed the finance ministry to restore a measure of financial control over EDF, though without preventing it from proceeding with its massive investment programme, its electro-nuclear investments amounting to 47 per cent of its turnover in 1979. Although the planning process as such has never done more than register the energy policy decisions taken elsewhere, notably by the EDF, Giscard's institution of the Central Planning Council resulted in greater presidential control over the setting of targets, which were closer to EDF's rather than to the finance ministry's. The fact that the Mitterrand presidency has not led to any appreciable cutback in the electro-nuclear programme was predictable, given that the Socialist Party's energy committee before 1981 had a majority of EDF and CEA members.[21]

The public image of the nationalized monopolies remained

*On the Atomic Energy Commissariat and defence policy, see below pp. 271-3.

*Table 19*
*Public opinion of major public services in 1980* (%)

| Public service | Works well | Works badly | Don't know |
|---|---|---|---|
| EDF | 93 | 5 | 2 |
| GDF (gas) | 80 | 4 | 16 |
| SNCF (railways) | 76 | 15 | 9 |
| Post and telecommunications | 71 | 28 | 1 |
| Television | 56 | 38 | 6 |
| Social security | 40 | 54 | 6 |

Source: SOFRES poll in March–April 1980 published in *Le Monde, Dossiers et documents*, Supplement, October 1980, p. 25.

consistently favourable from the late 1940s. Table 19 shows that a year before the advent of the Mitterrand presidency, their standing, especially that of EDF, was high, with the exception of social security and to some extent of television. Only 24 per cent of the public were inclined to give credence to the view that the electro-nuclear policy had been foisted upon the government by EDF while 64 per cent considered that it was simply carrying out the government's decision. When asked more generally whether EDF had the power to impose its will upon the government, 39 per cent agreed whereas 47 per cent disagreed, which suggests that the 'EDF state' slogan favoured by anti-nuclear environmentalists has made an impression without convincing a majority of the public.[22]

In the market economy public sector, the government generally left its wholly or partly owned firms much more to their own devices. There were exceptions to this rule, notably the petroleum enterprises, ELF–Aquitaine and TOTAL–CFP, which supply about 23 per cent of France's consumption, in competition with the major multinational enterprises. Like British Petroleum, they are joint public–private enterprises, but the contrast in national attitudes is exemplified by the fact that whereas the British government has not asserted its management rights despite majority ownership, the French government expected these public enterprises to set private business an example in entrepreneurial drive as well as patriotism. CFP, created in 1924, was deliberately designed to be, in the words of Foreign Minister Poincaré, 'a tool capable of achieving a national petroleum policy', working closely with the government's administrative instrument, which became the fuel division of the industry ministry. We shall see how this oil policy was to become entangled with French policy towards Algeria and more generally in French foreign policy.*

In addition to these petroleum enterprises, some major transport firms also came into this competitive sector, notably Air France and Air Inter (domestic flights) and two merchant shipping firms which accounted for half the French merchant navy. However, the market economy sector principally flourished in the three main industries outside power and transport. First the state acquired a firm grip on deposit banking and insurance when it nationalized, in addition to the Bank of France, the four major banks and thirty-four insurance companies (since amalgamated into three) doing 36 per cent of the business, to neutralize the political as well as the economic influence exerted by private financial interests. In 1966 the number of state deposit banks was reduced by amalgamation to three. They were instructed to invest directly in industry and to establish merchant bank subsidiaries and generally to use public money for the promotion of industrial mergers and competitiveness. The three state banks, *Banque Nationale de Paris*, *Crédit Lyonnais* and *Société Générale*, controlled 59 per cent of all bank branches and deposits. In addition SNCF (railways) and the nationalized insurance companies created their own banks. Secondly, the state owned half the aerospace industry, paradoxically the civil aviation half, through SNIAS, a 1969 amalgamation into a joint enterprise (two-thirds public). Finally, the French motor car industry was lead by Renault, which moved from third place when it was privately owned to first place after nationalization.

The case of Renault is particularly important because the relative managerial freedom with which it operated, its striking commercial success and the vanguard role it played in improving pay and conditions of work, made it a model for the new style nationalization planned by the Socialists. This was symbolized by the appointment of Pierre Dreyfus, director-general of Renault from 1955–75, as minister of industry in the Mauroy Government from 1981–2. He recalled that he had only once

*See below, p. 262.

been summoned by a minister (Prime Minister Pompidou) during his years in office, it being understood that the initiative for meetings should be his. 'Never, in twenty years at the head of Renault, did I receive an order from anyone.'[23] Though he met the president, the industry minister and treasury officials regularly, the profitability of Renault and its commercial prestige meant that it was not at the mercy of the finance ministry. 'It is impossible to prove that the industry has performed better than it would have if Renault had remained under private ownership, but those respects in which the firm's choices differed from the private companies' were consistently in directions favourable to consumers and to the expansion of the French economy.[24] As well as its impressive record in product innovation and increasing exports, Renault played an important role in improving working conditions. It pioneered the concession of a third and then a fourth week's paid holiday to its employees, against the opposition of both private business and the government, which correctly anticipated that longer holidays would quickly spread throughout French industry. In most respects, Renault operated commercially like a private firm, though it pursued public interest priorities in terms of export promotion, industrial location, labour relations (the contrast with Peugeot, Citroën and Talbot was especially marked) and keeping its prices and profit margins down. It rapidly expanded even during recession, using its network of over two hundred subsidiaries in France and abroad to develop its market penetration. With its successful takeover bids, it seemed to have all the virtues of a successful conglomerate capitalist enterprise to which it added those of public enterprise.

The last thing that the CGT pioneers of nationalization wanted to bring about was state capitalism. Their 1919 Programme was a functionally representative version of the anarcho-syndicalist vision of workers control in which the miners, not the minister, would run the mines. However, the attempt to create autonomous public corporations after the Second World War quickly succumbed to political and administrative pressure for a reassertion of state control. Characteristically, it was Debré who gave the most frank and forceful expression to the view that only the government was entitled to act in the general interest:

The state must not be divided up. There cannot be nationalized industry policies independent of state policy. One might even say that the existence of a nationalized sector imposes on the state, if for no other reason, a transport, credit, fuel, insurance, social security and public employees policy. A significant part of the faults attributable to the nationalized sector is due to the fact that the state, represented by the government, has not been sufficiently conscious that being 'boss' it should deliberately formulate a policy and guide the enterprises over which it has assumed responsibility.

Debré was proud of the fact that when he was in office he had increased the prime minister's control over managerial appointments in nationalized industry and set up an interministerial committee which was consulted before any wage agreement was concluded in a nationalized industry. His rejection of the idea of a nationalized industries ministry was based on the view that 'it is indispensable to maintain and even reinforce [the nationalized firms'] allegiance to the ministry for whose policy they should be an instrument and sometimes the main instrument.'[25]

Most of the nationalized industries lost their autonomy long before Debré became prime minister. The fears that they would become 'states within the state', and that their deficits would impose an excessive financial burden on the government, were utilized by those who wished to reassert traditional state control. The managements are now so curbed by regulations and supervision that one is reduced to speculating whether their profusion indicates a lack of autonomy or really signifies the failure to impose effective state control. Superficially, it would appear that interventions by various state agencies 'are so numerous and direct in all matters concerning investment, finance, charges, remuneration, production and sales objectives, that managerial discretion is better defined by subtraction than by enumeration'.[26] Although the nationalized enterprises are subject to a variety of checks, these usually concern detailed operations rather than the enterprise's strategy. Furthermore, public enterprises generally do not supply enough information to government departments about their activities, Renault justifying its taciturnity by a desire not to forewarn its competitors. Government control is exerted both from outside and from inside each nationalized industry. Externally, a few officials in the finance and budget ministries, together with the relevant

sponsoring ministry, seek to influence most of the public enterprise's major decisions. They do so to suit national economic
policy rather than the objectives of the enterprise, whose management has suffered as a consequence. Public enterprise investment is often the victim of the finance ministry's short-term
economic management, being speeded up or delayed to suit the
need to reflate or deflate the economy. Prices and wages in the
nationalized industries are also an important part of the government's anti-inflation armoury. The sponsoring ministries are
much more sympathetic to 'their' public enterprises, officials
and managers generally having both been trained at the *Polytechnique*, but they are in a weak position compared to the budget
division, which plays the crucial part if a subsidy is to be
granted, whilst the treasury division decides if an investment
loan is requested.

Inside the public enterprises, there are two kinds of state
surveillance. In a few corporations there is a government commissioner, usually the director of the relevant division in the
sponsoring ministry, who provides liaison and exercises on the
spot supervision, as well as representing the sponsoring ministry
on the board. More generally, there are either state supervisors
or supervisory commissions, loosely linked to the finance ministry, who tend, however, to become spokesmen for the enterprise to which they are attached for a long time. Actual ministerial interference in the running of a nationalized industry
generally depends upon two factors other than whether or not
they are public service monopolies: the size of the corporation's
income and capital, in absolute terms and as a proportion of its
total revenue and investment programme, provided by the
government; and the volume and intensity of the political pressures by business, trade unions and local authorities, directly or
through members of parliament. Under the Fourth Republic,
sub-committees of both Assembly and Senate finance committees tried to exercise parliamentary control but from 1958
until 1971 this practice was virtually discontinued. Since then,
there have been some searching reports, notably that of Senator
Bonnefous in 1977. From 5-10 per cent of parliamentary questions concern public enterprise. Parliament annually received
the general report of the Public Enterprise Accounts Audit
Commission but its searching comments seldom result in severe

sanctions. The debates on the sponsoring ministries' budgets provide the main occasion for parliamentary scrutiny of the nationalized industries.

The attempt to nationalize whilst avoiding state management was to be achieved by confiding power to a tripartite board where functional representation was to express the aspirations of the interwar CGT towards economic democracy. In 1919 the CGT, considering that it could not realistically demand outright workers' control, accepted a formula coined by the economist and co-operative propagandist, Charles Gide: a board equally representative of the state, the workers and the consumers, a formula which directly challenged the view that the sovereign state alone represented the national interest. The functionally representative boards of directors established after the Second World War failed to achieve the aim of autonomous management for a variety of reasons, including the fact that each of the three 'interests' to be represented raised problems even before the question of their co-operation in decision-making arose.[27] The most paradoxical case is that of the government nominees, given the view that the state alone represented an indivisible general interest, which was the pretext for the restoration of total government control after 1953. In practice, state representation was divided between the 'interested ministries', who became accustomed to regarding their nominees as instructed delegates representing their separate ministerial viewpoints, although they often attempted to reach advance agreement. Consumer representation, which was meaningful in terms of Gide's vision of a co-operative republic based on powerful consumer organizations, was reduced to the representation of local authorities, consumer industries and family associations; the government in 1953 taking over the choice of consumer nominees to give it an unchallengeable majority on the board, including choice of the chairman. Finally, by the time the CGT's diluted conception of workers' control was attained, the leading trade union had been captured by the Communists, who did not believe that it was possible to undertake socialist experiments in a capitalist context. The attempt by Communist ministers and the CGT in 1946–7 to assume control of the nationalized industries provided an early pretext for extinguishing the hope of a socialist-style autonomy which re-emerged in 1981.

Even before the government acquired both majority control and a suspensory veto over the decisions of the public enterprise boards, such power as remained after ministerial direction, authorization and surveillance had passed to the full-time management and particularly to the chairman–managing director, who embodies the Napoleonic style of managerial authority. The board members, composed of busy part-timers, generally delegate all their powers to the chairman–managing director, retaining a residual advisory and supervisory role. The appointment of chief executives, like that of the government board nominees, provides ample scope for political patronage. This ensures that the propensity to technocracy is based upon a combination of expertise and political reliability. The transfer by *pantouflage* of technocrats from the civil and military *grands corps* of engineers and finance inspectors (the latter dominating the state banks) has provided the personnel to run the nationalized industries with a high degree of efficiency, although the osmosis between the supervising ministries and the management that sometimes results has its dangers.[28]

Public enterprise, through the severance between ownership and control, has allowed an executive élite to subordinate these large-scale organizations to the discipline of efficiency defined in terms of technical criteria, making it the best example of techno-bureaucratic management. A new sort of autonomy has developed, a technocratic autonomy, in which princes of petroleum, earls of electricity, counts of railways or Renault have become more powerful than some ministers. Pompidou said as much to Roger Gaspard, director general of EDF from 1946–62, who briefly became chairman before going to run the celebrated firm of Schneider, responsible for producing nuclear equipment for the public sector. Gaspard declared that there was not much difference between the role of management in the two cases, except that on major policy matters he had enjoyed more freedom of action from government when he was in the public sector.[29] An even greater influence on French energy policy than Gaspard was Pierre Guillaumat, appointed by de Gaulle as head of the fuels division of the industry ministry (1944–51), head of the Atomic Energy Commissariat (1951–8), minister for war but informally minister of oil in the early years of the Fifth Republic, before taking over as first head of ELF-

Aquitaine from 1966–77. A fuels division official is reported as bluntly asserting 'No one could say Guillaumat was controllable.'[30] His influence was perpetuated by his protégé, André Giraud, like him director of the fuels division before heading the CEA and becoming industry minister under Giscard. We shall see in the next chapter how, when at the Atomic Energy Commissariat, Guillaumat was able to use its autonomy to conceive and implement a nuclear policy which was foisted upon a succession of indecisive governments under the Fourth Republic.

## Public enterprise since 1982

As we saw earlier, the PCF had been unenthusiastic about nationalization immediately after the Second World War but by the late 1960s it had developed a new theory of state monopoly capitalism. The PCF now saw in extensive nationalization a way of preventing the capitalist state from surviving an economic crisis and securing a peaceful transition to 'socialism'. The PS did not have the same theoretical problems but it required the left-wing turn that the party took especially after 1971 for nationalization to become a prominent policy objective. The 1972 Common Programme dealt with the subject under the heading 'Democratization and extension of the public sector' and because the 1982 legislation was close to it both in spirit and substance, it is worth quoting its minimum commitments. 'To break the domination of big capital and implement a new economic and social policy, the government will gradually bring about the transfer to the community of the most important means of production and finance currently in the hands of the dominant capitalist groups. The public sector will be extended, democratized and restructured. Nationalized enterprises, provided with wide managerial autonomy, will respect the Plan's guidelines.'[31] It promised to nationalize virtually the whole of the banking and commercial insurance sectors, as well as enumerating a list of industrial firms corresponding broadly speaking with those nationalized in 1982. In 1982 it was decided not to proceed with nationalizing the remainder of non-friendly society insurance, and the promise that the workers in a firm could request its nationalization was dropped before the 1981 presidential election.

However, the main difference ten years later was that whereas in 1972 nationalization was advocated primarily to shift power from capitalists to workers, in the wake of the 1970s economic recession nationalization was presented as a major instrument for overcoming under-investment and unemployment. Less emphasis was placed upon ideological imperatives and more weight was given to practical concerns, though nationalization as protection against multinationalization conveniently combined both preoccupations. Mitterrand appealed openly to the patron saint of industrial patriotism: 'We must achieve through nationalization what de Gaulle achieved in nuclear strategy, provide France with an economic strike force.'[32] The explanatory memorandum to the 1982 Nationalization Act stressed the practical arguments aimed at reviving French economic growth. The banking system, even the nationalized parts of which had never come properly under public control, would be required to conform in their actions with the National Plan's guidelines and the directives of the government, as one of the means of dealing with the economic recession by providing risk capital for planned reflation. The general argument in favour of nationalizing industrial firms was supported by comparing the recent investment record of the public and private sectors. Between 1974 and 1980 public enterprise had counter-cyclically increased its investment by 91 per cent (especially the electro-nuclear and telecommunications programmes) while private sector investment decreased by 5 per cent.

Why were the banks and industrial groups expensively nationalized 100 per cent and why were their subsidiaries not acquired? These matters had been hotly debated by Socialists and Communists in the 1970s and unresolved disagreements had been the pretext used by the PCF for breaking its alliance with the PS. Total nationalization did not only have ideological and symbolic significance. As long as there are private shareholders, a firm is under an obligation to consider their interests, so that it may have to sacrifice the requirements of the general interest as conceived by the government or their management. Furthermore, the management would have a freer hand in restructuring the public sector in pursuit of the government's economic strategy and in giving the workers' representatives a bigger share in running the enterprise. The PS refusal to nationalize the subsidiaries – even the strategic ones, as defined by the government's policy statements – contenting themselves with only the holding companies, was a backward step compared to the 1977 renegotiation of the Common Programme, when the PS had agreed to 295 subsidiaries being nationalized as against the 729 proposed by the PCF. The reasons were essentially practical. Nationalizing hundreds of firms, which would be controlled through the holding companies, would be very expensive; it would involve an enormous legislative effort, as well as the problems of preparation and implementation; it would risk fragmenting the groups by creating many separate public enterprises. The result has been an enormous increase in the joint public–private sector of the economy, with public holding companies playing the role of senior partner.[33]

The public sector had been moving increasingly out of the public utility services and into competitive high technology industry in the post-war period. The 1982 nationalizations gave this trend enormous acceleration. In terms of comparative size, as measured by the number employed or its share of gross domestic product, the French public sector grew to about one and a half times the public sector in Great Britain and Italy and even exceeded that of Austria. The number employed in approximately five to six thousand firms that make up the public industrial sector more than tripled from just under 300,000 to over 900,000, increasing the total employed in the public enterprise sector from 1·7 million to 2·4 million, accounting for 11 per cent of the active population. Public enterprises produce a sixth of the gross domestic product (17 per cent) and over a third of investment (35 per cent).[34] Since 1982, they account for 91 per cent of bank deposits, 95 per cent of steel, 84 per cent of aircraft manufacture, 75 per cent of arms manufacture (acquiring control of the Dassault military–industrial complex) but also 44 per cent of electronics, 35 per cent of glassware, 28 per cent of pharmaceutical production and 25 per cent of household appliances. The state had undoubtedly become a super-conglomerate, a holding company of holding companies. How is it to control them?

We have seen that despite the numerous formal controls over

public enterprises, those in the competitive sector especially have enjoyed a substantial and increasing measure of *de facto* autonomy. Former President Giscard is reliably reported as saying in 1979 that 'The power to appoint is virtually the only influence that one can have over the policy of these enterprises' as the justification for shortening the chairman-managing director's term of office to three years.[35] The 1982 Act's explanatory memorandum specified that the newly nationalized firms would not be subject to the usual controls, so that they could operate on equal commercial terms with private firms. 'The government intends to give these firms real managerial autonomy which will be exercised within the framework of contracts with the government for the duration of each Plan.' This approach was inspired by the Nora Report and the not wholly convincing experience with programme contracts (early 1970s) and enterprise contracts (late 1970s) which ran into difficulties because the finance ministry resisted attempts to bind it for several years in advance. The *lettre de mission* which the industry ministry sent to the heads of the newly nationalized industries asked them to prepare a draft corporate plan that would form the basis of a medium term contract, taking account of the priority goals of industrial policy: job creation, investment and sales at home and abroad. To reduce governmental interference with their freedom to manage, the newly nationalized firms would all be sponsored by the industry ministry while all the banks would be sponsored by the finance ministry. In practice their independence would be subject to the operation of bodies like the Central Wages Committee that would influence decisions about wage agreements, in which the prime minister always takes a close interest. The lessening of public control in advance of decisions increases the importance of control by the Court of Accounts, which would be spending nearly a third of its time on checking the accounts of the nationalized sector. To make up for the past inadequacies of parliamentary control, a new body, the High Council of the Public Sector, was established to monitor the activities of the nationalized enterprises and report every two years. It is comprised of six deputies, four senators, five government nominees, five trade union representatives and five experts co-opted by the twenty others.[36] The chairmen and managing directors were generally agreed to have been chosen for their competence rather than their political pliability. This was crucial if, as Georges Vedel (who wrote the decision of the Constitutional Council on the 1982 Nationalization Act) had said twenty-eight years before: 'Nationalizing is changing the managers.'[37]

The danger of making public enterprises as like private enterprises as possible is that it undermines the case for nationalization and strengthens the case for privatization. While the French approach was to avoid 'statization', it sought to give the publically owned firms a socialist character, notably through the tripartite composition of the boards of directors. In the case of the five major industrial firms wholly nationalized in 1982 (*Compagnie Générale d'Electricité, Saint-Gobain-Pont-à-Mousson, Pechiney Ugine Kuhlmann, Thomson–Brandt* and *Rhône–Poulenc*) the board will consist of seven state nominees, six worker representatives from the firm and its French subsidiaries and five appointed as users of the firm's products and services or because of their expertise. In the case of the banks, the board consists of five representatives of each category, except that 'depositors and borrowers' replaces 'consumers' in the third category. Of the state's representatives in the five industrial firms, at least three are nominated by the industry minister and one each by the finance and budget minister. For five of the banks and the two finance companies, two of the state representatives are nominated by the finance minister and one each by the ministers of industry and the budget and one jointly by the ministers of external relations and external trade. In the case of the other banks, at least three board members are nominated by the finance minister. One should note the fact that the planning minister does not make any nominations. The worker representatives were initially nominated by the trade unions but will subsequently be elected by the workers, as was promised by Mitterrand when he was a presidential candidate. (Worker participation will also be developed at workshop level.) Finally, the 'consumers and experts' category will continue to be recruited on a rather arbitrary basis, except that it will allow the government to ensure that it usually has a majority on the board. In case of any difficulties, the fact that the state is the sole shareholder means that the government can assert control over the board.[38]

Unlike the 1945 nationalizations, which were carried out with minimal opposition, the 1982 nationalizations were the subject of acrimonious parliamentary opposition, with a flood of nearly 1,500 amendments intended to delay rather than change the legislation. Reference to the Constitutional Council only increased the compensation given to the expropriated shareholders, so if a motivation for nationalization was to deprive the right-wing parties of financial support, this was not achieved in the short run! A personal commitment was made by Jacques Chirac in December 1981 that if and when he had the power to do so he would privatize all that he could. Given that France has not hitherto faced the British problem of nationalization, denationalization and renationalization, this statement has ominous implications. Pierre Mauroy's claim in the November 1981 Senate debate that 'nationalization is a form of the French genius' is reinforced by the colossal cost of privatization. A more serious consideration is, perhaps, that in an increasingly interdependent world, there is only limited scope for nationalized firms to act in accordance with national needs rather than at the dictates of the international market. More positively, their activities are increasingly inseparable from France's economic foreign policy and become instruments of that policy.

# 8 National Independence and International Mission

While de Gaulle was at the helm, the primacy of international concerns was such that the Fifth Republic could be character-ized as pursuing 'depoliticization in domestic affairs, plus a foreign policy'. However, he was well aware of the interdepend-ence of France's international standing with her internal polit-ical stability and economic strength. He deliberately used each in the service of the other. His first priority was to construct the political and economic springboard from which to launch an ambitious foreign policy, but he was convinced that without the restoration of patriotism and national pride, France would re-main prey to the divisions that had wrecked her polity and economy, thereby reducing her international stature. His ability to adopt a more assertive and independent role in foreign policy reflected the greater strength which France had already begun to acquire under the Fourth Republic, assisted by the conclusion in 1962 of the main decolonization process and by the changing nature of Soviet–American relations. He exploited these new opportunities with great skill until the domestic crisis of 1968 compelled him to assume a more modest posture.

De Gaulle combined an unswerving commitment to a few principles with complete flexibility in the way in which circum-stances required that they be applied. Inter-state relations had power and cunning as their means and the promotion of national interests as their objective. France must be restored to her rank as a great world power, albeit not a super-power, and to this end all else should be subordinated. To avoid domination by the two super-states, the smaller nation states should co-operate by forming confederations and alliances to preserve the balance of power. In particular, France should repudiate her relative international self-effacement and assert her 'immemorial vocation for influence and expansion'.[1] Alliances were seasonal, dictated by the opportunism of a government determined to preserve the sovereignty of the state in an international environment which threatened foreign penetration and domination. What was personal to de Gaulle was the style and range of intervention rather than the substance of this foreign policy, so one should not be surprised at the continuity between the Fourth Republic and de Gaulle, as well as between de Gaulle and his successors. The phrases may be less grandiose and the gestures less offensive (in both senses of the word) but the task of defending French interests in the context of internal and external pressures persists.

## Foreign policy: process and objectives

In domestic affairs, the policy process is discussed frequently but the policies themselves are generally neglected, whereas in foreign affairs the policies are described and assessed *ad nauseam* but the policy process is seldom investigated. French foreign policy in the de Gaulle era was described as being 'made in three admirably synchronized steps: it is prepared at the Quai d'Orsay, decided on at the Elysée and implemented nowhere. . . .' As well as emphasizing the extent to which the president dominated foreign policy-making, this statement draws attention to the fact that because de Gaulle's ambitions exceeded the strength he was able to mobilize, the actual successes achieved were few, even if one bears in mind that such success is rare. Pompidou, by contrast, respected the ' "Micawber rule" – never allow commitments to outrun strength'.[2] From the very start of his presidency, he took a firm personal grip on the conduct of French foreign policy, publicly symbolized by his role in the 'summit' meetings at which the major understandings are reached and in the bi-annual press conferences at which he stated France's foreign policy.

French foreign policy is controlled by a triumvirate, headed by the president, who is responsible for setting the policy guidelines and taking the decisions of major national and international consequence. The second-in-command is the prime minister, whose main task is to co-ordinate foreign policy with the decisions of all government departments other than the external relations ministry (especially defence and finance) and to defend the president's policy in parliament. Under earlier regimes, the office of foreign affairs minister was frequently combined with that of premier. From 1871 to 1918, 28 per cent of premiers were also foreign ministers; between 1919 and 1939, 53 per cent held both offices simultaneously, but from 1944 to 1958 the proportion fell to 15 per cent. Under the Fifth Republic, the prime minister has held no other office, so it is necessary for a minister of foreign affairs to make up the triumvirate. He is responsible for the detailed implementation and defence of the president's policy, the conduct of relations with countries in which the president takes only intermittent interest, and for routine diplomatic work. In describing the formation of his 1958 government, de Gaulle stated that he had entrusted four posts to former civil servants who 'would be more directly under my wing', including 'ambassador Couve de Murville at foreign affairs [and] engineer Pierre Guillaumat at the war office'.[3] While Couve was not a merely impassive executant of presidential directives, he has stated that during his tenure (1958-68) of the foreign ministry, he shared 'a sort of spontaneous agreement' on aims with de Gaulle and at their regular Friday morning meetings they only discussed 'ways and means and timing'.[4] Charged by Article 13 with the appointment of ambassadors, de Gaulle interpreted these provisions to mean that French ambassadors abroad were his personal representatives.

The Cabinet seldom discusses foreign affairs but receives a weekly review of the international situation from the external relations minister. The president will usually have consulted the prime minister and external relations minister before any major decision is made and when the decision has important military implications – such as the 1966 withdrawal from the North Atlantic Treaty Organization – the defence minister will also be involved. So, apart from reminding cabinet ministers of the official position on all foreign policy issues, and hinting at such shifts in these positions as are contemplated, the Cabinet's function is to ratify decisions settled beforehand[5] by the triumvirate or at interministerial councils or committee meetings. To prepare the ground for interministerial meetings, there is close contact between the diplomatic advisers of the president and

prime minister, who receive copies of the foreign ministry telegrams, and the personal staff of the foreign minister. The need
to follow up and co-ordinate the implications of foreign policy
for other ministries has increased considerably, especially since
the establishment of the EC, strengthening the role of the prime
minister as chairman of such interministerial meetings. However, when it comes to overseas visits, the president travels to
the political summits, leaving the prime minister to perform the
role of France's commercial traveller in the foothills. There are
two other ministers attached to the foreign ministry, one of
whom is concerned with European affairs while the other one is
specifically responsible for co-operation with developing countries.

The existence since 1915 of a powerful secretary-general, the
only such office to have survived all political vicissitudes since
that date, has reinforced the foreign minister's *cabinet* in the co-
ordination and checking of the civil servants' work. The reasons
for the survival of the secretary-general in the foreign ministry
appear to be the desire to maintain continuity in the conduct of
foreign policy; to compensate for the frequency with which the
foreign minister has to travel abroad; and finally, the small and
relatively homogeneous nature of the ministry. The secretary-
general co-ordinates all the work of the ministry through his
control of the communications network, his meetings with division directors and with the minister and his personal staff. The
incoming diplomatic telegrams are channelled four times a day
through the director of the secretary-general's *cabinet*, who sorts
them and selects the most important ones for the secretary-
general's attention. Whilst the minister signs the most important
telegrams sent, the secretary-general signs those of lesser importance. Each morning, he holds a meeting with the directors of
the political, economic and cultural affairs divisions, at which
the director or assistant director of the foreign minister's *cabinet*
is present. At these meetings the secretary-general comments on
the telegrams received, gives instructions for outgoing telegrams
and allocates the day's work. They also provide an opportunity
to assess the state of all pending issues and for views to be
exchanged. Once a week this meeting is also attended by the
director of personnel, the head of protocol, and representatives
of the prime minister's *cabinet* and of the defence minister. The

secretary-general has frequent formal and informal contacts with the directors of all the ministry's divisions, personally or by telephone, to ensure overall administrative co-ordination. Finally, every evening the day's business is reviewed by the foreign minister, the director of his *cabinet*, the secretary-general and the director of political affairs.[6] The secretary-general is an unusually powerful official, who remains in office for long periods and exercises real influence on policy over political and diplomatic as well as administrative matters.

France has always given an especially high priority to projecting its culture abroad, reflecting the eighteenth-century reality that France was the cultural centre of the universe and French was the language of diplomacy. Since then the pretence of French cultural pre-eminence has become increasingly difficult to maintain and the civilizing mission has appeared to be as unrealistic as it is arrogant. French foreign cultural policy is officially organized by the foreign ministry's cultural relations division, rather than through a semi-autonomous public body like the British Council. The contrast, for once, is more apparent than real because French cultural and educational establishments abroad are staffed by secondment from the education ministry and call on the services of independent-minded French intellectuals, while the British Council is very much under the thumb of the Foreign Office cultural relations department. However, France is the country which maintains the largest number of educational establishments outside its borders, employing thousands of teachers. These institutions are regarded as the cultural equivalent of consulates in the commercial sphere.[7] We shall return to this subject in dealing with France's relations with the French-speaking world in general and its former colonies in particular.

Most of the external relations ministry's staff are accredited to particular countries, where their function is twofold. They collect information that will be telegraphed back to Paris and which forms the basis on which policy decisions are made. About a thousand telegrams arrive daily at the Quai d'Orsay of which the most important are selected by the minister's personal staff for his attention. They protect French interests and citizens (of whom a million and a half live outside the country), promote trade (including, in the case of military attachés, the arms trade) and conduct relations with the Government of the country in which they are located. Embassy work is political, military, commercial and cultural, the military and commercial attachés reporting back to their parent ministries (defence and finance). Diplomats are now sent on courses devoted to trade, science, strategy and armaments. The prestigious political work has declined in relative importance owing to the greater centralization of control at the Quai d'Orsay and more frequent direct summit dealings. There are also the very important permanent missions abroad, notably those attached to the United Nations and the EC. French membership of the Security Council renders a permanent UN mission essential, the work – contacts in the corridors, speechmaking – being parliamentary rather than diplomatic in character. The permanent representative at Brussels not only provides liaison with the EC but also plays a direct part in running the EC through the Committee of Permanent Representatives. The French diplomatic corps does not enjoy the British foreign service's higher status relative to the home civil service. Its top echelons are recruited from ENA but it is below the Finance Inspectorate, Council of State and Court of Accounts *corps* in the pecking order, owing to the more limited opportunities to transfer to remunerative positions in public or private corporations or to membership of the personal staff of a minister.

Because foreign policy is conducted in the 'closed politics' context of discreet negotiation rather than the open debate characteristic of legislation, parliaments have generally been unable to intervene effectively in this part of the policy-making process. Even under the Third and Fourth Republics, when executive–legislative relations were dominated by the legislature, foreign affairs – except for isolated cases like the 1954 Assembly rejection of the European Defence Community Treaty, when the Government was neutral – have always been a special case of almost undisputed executive control. So the Fifth Republic's reversal of the previous relationship in the executive's favour has merely served to bring the formal position into line with the real situation. Parliament has generally been content with an *a posteriori* oversight, leaving the initiation and conduct of foreign policy to the government. Apart from the anodyne provisions for asking parliamentary questions or debating a government foreign policy declaration (where no vote is taken) parliament may be asked to ratify a treaty, unilateral amendment of which is, however, impossible. The main instruments for a more searching investigation of the government's foreign policy are the foreign affairs and finance committees of the Assembly and Senate. The external relations minister or a junior minister testifies several times each year before the foreign affairs committees, and the chairmen of these committees may enjoy close contact with the minister and the ministry, having access to incoming but not outgoing telegrams and so being better informed about foreign developments than about French policy. Annually, the discussion of the foreign ministry's budget provides an opportunity for the finance committees to raise policy matters, but although foreign affairs and finance have traditionally attracted the most eminent parliamentarians into their ranks, they are likely to be little better informed than are the readers of *Le Monde*.

It is the president of the republic, not the external relations minister, who holds press conferences to survey current international problems and announce major policies, providing the best source of information in a field where publicity is the public relations facade that conceals rather than reveals the serious discussions between the select few. Whereas de Gaulle openly confessed that the questions were arranged in advance by his press officer and answered so that the press conference replies 'added up to the affirmation of a policy' calculated to 'rouse the national spirit',[8] his successors have allowed the journalists to choose the questions they ask; but the purpose of the exercise has remained unaltered. From time to time, when he wishes to put the French position on an international issue of current concern, the external relations minister receives a handpicked group of French or foreign journalists for a confidential chat. More routine contacts with the diplomatic press are left to the head of the ministry's press service, who holds a daily press conference. The press resent the fact that the Fifth Republic's accentuation of the tendency for foreign policy decisions to be concerted in private rather than debated in public has weakened their informative role. For the journalist there are two kinds of diplomat: those who know but don't tell and those who tell but don't know. Whereas the government would like the press to act as a formative influence, mobilizing public support for national policy, the press interpret the news in partisan ways. The newspapers polarize attitudes through controversy rather than promote an acquiescent consensus.

Until the Second World War, France, unlike Britain and Germany, tried to be both an imperial and a continental power. Under the Fourth Republic, although she made a remarkable recovery from the national and international consequences of defeat and occupation, France accepted a more modest role based upon a reluctant acquiescence in three 'necessities'. First, the cold war between two coalitions led by the United States and the Soviet Union persuaded all except the Communists and Gaullists to accept American leadership within an Atlantic Alliance. The resentment of an Anglo–American (with an increasing emphasis on American) directorate over NATO predated de Gaulle's return to office, but the Fourth Republic Governments felt powerless to challenge this subservience. However, to the extent that they attributed French subordination to the lack of nuclear weapons, steps were taken to equip France with the means to assert herself, it being assumed that this would be primarily within an integrated NATO alliance. Secondly, Franco-German reconciliation was only possible within the context of an integrated Western European Federation in which France would play the dominant role as long as Britain was not present to counter-balance potential German hegemony. Several factors dictated French policy on the European continent: the Soviet danger, which dwarfed the fear of a partitioned Germany's military power; the elimination in 1955–6 of the one remaining Franco-German territorial dispute in the Saar; and the hope that European unity would help solve France's economic troubles, end her industrial inferiority complex and prepare her to face international competition. In the process, Germany ceased to be France's main enemy and became her principal ally, well before de Gaulle explicitly adopted this policy as an expedient in the early 1960s. Finally, France's defeat in Vietnam pointed to the necessity of decolonization but this policy proved difficult to reconcile with the ideology of assimilation. It was the Fourth Republic's indecisive move towards Algerian independence that led to its demise and de Gaulle's return to power. This in turn accelerated the process of decolonization, except temporarily in the case of Algeria, and shifted the French position *vis-à-vis* the United States and Europe to an assertion of France's independence rather than an abdication from it through acceptance of a one-sided interdependence.

It was this more vigorous affirmation of French national interest – conceived as a self-evident truth vouchsafed only to him – coupled with the 'realistic' approach to inter-state relations recalled at the outset of this chapter, that were the hallmarks of de Gaulle's conduct of foreign policy, rather than any reversal of the Fourth Republic's legacy. The bewildering contrast between the obstinacy with which he clung to fundamentals and the pragmatism with which he rung the tactical changes, should not blind one to the calculated mixture of brutality and subtlety in his statecraft, or to the resourcefulness with which he used his limited resources to achieve a 'great power' status for France as an end in itself. The appearance of inconsistency and the reality of limited success in attaining his grandiose objectives did not worry the general public unduly. They were content to be 'spectators of French prestige achieved by a single man', particularly as they thought they were not required to make any effort and that de Gaulle would provide them with a flattering prestige on the cheap.[9] However, when they began to grasp the fact that there was a stiff price to pay in foregoing personal well-being, they showed in 1968 and 1969 that they placed their standard of living well above humiliating the United States, and welcomed Pompidou as president in the belief that he would conform more closely to their order of priorities.

The pro-American sections of the élite and France's allies were flabbergasted at the severance of the military connection with NATO and 'the implementation of new relations with the so-called Eastern European states, towards *détente, entente* and co-operation' as de Gaulle put it in his 1966 Kremlin speech. De Gaulle's failure to institutionalize political co-operation within an EC led by France, and Germany's demonstration that she was willing to act as America's 'Trojan Horse' in Europe as the price of support against the Soviet Union, resulted in acceptance of a *rapprochement* initiated by the Soviet government in 1964–5. This move was attractive to France as a lever to be used against

America and Germany, while to the Soviet Union the French rejection of nuclear armament for Federal Germany and her recognition of the Oder–Neisse frontier (although not of Eastern Germany as a permanent fact) made her a valuable friend within the capitalist camp. France and the Soviet Union shared a common interest in reducing the economic and military dependence on the United States to which many European politicians had accustomed their countries under the guise of anticommunism. Rejecting an ideological vision of world conflicts, de Gaulle regarded Soviet Russia as part of privileged Western civilization confronted by the underdeveloped East, of which China was the formidable potential leader. In the long run, Eastern Europe would recognize its vocation as part of a 'European Europe' and meanwhile bilateral contacts of all kinds ought to be increased to facilitate this process. This strategy led to a substantial increase in commercial, cultural, scientific and technical co-operation, underpinned by regular meetings of the Franco–Soviet commission and twice yearly political consultations at foreign minister level. Whilst this policy has been especially applauded by the French Communist Party, it was popular and led to an improvement of the Soviet Union's image in France, up until the Soviet military intervention in Afghanistan since when there has been a cooling of relations, especially during the presidency of Mitterrand.

One of the most striking contrasts in foreign affairs between Mitterrand's attitude and that of his predecessors was in France's relations with the two super-powers. While part of the reason for this can be attributed to the change from *détente* to renewed tension in East–West relations, there is an interesting relationship between domestic and international politics that operates. The 1976 Puerto Rico Agreement, in which the USA secretly agreed with Giscardian France, Britain and West Germany that financial assistance would not be granted to governments that included communist ministers, is an interesting example of this linkage. This policy had serious implications for the French Socialists, who had in 1972 allied themselves with the PCF, even though the more immediate target of the 1976 agreement was Italy. Whereas de Gaulle, Pompidou and Giscard cultivated the Soviet Union as a way both of avoiding excessive dependence upon the USA and of placating the PCF at home and neutralizing its capacity to exploit popular anti-Americanism, Mitterrand was in a different situation. Because he wished for domestic political reasons to have Communist ministers in the government, he needed to emphasize his firmness *vis-à-vis* the Soviet Union, with the result that in his first year of office he met President Reagan four times and President Brezhnev not at all. In other respects, notably in his controversial support for liberation movements in Latin America, Mitterrand has shown that he has been prepared to brave United States official displeasure, so it is not a case of subservience to Uncle Sam. However, Mitterrand showed on the issues of buying gas and constructing the East–West pipeline (strongly opposed by the US) that he was prepared to develop *economic* links with the Soviet Union, whilst suspending the summit *political* dialogue between the two countries. The fact that Communist ministers (rather than the party as such) have been prepared to subscribe to the tough French policy towards the Soviet Union and Eastern Europe on sensitive issues such as the military coup in Poland, merely confirms that they are also prepared to pay a price in terms of international policy so that they can secure domestic political benefits.

Despite certain changes of emphasis and direction in French foreign policy, the coming to presidential office of a Socialist has been accompanied by much more continuity than change. Continuity is especially evident in the concentration in the hands of the president himself of the conduct of external relations. Giscard's development of direct summit contacts, both bilateral and multilateral, has been continued, with institutionalized annual meetings such as the European Council, the meetings with African heads of state and of the leaders of the seven advanced non-communist industrial countries. Mitterrand, like his predecessors, has clearly seen the advantages of giving prominence to the president's international role, where he is seen in the statesmanlike stance of champion of the national interest rather than as the leader of a victorious faction within a divided nation, which is the way his domestic opponents are tempted to portray him. There has been a price to pay for this increasing reliance upon personal diplomacy because there are no minutes of many of these meetings, with the result that the rest of the foreign policy machine is not always fully informed about the

line the president is taking and cannot therefore give it maximum implementation. This task falls to the secretary-general of
the presidency and it is not pure chance that two foreign minister in the 1970s (Michel Jobert in the Pompidou presidency
and Jean François-Poncet under Giscard) were former heads of
the president's secretariat. With certain conspicuous exceptions,
such as the Heath–Pompidou negotiations on the United Kingdom's entry into the European Community, the external relations ministry is properly informed about the president's policy
and plays a full part in carrying it out.[10]

### A confederal Europe: an ideology and a strategy

In his 1950 memorandum to the French premier that inspired
the creation of the Coal and Steel Community, Monnet argued
for what de Gaulle was to call a 'European Europe' under
French leadership, but maintained: 'It is not by an addition of
sovereignties meeting in council that an entity is created.' However, subsequent experience showed that as long as national
governments retained real power and responsibility, the supra-
national high authority was unable to deal with serious problems, leaving member states to act in their national interest
outside the ECSC framework. Ten years later, de Gaulle substituted an institutional emphasis on confederation based upon
inter-state co-operation as the only realistic basis for a harmon-
ization of national policies going beyond the limited, technocratic ECSC, Euratom and EEC treaties (inherited from the Fouth
Republic) to a separate political union. For the foreseeable
future, power would be concentrated in the Council of Ministers
representing the member states, decisions being subject to unanimity. De Gaulle's 1960 scheme, which came to be known as
the Fouchet Plan, foundered in 1962 on Belgo–Dutch opposition and Italian hesitation, inspired by the desire for prior
British entry into the EEC as a safeguard against Franco–German hegemony.[11] In January 1963 de Gaulle counter-attacked
by unilaterally terminating negotiations on Britain's application to join the EEC and concluding a treaty providing for closer
political co-operation with Germany as the basis for a Franco–
German condominium over the EC. The treaty transposed the
Fouchet Plan provision for regular meetings of heads of the

executive and foreign ministers on to a bilateral plane. It established an interministerial secretariat run by senior foreign ministry officials in the two countries to co-ordinate consultations at all levels. The refusal of her EEC partners to accept French leadership led de Gaulle to press forward his policy of *détente* with Eastern Europe. Within the EC he secured, through the boycott of community institutions in the latter half of 1965, the abandonment of majority voting in the Council of Ministers, a curb on the power of the EEC Commission, and the replacement of its supra-nationalist president (Walter Hallstein), who was accused of usurping the functions of the national governments.

To establish the fundamental continuity between the conception of Europe championed by Pompidou as de Gaulle's prime minister and as president in his own right, some comparisons are useful. In a speech to the National Assembly just before the June 1965 EEC crisis came to a head, Pompidou asked:

What can the goal of a European policy be? Federation? Confederation? Let us not quarrel over words. In any case, no one can claim ... that all the conditions have at this time been met for a true federation ... with a single government, a common parliament, one foreign policy, one military policy, and one financial, economic and social policy. At the present stage, there is no possibility other than to encourage a gradual *rapprochement* among the European states which will lead them little by little to harmonize their policies ...

Accusations of French nationalism ignored the fact that because France alone defended her own and Europe's independence, the French were the real 'Europeans'. Destined by history and geography to be the motive force of Europe, Pompidou claimed in 1967 that France was 'not its administrative, technical or institutional but its ideological motive force'.[12] The ideology was that of national independence, conceived increasingly within a European framework; an extension that was tolerable only so long as France was able either to get her own way on all major points at issue or remain free to opt out or veto any proposals to which she objected. In his January 1971 presidential press conference, Pompidou met the question 'What kind of Europe?' with the reply: 'It can only mean building, on the basis of what exists, a confederation of states that have decided to harmonize their policies and to integrate their economies.'

In line with the Monnet approach, Pompidou believed that political union, and agreement on foreign and defence policy, could only come after piecemeal, pragmatic economic *integration*, the word de Gaulle shunned like the plague. However, he remained faithful to the Gaullist view that all these decisions would have to be based on intergovernmental agreement. The Gaullist fear of a European 'government by Assembly' emerged clearly from President Pompidou's postponement of the creation of a 'true European parliament' – directly elected and with increased powers – until after the establishment of a 'true European government'. Confronted by governments that often seemed not to have any clearly thought out objectives or strategy to attain them, France had the advantage of knowing what it did and what it did not want.

Although the interrelationship between national and EC officialdom has been fostered by hundreds of specialist working groups in Brussels, the French government has maintained close control over the experts who represent it, allowing them ever less discretion as the stake involved in EC decisions increased and propensities towards technocratic decision-making had to be curbed. Instructions were more frequent and precise and were issued earlier in the policy formulation and negotiation process by the general secretariat of the interministerial committee for European co-operation. This secretariat is headed by a finance official responsible to the prime minister, receiving most of his directions from the external relations ministry. Co-ordination is achieved notably through weekly meetings called by the secretary-general, attended by ministerial *cabinet* members, senior finance and external relations ministry officials, and representatives from other ministries particularly concerned with the EC, e.g. agriculture. A separate meeting is held each week attended by the secretary-general and the directors of the treasury and foreign economic relations division of the finance ministry and the economic affairs division of the external relations ministry (which controls the permanent delegation in Brussels). The secretariat has been 'the most organized and most effective co-ordinating mechanism' between a national government and its EEC agents, giving 'maximum manoeuvrability to the political leadership'.[13]

Under the president, the prime minister seeks to assert control over European policy through the interministerial committee for European co-operation which deals with high policy. However, the finance minister chairs the interministerial committee for the implementation of the European treaties, concerned with detailed application, while the external relations minister has sought to monopolize supervision over the relations between the EC Commission and all French ministries. The external relations ministry plays a decisive role in the key EC decision-making bodies, the Council of Ministers and the Committee of Permanent Representatives, through the monthly meetings of EC foreign ministers and its influence over the preparation and exposition of agreed national positions through France's permanent delegation. (The Committee of Permanent Representatives meets weekly to prepare the monthly discussions of the Council.) Couve de Murville recalled how much he relied on the director of economic affairs at the Quai d'Orsay and France's permanent representative in Brussels during his ten years as foreign minister, but his regular presence at EC council meetings was essential to gain the mastery necessary 'to make France the community's motive force that she intended to be'.[14] Under intense French pressure, it has been accepted since January 1966 that all important actions by the EEC commission should be preceded by consultation with national governments through their permanent representatives, thereby placing the external relations ministry at the intersection of the French and the EEC decision-making processes. Although a few top officials in the finance, agriculture, labour and transport ministries should be included among the national actors involved in the Community process, the dominant position of the external relations ministry in deciding strategy and tactics has largely insulated the European aspects of French policy from the rest of national politics, promoting 'the minimalist strategies pursued in Brussels and the minimizing of participation at the national level'.[15]

Especially since the resignation of President de Gaulle in 1969, there has been 'a great discrepancy between a declaratory policy of independence and autonomy and the circumscribed policies taken by the Pompidou Government – and later by the Government of Valéry Giscard d'Estaing. Increasingly, French foreign policy has focused on economic matters and has been formulated more as a function of domestic economic imperatives than as a result of a coherent foreign policy orientation.'[16] This has been especially clear in the EC where, despite institutional developments like the directly elected European parliament or the regular European summit meetings and the close personal understanding he achieved with Federal Chancellor Schmidt, Giscard made little progress during his seven years from 1974–81. Attempts at European monetary co-operation to restrict exchange rate fluctuations, notably since the 1979 creation of the European monetary system, were slowed down by the French need to protect its own currency, a problem that has continued during the Mitterrand presidency. Mitterrand unsuccessfully attempted to move away from the Paris–Bonn axis towards a *rapprochement* with Britain and has had to fall back on the staple French West European policy since 1950. His wish to develop a 'social Europe', notably by a concerted move to a higher rate of economic growth and shorter working hours to reduce unemployment, met with no response from his EC 'partners'. The EC has been ineffective even at defending its collective interests, notably over US restrictions on steel imports from Europe, the pursuit of national interest taking priority over collective action.

The revival of mercantilist policies of economic patriotism in the early 1980s has deprived the EC of such residual impetus as it still had, while neither the EC commission nor the European parliament (directly elected despite Gaullist reticence in 1979) have been able to overcome the inertia resulting from a deadlocked Council of Ministers. Even when a British veto was overruled in 1982 – Mitterrand reversing Giscard's defeat at the hands of Margaret Thatcher – this was not a step towards restoring majority voting but a desperate act to prevent total paralysis of the Community institutions and satisfy the demands of irate French farmers. The fact that France has been the worst offender in the matter of confirmed Rome Treaty infringements, with a tally of 40 cases in 1981, way ahead of Italy (27), Germany (17) and more recent members such as the United Kingdom (9), suggests that the pressures towards national protectionism will be especially irresistible in France. French opposition under Giscard and lack of enthusiasm under Mitterrand to the admission of Spain into the EC is due to a fear of the domestic economic consequences, even though it is realized that admission would politically assist a fragile democracy.

## Imperial aftermath: from colonization to co-operation

French overseas expansion was inspired by the same unitary political ideal as reigned at home. Boissy d'Anglas expressed the peculiar mixture of chauvinist pretentiousness and universalist egalitarianism characteristic of the French colonial ideology of assimilation when he declared in 1794: 'The Revolution was not only for Europe but for the Universe.... There can only be one right way of administering: and if we have found it for European countries, why should [the colonies] be deprived of it?' The sense of cultural superiority, the stress on the cultural aspect of colonialism (the French language being the instrument of France's 'civilizing mission') over and above the crude appetite for economic exploitation, was very clearly stated in the 1880s by the principal architect of French colonial expansion, Jules Ferry. The cultural self-confidence that subsumed the French belief that, just as she had assimilated the many diverse peoples that made up metropolitan France, she could convert any people in the world into French citizens, was more genuinely Roman than anything the British Empire had to offer. However, assimilation never really applied to more than a tiny élite. When they moved from principles to practice, the French were all too conscious that if they granted their overseas subjects equal democratic rights to representation in a unitary parliament in Paris, they risked becoming the colony of their colonies. So, while the ideal of assimilation was publicly proclaimed, evoking the enthusiasm of a privileged minority overseas, a select few becoming deputies and even ministers during the Fourth Republic, the promise of equality through integration proved to be a hollow mockery. Those territories (Vietnam, Morocco, Tunisia) that could envisage creating a viable state independent of France, did so by force of arms or through negotiation under the Fourth Republic. Because of the large number of European settlers in Algeria, decolonization proved a more prolonged and agonizing process, destroying the Fourth Republic and unsettling the early years of the Fifth Republic. France thus paid a high price for trying to absorb and assimilate

257

her colonies, the absence of a tradition of colonial self-govern-
ment making a peaceful transition to independence especially
difficult.

In 1958 de Gaulle made one final attempt to rescue the old
assimilationist relationship based on a common citizenship,
common language and common control of foreign, defence,
economic and financial policy, it being understood that 'common' was a euphemism for 'French'. The confederal 'Community', established by Articles 1 and 77–88 of the Fifth Republic
Constitution, was intended to maintain a close association between France and her former black African colonies, most of
whom were dependent upon financial, administrative, technical, military and educational assistance from France. This
dependence was accentuated by the dismantling of the West
and Equatorial African federations, owing in part to de Gaulle's
hostility towards federations. Another factor was the desire of
the leaders in each colony to acquire the trappings of independence, accentuated in the case of the relatively wealthy Ivory
Coast and Gabon by a reluctance to combine with impecunious
neighbours. Although Guinea alone voted against any further
association with France, the Community, with its elaborate
political institutions, became a dead letter in 1960 as all its
twelve members successively obtained formal independence.*
France secured as a precondition the signature of bilateral co-
operation agreements in all or some of the following fields: prior
consultation before taking major foreign policy decisions; defence assistance against internal or external threats, French
troops occupying military bases to facilitate offering such assistance; access to raw materials and strategic products (notably
the uranium of Niger); a common monetary policy through the
franc area; reciprocal preferential trade relations, extended by
the Yaoundé and Lomé conventions to include the EC, which also
provides financial assistance through the European Development Fund whilst French aid is channelled through the Aid and
Co-operation Fund; and technical and cultural co-operation,
mainly through the provision of personnel. The transitory Community, although it survives meaninglessly in the Constitution,

---

* These states were the Central African Republic, Chad, Congo-Brazzaville, Da-
homey, Gabon, Ivory Coast, the Malagasy Republic, Mali, Mauritania, Niger, Senegal
and Upper-Volta.

is just an indistinct memory, but the relations of unilateral dependence upon France have remained.

Many of France's former colonies, including Cameroun and Togo (previously UN trusteeship territories) remain in monetary union with France through the franc area. The currencies of member countries are mutually convertible at fixed parities in unlimited amounts. Foreign exchange receipts are pooled, all central banks holding their reserves in French francs in French treasury accounts. Foreign exchange dealings are made through the Paris money market, giving it an international standing that it would not otherwise have. These countries offer reliable and expanding markets for French goods, France's favourable trade balance with them being compensated by their excess of exports to other countries, providing the common foreign exchange pool with a useful injection of funds. The advantage of securing a French guarantee for their currency and the reward of French aid involves acceptance of French influence over their internal monetary policies exercised notably through Frenchmen sitting on the boards of their central banks.

The work of conducting 'co-operative' relations with France's satellite states operates at two levels: overtly, through a minister for co-operation and development attached to the external relations minister, who conducts the formal relations between governments; covertly, through the adviser on African affairs, attached to the president of the republic, through which the more important informal relations between heads of state are conducted. A conflict over 'co-operation' policy led in December 1982 to the resignation of the minister, Jean-Pierre Cot. The junior minister is responsible for cultural and technical co-operation with all sub-Saharan French-speaking countries. It is through this agency that co-operation agreements are signed and aid missions set up to organize a substantial programme of assistance through the provision of personnel: judicial, police and administrative officials in the early 1960s, predominantly secondary and higher education teachers since then. The main beneficiaries have been the Ivory Coast, Malagasy and Senegal although North Africa has remained a very important user of French teachers. Cultural centres, financed by the Aid and Co-operation Fund, have been established in the capitals of former French colonies, helping to foster the 'cultural presence' to which France and the local French-trained élite attach great importance. In 1970 a French-speaking countries cultural and technical co-operation agency was established in Paris by twenty-one countries, including (in addition to nine of the twelve former Community states and France) Belgium, Burundi, Cameroun, Canada, Luxembourg, Monaco, Ruanda, Togo, Tunisia and South Vietnam. France supplied 45 per cent of its modest budget, Canada 33 per cent, Belgium 12 per cent, the remaining 10 per cent being shared amongst the other signatories of the agreement. Its birth was characterized particularly by the struggle over whether Quebec should be recognized as an equal signatory with the other member states, a problem resolved by the equivocal compromise of counter-signature.

'Co-operation has become an integral part of our foreign policy,' asserted France's former foreign minister, Couve de Murville, even though he had little say in post-colonial policy with Africa. 'There is such an interconnection between our political relations and our co-operation relations that it would be impossible to separate the two. . . .'[17] During the de Gaulle period, there were especially close links between Jacques Foccart, head of the general secretariat for African and Malagasy affairs, and the president. Foccart reported daily to de Gaulle, in his capacity as the president's adviser both on African affairs and on secret service matters. Foccart has been described as 'the president's right-hand man in the arcane cloak-and-dagger upper reaches of French politics and the trusted confidant of a dozen African presidents, many of whom owed more to him than they did to their electorates.' In addition to the 'day-to-day supervision, execution and quite often initiation' of policy in relation to France's ex-colonies, Foccart's secretariat rather than the foreign ministry was the communications centre for these matters. This was due to the fact that in addition to numerous unofficial sources of information, 'many key ambassadorial posts in black Africa were held by non-career diplomats, many of them Foccart's colleagues and leading Gaullists'.[18] Furthermore, Foccart was able to place advisers on the personal staff of several African presidents and in at least one case the person in question was at the same time a member of Foccart's secretariat. After a brief eclipse during the interregnum following de Gaulle's resignation, Foccart was restored to office by President Pompidou, a testimony to his standing both in the Gaullist hierarchy and with France's African client states.

In 1974 Giscard wound up the secretariat for African affairs, whose staff were transferred to the ministry for co-operation, but he replaced Foccart by appointing to his staff Foccart's deputy, René Journiac. Giscard clearly did not feel able to do without the assistance of someone who would act as the president's discreet personal emissary in Africa, although he was determined to eliminate a man like Foccart who was closely identified with Gaullism and with the secret service manipulation of ex-colonial leaders. Until his death in an air crash in 1980, Journiac played a crucial part in Giscard's active African policy, involving military as well as financial support for threatened presidents. He may have had 'no decision making power but his advice could sometimes decide the fate of certain African regimes.'[19] He was replaced by another of Foccart's former collaborators but in 1981 the advent of Mitterrand meant that a new way of handling relations with France's post-colonial successor states might develop. While there has been an undoubted desire to move to more normal relations, Mitterrand felt it necessary to appoint to his presidential staff a person (Guy Penne) to act as his itinerant ambassador in those African countries that still look to France for help in their hour of need. Apart from the economic benefits that French firms derive from the bilateral contractual ties that exist, France secures greater support in the United Nations, notably tolerance in the 1970s when it was supplying arms to South Africa, than it would otherwise have enjoyed. It maintains, thanks to a network of client states, a semblance of great power status. However, these states often show their identification with the Third World rather than their patron by voting differently from France at the UN.[20] President Mitterrand has assiduously continued to cultivate France's African clientele, some forty delegations (nineteen representing full members) attending the eleventh conference in Kinshasa of French and African heads of state in 1982.

The Algerian rebellion played a decisive role in the decolonization process. It accelerated the movement towards independence in Black Africa after de Gaulle had established a Community that he hoped might preserve Algeria within the

French fold. The 1962 peace agreement, whereby France granted independence to Algeria in return for a commitment to co-operate with France and guarantee the rights of the French settlers, was quickly undermined. The mass emigration of the French settlers was due in part to their own extremists and partly to the pressures of the Algerian government wishing to get rid of all the vestiges of French colonialism as soon as possible. Throughout the 1960s the Algerian government gradually eliminated France's economic and military presence in Algeria. It took advantage of the importance the French government attached to relations with Algeria, regarded as a passport to good relations with the developing countries in general, and the Mediterranean countries in particular.[21] So, despite measures of nationalization without compensations in 1971 and the cancellation of two-thirds of Algeria's debt to France, Algeria continued to receive a large share of French aid, nearly as much in 1970 as the aid granted to the whole of French-speaking Black Africa. The 1970s marked a period of difficult Franco-Algerian relations, with oil and migrant labour playing a prominent part in their dealings. Though the oil issue received much prominence, especially after the 1973 Arab oil price rise, the labour question was a festering sore. As one French observer put it with some vehemence, 'on the whole the workers who come to France illiterate, unskilled and healthy leave it illiterate, unskilled and sometimes sick or injured. Who, then, is giving aid to whom?'[22] By the late 1970s, France having moved from a situation of labour shortage to increasing unemployment, the French government was actively seeking to reduce such migration. Things were not helped by Giscard's diplomatic and military support for Morocco and Mauritania in the Sahara against Algeria and, although some *rapprochement* subsequently occurred, it was not until Mitterrand became president that a new start was made. The nub of the 1982 Franco-Algerian Agreement was an artificially high price for oil, justified as a way of aiding a Third World country which had historic ties with France and would provide a vital element in the ambitious North–South strategy that both Giscard and Mitterrand have followed.

A small part of France's overseas empire has survived as an integral part of the republic. These imperial residues are of two types: overseas departments and overseas territories, the joint responsibility of a junior minister in the French government. The former consist of 1·2 million people living in two Caribbean islands (Martinique and Guadeloupe), French Guiana on the South American mainland, the Saint-Pierre and Miquelon islands off Canada's east coast and the island of Réunion in the Indian Ocean. They are represented in the French parliament and the official fiction is that they are treated in all respects as though they are part of metropolitan France. The attempt to assimilate them has resulted in absurd consequences, notably an inflated administration, a lopsided economy and an inappropriate educational system, which renders them financially dependent on metropolitan France. The local leaders are torn between political pressures favouring autonomy and economic pressures requiring integration. So, despite the occasional eruption of violence and repression, France will continue to enjoy the use of the Kourou rocket launching site and space centre in Guiana, while an electorally corrupt Réunion will continue to provide a safe seat for defeated metropolitan politicians such as Michel Debré. The three remaining overseas territories, whose population amounts to 300,000 people, have varying degrees of autonomy but share the characteristics of being remote from and economically dependent upon France. French Polynesia is militarily important as the location of the Pacific Experimental Centre at which France explodes her nuclear bombs. The economies of New Caledonia and the Wallis and Futuna islands are dominated by the Rothschild-controlled firm *Le Nickel*.

French ministers make great play with the size of French aid to developing countries, which amounted in 1981 to 0·46 per cent rather than the OECD target of 0·7 per cent of the gross domestic product, to which it rose only if one included aid to French overseas departments and territories, which absorb nearly one-third of the total. The Mauroy Government agreed that France should increase its aid, excluding its own overseas possessions, to 0·7 per cent by 1988. The beneficiaries submit annual investment programmes to the local aid and co-operation mission, then to the officials of the co-operation ministry and finally to the French Aid and Co-operation Fund which allocates the assistance. The treasury division of the finance ministry plays a decisive role in authorizing loans. Although

France has increased the share of aid going to countries outside the franc area, most of French aid is allocated to countries with under 1 per cent of the underdeveloped world's population. Successive reports on the French policy of co-operation with the developing countries have acknowledged the deliberate neglect of industrialization, arguments which had been advanced earlier by Réné Dumont in *False Start in Africa,* chapter 6 being entitled 'Independence is not always "decolonization" '. Appreciation of this fact led some of France's client states to renegotiate their 'co-operation agreements'.[23]

The French government has engaged in both covert and overt military intervention in Africa. It was Giscard who played a particularly active role in the affairs of African states and not just former French colonies. Thus in 1977 and again in 1978 he went to the help of President Mobutu of Zaire, on the first occasion by airlifting Moroccan troops and on the second occasion by dropping parachutists of the French Foreign Legion in an even more direct intervention at Mobutu's request. In 1977–8, French aircraft were deployed against the Saharan Polisario tribesmen at war with Mauritania and Morocco, whilst in Chad French troops were used in support of a succession of leaders in the civil war and to deter Libyan intervention. The most flagrant example of the use of military force, first to support an African head of state in power and then to remove him, was the case of Bokassa. France helped to crown him emperor of the Central African Empire in 1977 and subsidized his extravagances while Giscard had close personal relations with him, involving the controversial acceptance of gifts of diamonds. After it became clear that Bokassa was directly implicated in a massacre of schoolchildren, Journiac was personally charged by Giscard with the military operation to overthrow Bokassa and replace him with a more respectable nominee, work for which he was formally thanked at a Cabinet meeting on 24 September 1979.[24]

In the post-Vietnam era, when the USA was reluctant to become militarily involved in farflung places, Giscardian France seemed to be the West's answer to the Cuban catspaw of the Soviet Union, though there was no direct confrontation because they intervened in different parts of Africa. France still has about 9,000 troops stationed in Africa (mainly in Djibouti) with a further 4,000 military advisers. As Louis de Guiringaud, Giscard's second foreign minister, effusively put it, Africa was the only continent where France 'can still, with 500 men, change the course of history.'[25] Whilst Mitterrand will also wish to promote France's economic interests and protect its sources of uranium, he is unlikely to play the *gendarme* in Africa as readily, or with the same relish as his predecessor used the 'intervention forces' especially prepared for this task. Mitterrand has, however, used French forces in the Lebanon, on behalf of the United Nations, although his 1982 visit to Israel did not allow France to become the influence in the Middle East she once was. Her dependence upon Arab oil and Saudi support for the French franc has circumscribed Mitterrand's room for manoeuvre.

## National defence and nuclear deterrence

Although a combination of indecisive government and colonial war led to a military usurpation of civil power under the Fourth Republic, the re-emergence of General de Gaulle in 1958 was to establish strong government, terminate the Algerian war and restore civil control over the military. The disastrous 1940 experience of confiding the conduct of war to the army convinced de Gaulle that the chiefs of staff should be reduced to advisers of the civilian authorities and he embodied this principle in the decrees of 1946 and 1959 determining defence organization. Despite the importance he attached to military power as the instrument of national independence (declaring at the *Ecole Militaire* in 1959 that France and Germany had never achieved anything great without a large measure of military participation), de Gaulle did not have a flattering opinion of the political capacities of his former comrades in arms. In any case, 'national defence' was not just a euphemism for the old title 'war' or a concession to the need to co-ordinate the three services. The traditional distinction between peace and war had been blurred by involvement in prolonged colonial wars and in the 'cold war' in Europe, communism being both the domestic and foreign enemy. Given the 'total' nature of modern warfare, defence embraced civil as well as military matters, necessitating wide-ranging interministerial co-operation. This involved the ministry of the interior for civil defence, police and the prefects, the finance and industry ministries on the economic side – especially important as the cost of modern weapons escalated – and the scientific and technological research necessary to perfect this weaponry. National defence of such a comprehensive kind could not safely be entrusted to the military, who formed a world apart, with their own laws and (until 1981) courts, their peculiar values and professional code, frequently incomprehensible if not repugnant to the civilian population.

The uneasy relationship between the civil government and its military subordinate is reflected in the fact that from 1945 to 1965 there were twenty-five major reforms of defence organization. All accepted the spirit of St Just's assertion in 1793: 'There must be only one will in the state, the lawmaker must command war operations.' But who was the 'lawmaker'? In 1946 de Gaulle asserted the unity of defence by eliminating separate service ministries and placing defence firmly in the premier's hands. Within a year of de Gaulle's resignation, the logic of the Fourth Republic led to the delegation and dispersal of power to other ministers, to the Assembly and to the generals. Apart from the integration of French defence with NATO, and the denial to the French defence minister of responsibility for the Indo-Chinese and Algerian war efforts which weakened political control, the confusion and paralysis within the inter-ministerial defence committee produced by quarrelling coalition partners left the way open for the military leaders to take the political initiative, choosing whom to obey as between ministers and finally refusing to obey at all. A situation in which a general could declare: 'Each party, each politician has a clientele and candidates in the army', was ripe for revolt, particularly when members of the defence minister's personal staff were plotting to overthrow the republic.[26]

The French system of total integration of the three services within a single ministry, combined with the elimination of separate junior ministries for each service, instituted by de Gaulle in 1958, has its advantages and its disadvantages. It has facilitated budgetary economies at a time when military technology renders this especially necessary, as well as undermining the independence of the three services. However, owing to the inability of a single minister effectively to control all aspects of defence, the military are likely to enjoy greater political autonomy unless there is strong administrative backing to the ministerial integration. During de Gaulle's presidency, the armed forces minister, as he was called (to denote his more limited function) was a non-politician, whose role was simply to implement the president's policy. The key 1959 Defence Ordinance was deliberately vague, to allow maximum scope for regulatory discretion in defence organization. Following up Article 20 of the Constitution, which described the prime minister as 'responsible' (a strong but vague epithet) for defence, the 1959 Ordinance entrusts the making of defence policy collectively to the government, while policy co-ordination and implementation as well as the oversight of military operations is confided to the prime minister. However, if the prime minister is *generalissimo* on paper, de Gaulle saw to it that the president embodied the indivisibility of military power in practice. Using his chairmanship of the defence council, President de Gaulle assumed control of defence policy, reducing his prime minister and defence minister to executants of his edicts.

In the early 1960s, by a combination of presidential practice and of decrees, the prime minister's defence powers were delegated to the armed forces minister for day-to-day matters and to the president of the republic for major decisions.[27] Prime Minister Pompidou reduced Debré's large military *cabinet* to one officer and was content to leave his defence functions to the armed forces minister who was directly answerable to the president. A 1964 decree increased the role of the defence council, composed of the president, prime minister, foreign, interior, finance and armed forces ministers, the chief of the defence staff and of the three services, the secretary-general of national defence and the head of the president's military staff (who acts as its secretary) which meets five or six times a year and is responsible for general defence policy, including diplomatic, economic and nuclear matters as they relate to defence. The defence committee is concerned with more detailed matters such as military plans and the allocation of forces. The president treated these bodies as he did the Cabinet. The main function of the secretariat general of national defence (SGND) was to prepare the meetings of the defence council and committee and see that their decisions were implemented. It worked to presidential directives rather than for the prime minister to whom it was formally attached. Should anyone have doubted the president's dominance over defence policy, the 1964 decree giving him control over France's strategic nuclear deterrent provided a formal acknowledgement of the realities of power. Military predominance in the SGND made it amenable to armed forces influence even before it was attached to the defence minister in 1969. The SGND was de Gaulle's instrument for the general oversight of defence negotiations, the collection and communication of political, economic, scientific as well as military intelligence and the export of arms. Consequently, when Debré secured the SGND's transfer to the defence ministry he achieved a major shift in power.

Although Debré's resumption of the Fourth Republic title of defence minister and his acquisition of a junior minister (until 1972) seemed to mark the reversal of the policy of confiding defence policy nominally to the prime minister and in fact to the president, the ground had been prepared by the twenty-three decrees reorganizing the armed forces ministry in 1961. The minister emerged with his capacity to secure information and exert direct control substantially increased. Not only did he acquire control over promotion through his direct responsibility for military personnel. Through the new general supervision of the armed forces corps, he obtained a super-inspectorate over all administrative and financial matters. Legislative and regulatory proposals having administrative, economic or financial consequences had to be approved by members of this body, which could be overruled only by the minister. However, the minister's authority was based on three main pillars: the secretary-general (administration), the ministerial delegate (armament), and the chiefs of staff committee. Unlike the secretary-general in the foreign ministry, the defence secretary-general has only a partial co-ordinating role and was created to achieve unity of administrative and financial management to counterbalance the power of the service chiefs and of the armaments delegate. The secretary-general (administration) works in close contact with the minister, the director and members of the minister's *cabinet*. He is the minister's main adviser on budgetary matters. About half the secretary-general's time is spent with the division directors, co-ordinating budgetary, personnel and purchasing policy.

He is an important factor in securing civilian control over defence.[28]

The 1961 creation of the ministerial delegation (armament) initiated a US, McNamara-style centralization of authority over the military research and development programme, all the more remarkable because until then the separation between science and defence was, with the exception of nuclear research and development, almost complete. It established, alongside the secretary-general (administration) and the service chiefs, a ministerial delegate responsible for the management and co-operation of arms research and production who would supply French-designed weaponry rather than rely on American arms. The delegation's research and testing directorate brought university scientists, engineers and officers together for the first time within one organization to achieve a highly centralized focus for science research policy-making, notably through the selective award of research grants and contracts. Thus the French space programme, third only to those of the United States and Soviet Union, is like the proverbial iceberg, the civilian component being the tip, the hidden portion being made up of the delegation's military projects. On the nuclear deterrent, the delegation works closely with the Atomic Energy Commissariat's military applications division. In the belief that it would encourage a 'spillover' into the civil economy and alter its 'unproductive' image, French military research, development and production was contracted out to private firms, some of which were nationalized in 1982. While as yet there has been little evidence of a 'spin off', the policy of subsidizing advanced technology industries with military funds encouraged the development of a mini industrial-military-scientific complex on the American pattern.[29]

Arms exports are primarily the responsibility of the delegation's international affairs division, which makes the preliminary appraisal of 'whether a proposed export sale falls within France's *armaments* policy'. If it does, the matter goes to the interdepartmental arms exports committee, serviced by the defence secretariat, which meets under the chairmanship of a defence secretariat official, with the foreign and finance ministries represented. If the decision is not unanimous, the matter is referred to an interministerial arms exports committee, which 'determines whether the proposed sale fits into France's *political* policy. If the sale is a particularly delicate one, the request will end up at the Elysée palace for decision.'[30] The president, defence and external relations ministers are the main people involved in a policy which was primarily politically motivated under de Gaulle – to diminish Anglo-American influence compared to that of France – but has switched to a more economic emphasis under his successors. While France re-established herself as a major arms exporter under the Fourth Republic, her sales decreased fourfold (in money terms) between 1958 and 1968. Whilst both Giscard and Mitterrand proclaimed on taking office that it was their intention to reduce arms sales, though some redirection has occurred, the volume of arms sales has continued to increase, fuelled by the need to counterbalance the foreign exchange drain of increasingly expensive oil imports. France has become the largest arms salesman in the world per head of its population, though behind the USA and the USSR in terms of the volume of its arms exports. Although in 1978 Giscard abandoned de Gaulle's sixteen-year-old policy of the 'empty seat' in the Geneva disarmament committee, French governments have continued to argue that French arms sales provide a safeguard against dependence upon the two superpowers, a clear case of rationalizing national self-interest. The armaments industry employs 300,000 people and in 1980 exported 40 per cent of its production (which represents 6 per cent of all French exports and 12 per cent of the international arms trade). Forty-five per cent of French arms went to the Middle East.[31] Because this export drive is essential if the burden of French arms expenditure is to be shared with foreign purchasers, defence ministers have instructed the chiefs of staff and armaments delegation to equip French forces, as far as possible, with weapons that could also be exported.

In 1967, Messmer (de Gaulle's armed forces minister from 1960–69 before becoming Pompidou's prime minister from 1972–74) exposed the unreality of ministerial accountability to parliament over defence expenditure when he declared: 'There are military secrets which are reflected in budgetary silences.' In no area of the military budget is this admission more relevant than in the matter of the nuclear deterrent. While it is not surprising that the nuclear weapons policy should be secretive, the striking contrast between France and either Britain or the United States is that the French atomic programme was militarized in the 1950s by a series of incremental steps in which the political leaders responded to technocratic pressures rather than made deliberate decisions. 'Guidance and direction for nuclear policy came not from the French government or the French parliament, but from a small dedicated group of administrator-technocrats, politicians and military officers' whose activities centred on the Atomic Energy Commissariat; while '... it was the commissariat cadre which provided the element of continuous advice and support for a military atomic programme and which assured continuity in French nuclear progress, even in the face of disinterested and unsympathetic political leadership.'[32] The interplay between the techno-bureaucrats and the politicians, with individual army officers and industrialists playing an accessory role, is most instructive about the way policy is made in situations where the government is divided and insufficiently interested and therefore indecisive, allowing those with a clear objective to get their way.

The Atomic Energy Commissariat, established by de Gaulle in 1945, enjoyed the unique situation of state financial support without supervision by any ministry or budgetary surveillance by the finance ministry. The explanatory memorandum creating it explained that it would be attached to the prime minister so that it would be 'very close to the government and, so to speak, mingled with it, and nevertheless vested with great freedom of action'. It had two heads, a high commissioner on the research side and an administrator-general who as 'government delegate' was the link with the prime minister's office. Although in the first, pure research, phase of the Commissariat's work, it was the high commissioner who was in effective command, the removal in 1950 of Joliot-Curie on the grounds of his Communist affiliations and his refusal to accept the possibility of a military orientation of the Commissariat's work prepared the way for dominance by the administrator-general on the classic French pattern. This in turn led to a change in the early 1950s towards an industrial and military emphasis, as the pacifist and left-wing scientists were purged and administrative leadership was assumed by *polytechniciens* with Gaullist sympathies. In 1951 *polytechnicien* Louis Armand refused the succession of *polytechnicien*

271

Raoul Dautry and suggested *polytechnicien* Pierre Guillaumat who accepted the post of administrator-general. Guillaumat held this post from 1951 to 1958, when he was appointed armed forces minister by de Gaulle, which was both a tribute to his pre-eminent past role in fostering the development of a French nuclear deterrent and an indication of the central role it was to play in defence policy. It was left to André Giraud, *polytechnicien* and associate of Guillaumat, to convert the Atomic Energy Commissariat into an instrument of France's energy policy, before becoming Giscard's industry minister.[33]

The combination of a military and engineering *Ecole Polytechnique* training naturally inclined its graduates to think in terms of giving nuclear power a military application. Guillaumat was well aware that the majority of senior officers were wedded to reliance upon the American deterrent with the NATO alliance and he successfully prevented subordination of the Commissariat to military control. To help him achieve his aims, he nevertheless used well-placed *polytechnicien* army allies such as Charles Ailleret, in charge of special weapons at the defence ministry from 1952–8, and subsequently armed forces chief of staff and exponent of the ultra-Gaullist doctrine of 'all-round defence' in 1967. Another strategically situated ally was *polytechnicien* General Lavaud, nuclear arms adviser to the defence minister, Bourgès-Maunoury, in the Mollet Government of 1956–7. Lavaud worked with Guillaumat as armed forces minister and became armed forces chief of staff in 1959. The *polytechnicien* old boy network[34] extended to politicians like Bourgès-Maunoury, who played a key role as minister for atomic affairs, defence and as prime minister. With Premier Félix Gaillard (a former atomic affairs minister) he provided the political support that was indispensable if the techno-bureaucratic influence of Guillaumat was to be effective. It was pressure within his Cabinet, as well as from the Commissariat and the Assembly defence committee, that led Mollet to turn a blind eye to the development of an independent nuclear deterrent under his premiership. Nor must one forget Gaullists such as General Koenig. As president of the Assembly defence committee from 1951 to 1954 and especially as defence minister in 1954 and 1955, Koenig was able to smuggle into the 1956 budget substantial 'hidden' funds for the atomic programme, helped by

Gaston Palewski, atomic affairs minister in 1955 (who was to succeed Guillaumat as atomic energy minister in 1962). It is significant that when it was necessary to find Gaullist Olivier Guichard a post in 1955, he was appointed press attaché to the Atomic Energy Commissariat. So, the continuity between the nuclear policy of the Fourth and Fifth Republics was not a matter of chance. The latter unveiled and exploded a deterrent that had been furtively prepared by its predecessor.

The advent of the Fifth Republic was to lead to a decline in the influence of the Atomic Energy Commissariat as the nuclear deterrent became officially the centrepiece of French defence strategy. With the policy of diplomatic independence accepted, the Commissariat – formerly a state within the state, with Gaullists taking advantage of its technocratic status – could recede into the subordinate role of implementing government policy. De Gaulle kept close personal control over the Comissariat through frequent contacts with the administrator-general, the high commissioner and the director of the military applications division. In the mid-1960s, 60 per cent of the Commissariat's budget came from the defence ministry and three-quarters of its expenditure went on the nuclear weapons programme, but by 1969 a shift in emphasis led to its transfer from the prime minister to the minister of industrial and scientific development. It was no longer so necessary to pretend that France's nuclear energy programme could be achieved only with military assistance, whereas in fact this was not true. The military justification for nuclear weapons came after their production, the real motivation being to influence allies rather than to dissuade enemies.

The French nuclear deterrent makes greater sense if seen as a political symbol of national independence from America rather than as a military weapon directed at Russia. De Gaulle declared at the *Centre des Hautes Etudes Militaires* in 1959, in a statement which he quoted in his *Memoirs of Hope*, that 'France defends herself, by herself, for herself and in her own way'. He nevertheless appreciated that confronted by one super-power, France would have to rely on the support of the other; but such alliances were 'incidental not axiomatic' and to tie oneself simply to America would be fatal to French independence.[35] The French nuclear deterrent was the only hope of resisting a joint Russo–American hegemony and utilizing the United States to discourage any threat from the Soviet Union, while looking to the latter to prevent a resurgence of German (nuclear) militarism. Even the refusal to join in arms limitation talks made sense, as the value of the French deterrent was increased if other countries imposed restrictions which France could ignore. Since 1975 exports of nuclear material are co-ordinated by the external nuclear policy council, which meets two or three times a year and on which the external relations, defence, research and industry and foreign trade ministries are represented.

Because French nuclear policy is a logical corollary of French foreign policy, it was idle to hope that the former would change unless and until the latter did. Although Giscard and Mitter-rand have adopted a more co-operative attitude towards NATO and Mitterrand in particular has been firm in resisting the Soviet nuclear build-up in Eastern Europe, they both rallied in practice to a policy that was close to that of de Gaulle. In a June 1982 press conference Mitterrand went so far as to assert of NATO: 'we have tightened up the alliance, on which is based a large part of our security and in any case the world balance of power'. However, he went on to add that French policy involved not only 'tightening our alliance but reinforcing our own weaponry, the two pillars of our security', self-defence being placed on a par with *the* alliance rather than above it as de Gaulle would have done. It was a policy based 'neither on isolation nor alignment'. Whereas the education budget had overtaken the defence budget in Pompidou's presidency, this priority was reversed and the nuclear component of defence expenditure had increased to 19 per cent by 1981, with a particular emphasis upon France's five nuclear submarines. Although *Le Canard enchaîné* might poke fun at Mitterrand's defence minister Charles Hernu, dubbed *Hernucléaire*, the evidence is that the public appeal of nuclear nationalism has remained as powerful as ever, attaining the status of a subject on which there was a national consensus.[36]

Table 20 shows that there was a solid majority of 53 to 29 per cent in favour of the French nuclear deterrent in 1977 and while this support was strongest among right-wing voters (particularly the RPR) there was also a clear majority in favour among

Socialist voters. In the late 1970s, first the Communist Party and then the Socialist Party reversed their earlier hostility to the national nuclear deterrent, so that although there is some active environmentalist hostility to nuclear energy, there has not been a mass movement comparable to the British Campaign for Nuclear Disarmament. However, one should not exaggerate the reliance placed by the French public upon their nuclear deterrent. The same opinion poll indicated, in response to the question: 'What best guarantees France's independence?' that the army and its nuclear strike force were only supported by 22 per cent, while 38 per cent preferred France's neutrality in major international conflicts and 35 per cent thought that French economic power was the best guarantee of her independence.[37]

*Table 20*
*French public opinion on the desirability of a national nuclear deterrent in 1977.* (%)

|  | | Party support | | | |
| --- | --- | --- | --- | --- | --- |
|  | *All* | PCF | PS | PR | RPR |
| Strongly favourable | 20 | 9 | 16 | 30 | 35 |
| Rather favourable | 33 | 25 | 36 | 39 | 43 |
| Rather unfavourable | 17 | 18 | 22 | 8 | 12 |
| Very unfavourable | 12 | 31 | 17 | 2 | 2 |
| No reply | 18 | 17 | 9 | 21 | 8 |

Source: SOFRES, *L'Opinion française in 1977*, p. 294.

The French clearly put their trust in prudence and all-round strength rather than in sheer military power. They continue to bear the burden of conscription (conscripts account for about half of the 500,000 members of the three services) with fortitude, to allow France to maintain substantial conventional armed forces. This shows a shrewd appreciation of the fact that, once peripheral, international diplomacy and defence can less than ever be separated from the rest of national life. Each intrudes into the other, in an interdependence that is frequently disharmonious. The nuclear emphasis in French defence policy is reflected in the 1984–88 medium term military plan, which will coincide with the Ninth National Plan, to ensure that defence planning is no longer treated in isolation from general economic policy constraints. In this respect at least, there is a genuine deviation from the Gaullist conception of defence policy.

# 9 The Constraints on Political Will

An analytical problem which is seldom recognized in the study of French politics is how to embrace a number of dualities without either reducing them to a spurious unity or resigning oneself to infinite variety. There is always a more or less substantial gap between principles and practice, norms and behaviour, myths and realities, models and what they purport to represent. The French have underlined this dichotomy by the unspoken assumption that when something is the case in principle, this means that it is not so (partially or often wholly) in practice. In trying to transcend the two worlds of political reality and of meta-politics, one must both resist the temptation of dismissing the norms as mere fictions because they are not accurate descriptions of reality and avoid slipping into the assumption that the facts actually conform with official values and rhetoric. The attentive reader will have frequently been aware of the tension between the norms of unity and indivisibility on the one hand and the diversity and variety of behaviour. It is to be hoped that readers were not misled into supposing that the monolithic norm was meant to be a description of reality, any more than to describe France as a multiple and infinitely divisible republic would help one to understand the prevailing values of French society. What we have tried to show is that precisely because France has historically been in so many ways a fragmented society, the meta-political norms of the French state have sought to bring unity out of what is regarded as chaos. The fact that the state institutions are themselves riddled with division and dissensus merely means that the tension between norms and behaviour are not merely between state and society but within the component elements of society and the state.

Acknowledging, therefore, the precariousness of attempts at generalizing about the policy process in a whole society as complex and varied as France, particularly if one wishes to capture more than a moment of changing reality to comprehend very different kinds of public policy arenas, one may still wish to dwell upon what we have described elsewhere as 'the relatively stable set of semi-absolutes that constitute the normative framework within which the polity is deemed to operate.'[1] Because the French historical experience has elevated the state into a normatively superior position in French society, this has been a powerful and persistent force in shaping reality. Eugen Weber, a historian of enduring, provincial France, *la France profonde*, has warned against covering 'the intricate pattern of things as they were with a general mantle of things as they should be, as if a France become one and indivisible had thereby become uniform as well.'[2] He suggests the deliberately schizophrenic need to envisage France 'not as a given reality but as a work-in-progress, a model of something at once to be built and to be treated for political reasons as already in existence.'[3] The French statist drive to mould diverse society into an indivisible whole has produced an assertive, active policy style that pervades much of decision-making intention if not of implemented decisions. We have argued that while this 'active policy style does not in practice mean integrated or decisive action, it implies a *capacity* for policy initiative, a *potential* for far-sighted planning and a *propensity* to imposed (the state's) will when it is necessary to attain public objectives. Although French policy making may be characterized as having a predominantly reactive, short-term and piecemeal approach to problem-solving, at the summit of the French state there is an informal network or nucleus of executive power capable of challenging the routine norms and attempting to impose an active, longer-term and comprehensive style of policy making and implementation.'[4] It is the normative legitimacy upon which French leaders can rely in mobilizing élites and masses in the service of public ambitions that imparts an integrative impetus to the disparate forces that constitute French society.

We have seen that the Fifth Republic has become, with the sole exception of the Third Republic, the most stable political regime since the 1789 Revolution. Despite the resounding clash between left and right, the working of institutions and the content of policies have been discreetly marked by continuity rather than change, following the advent of the left to office in 1981 after twenty-three years in the wilderness. True, decentralization, planning, nationalization and worker rights have been advanced in bold legislative reforms. Prudence suggests that once the dust has settled, the traditional routines favouring centralization, incrementalism, *dirigisme* and managerial control will reassert themselves. In crucial areas like defence and foreign policy, continuity is virtually unchallenged, whilst in the others, such as education, change is considered with the utmost circumspection. There has been no major attempt to redistribute wealth, generally acknowledged to be highly inegalitarian. Attempts to cope with the immense burdens of social security are characteristically piecemeal and improvisatory. Yet if one compares French political and administrative practice with that of any other advanced industrial society, it still seems true that in the boldness of governmental policy innovation and the resolution with which it is implemented, the French state stands out as distinctively assertive. An ultra-nuclear strategy, whether in the civil field of energy policy or the military field of defence policy, is simply the most spectacular example of a policy style whose practice is shaped by the meta-political principles that endure.

France survived the strains of rapid population growth, economic expansion and modernization in the 1950s and 1960s, although the process of decolonization led to a change of republic and a drastic reorganization of the country's political institutions. In the 1970s, France dealt with greater success than most with the effects of the international economic recession, containing their impact upon living standards and sustaining a flagging economy by using public sector investment to compensate for the unwillingness of private business to invest when markets were shrinking. Thus, even before the coming to power of the left, French governments were adopting an offensive rather than defensive strategy towards the crisis, not sacrificing ambitious objectives but mobilizing national energies to overcome the challenge. However, by the early 1980s, the international pressures were exercising ever more stringent constraints upon France's capacity to follow an independent, 'odd man out'

279

policy of reducing unemployment even at the cost of higher
budget deficits and higher rates of inflation. With currency
devaluations not preventing further runs on the French franc,
firmness of national political will was simply not sufficient to
stem the scepticism towards the solitary sanity of French policy.
Though Mitterrand proudly began his June 1982 press conference with the affirmation: 'I will here express a will, a political
will, a personal will, a national will', a week later he was
humiliatingly forced against his will to devalue the franc. Even
Socialist France has, apparently, to resign itself to conformity
with a pattern of conduct fixed by international market forces,
largely mediating the effects of US policy. The nation's ability
to practice its principles is at the mercy of forces beyond its
control. It is a lesson in political modesty that is especially
difficult to accept for those whose values derive from the proud
French tradition which looks to those who control the state to
dominate external forces rather than defer to them. France
remains, as Rochefort described it more than a century ago –
although the population has meanwhile increased from the forty
million of his day – a country with fifty-four million subjects
... without counting the subjects of discontent.

# Notes

Chapter 1    *The Unwritten Constitution*

1    E. Weber, *Peasants into Frenchmen. The Modernization of Rural France, 1870–1914*, 1976, pp. 95, 112, 493.

2    See K. Dyson, *The State Tradition in Western Europe*, 1980, pp. 162–3; cf. 129, 137, 173–4.

3    J. Hayward, 'Presidential Suicide by Plebiscite: de Gaulle's exit, April 1969', *Parliamentary Affairs*, xxii/4, Autumn 1969, pp. 289–90, quoting J.-R. Tournoux, *La Tragédie du Général*, 1967, p. 437.

4    F. Mitterrand, *Politique*, 1977, pp. 543 and 283.

5    A. de Tocqueville, *Democracy in America* (1st edn 1835), World's Classics edn, 1959, ch. 4, p. 51.

6    See Blackwell edn of *Six Books of the Commonwealth* (1st edn 1576), book vi, chapter 4, p. 197, and book ii, chapter 1, p. 52.

7    Ibid., book iii, chapter 13.

8    E.J. Sieyès, *What is the Third Estate?* (1st edn 1789), 1963 English edn, p. 80; E. Thompson, *Popular Sovereignty and the French Constituent Assembly, 1789–91*, 1951, p. 6.

9    Quoted by J. Roels, *La Notion de représentation chez Roederer*, 1968, p. 83; cf. E. Thompson, op. cit., pp. 50–53. For J. de Maistre's castigation of the sovereignty of the nation concept, see his 'Considerations on France' of 1796, published in J. Lively (ed.), *The Works of Joseph de Maistre*, 1965, pp. 68–9.

10    Quoted in G.G. Van Deusen, *Sieyès. His Life and his Nationalism*, 1932, p. 130.

11    Reprinted in B. Constant, *Cours de politique constitutionnelle*, 1861 edn, vol. i, pp. 203–4.

12    Ibid., pp. 9–10; cf. J.S. Mill, *On Liberty*, 1859, chapter 2.

13    Ibid., p. 11. See also J. de Maistre, 'Study on Sovereignty', in *The Works of Joseph de Maistre*, p. 93.

14    Ibid., p. 12.

15    S. Hoffmann, 'Protest in Modern France', in M.A. Kaplan (ed.), *The Revolution in World Politics*, 1962, p. 69; cf. also pp. 72–4.

281

16  P.-J. Proudhon, *Idée générale de la Révolution au XIX<sup>e</sup> siècle*, 1851, epilogue.

17  F. Mitterrand, op. cit., p. 532. See also J. Hayward, 'Dissentient France: the counter political culture' and other contributions to P.G. Cerny (ed.), *Social Movements and Protest in France*, 1982.

18  P. Avril, *Politics in France*, 1969, part 1, chapter 2.

19  In S. Hoffmann *et al.*, *France, Change and Tradition*, 1963, p. 8.

20  A. de Tocqueville, *The Old Régime and the French Revolution* (1856), 1955 English edn, p. 202.

21  Ibid., pp. 210–11. It was Victor Hugo who so dubbed Louis Napoleon in his book on the 1851 *coup*.

22  S. Hoffmann, 'Heroic leadership: the case of modern France', in L.J. Edinger (ed.), *Political Leadership in Industrialized Societies*, 1967, p. 127 and *passim*.

23  M. Crozier, *The Bureaucratic Phenomenon*, 1964, p. 196; cf. Charles de Gaulle, *Le Fil de l'épée* (1944), 1962 edn, pp. 53–7. For reservations on the Crozierian crisis explanation of change in France, see Jack Hayward 'Dissentient France', *West European Politics*, I/3, Oct. 1978, pp. 54–5; and Roger Duclaud-Williams,'Change in French Society: a Critical Analysis of Crozier's Bureaucratic Model', *West European Politics*, IV/3, Oct. 1981, pp. 236–9.

24  S. Hoffmann, 'Heroic leadership', op. cit., p. 117.

25  M. Crozier, op. cit., p. 287; cf. p. 196.

26  R. Aron, *The Elusive Revolution*, 1969, p. 18. The translation of de Gaulle's comment has been amended slightly.

27  *Journal officiel. Assemblé nationale. Débats*, 12 December 1968, p. 5409.

28  V. Giscard d'Estaing, *Démocratie française*, 1976, translated as *Towards a New Democracy*, 1977, pp. 45–6. The passage quoted has been retranslated.

29  F. Mitterrand, op. cit., pp. 204 and 195.

*Chapter 2    Decentralizing the Indivisible Republic*

1  F. Mitterrand, *Politique*, 1977, pp. 525–6.

2  Quoted by G.G. Van Deusen, *Sieyès. His Life and his Nationalism*, 1932, pp. 85–6, 95.

3  *De la capacité politiques des classes ouvrières* (1st edn 1865), quoted in the Rivière *Oeuvres complètes* edn of 1924, p. 286.

4  G. Schubert, *The Public Interest*, 1960, p. 93.

5  E. Pisani, *La Région . . . pour quoi faire?*, 1970, p. 54.

6  C. Roig, 'Théorie et réalité de la décentralisation', *Revue française de science politique*, June 1964, pp. 463–4, and C. Roig,

'L'administration locale et les changements sociaux', in
*Administration traditionnelle et planification régionale*, 1964, pp. 13,
19–20, 33, 45. See also P. Grémion, *La Structuration du pouvoir au
niveau départemental*, 1969, pp. 29–32.

7   B. Chapman, *Introduction to French Local Government*, 1953, p. 225,
and B. Chapman, *The Prefects and Provincial France*, 1955, p. 16;
cf. P. Grémion and J.-P. Worms, 'La concertation régionale,
innovation ou tradition', in *Aménagement du territoire et développement
régional*, 1968, vol. I, p. 38.

8   *Vivre Ensemble*, September 1976, I, pp. 91–4; cf. II, pp. 12–14.

9   Octave Gélinier, 'Vers de nouveaux conceptes pour organiser
l'administration' in Alain Peyrefitte *et al*, *Décentraliser les
responsabilités, pourquoi? Comment?*, 1976, pp. 46–50; cf. p. 43 ff. and
*Vivre Ensemble*, op. cit., pp. 351–3. More generally, see Marc
Auffret, Edmond Hervé and Yves Mény, *La Déconcentration*, 1971;
Alain Peyrefitte, *Le Mal français*, 1976, pp. 441–3; 'Echange et
projets', *La Démocratie à portée de la main*, 1977, pp. 45–51.

10   *Le Monde*, 19 September 1981.

11   H. Machin, *The Prefect in French Public Administration*, 1977,
p. 128; cf. pp. 55–8, 75–7, 122–9, and C. Grémion, *Profession:
décideurs. Pouvoir des hauts fonctionnaires et réforme de l'Etat*, 1979,
Part I *passim*.

12   V.F. Gruder, *The Royal Provincial Intendants*, 1968, p. 3; cf. B.
Chapman, *The Prefects and Provincial France*, pp. 12–13.

13   P. Grémion, op. cit., pp. 45–7; cf. P. Grémion and J.-P. Worms,
*Les Institutions régionales et la sociéte locale*, 1968, pp. 227–8.

14   A. Mabileau, 'Les élections cantonales' in *Annuaire de
l'administration locale*, 1980, pp. 277–88.

15   M. Kesselman, *The Ambiguous Consensus*, 1967, p. 173; cf. B.
Chapman, op. cit., pp. 124 ff.

16   J.-C. Thoenig and E. Friedberg, 'Politiques urbaines et stratégies
corporatives', *Sociologie du travail*, 1969, no. 4, pp. 389–92; cf.
M.-F. Souchon, *Le Maire, élu local dans une société en changement*,
1968, pp. 240–1, 246–7.

17   B. Chapman, op. cit., p. 42.

18   M. Kesselman, op. cit., p. 75. See also L. Wylie (ed.),
*Chanzeaux: A Village in Anjou*, 1966, chapter 12.

19   B. Chapman, op. cit., p. 64; cf. S. Tarrow, 'The urban–rural
cleavage in political involvement. The case of France', *American
Political Science Review*, LXV, June 1971, p. 341 ff.

20   Club Jean Moulin, *Les Citoyens au pouvoir*, 1968, pp. 71, 136; C.
Alphandéry *et al.*, *Pour nationaliser l'état*, pp. 175–6.

21   *Vivre Ensemble*, op. cit., II, pp. 158–81.

22   Y. Mény, 'Financial transfers and local government in France' in
     D. E. Ashford (ed.), *Financing Urban Government in the Welfare
     State*, 1980, chapter 7.

23   M. Schain, 'Communist control of municipal councils and
     urban political change' in P. G. Cerny and M. Schain (eds),
     *French Politics and Public Policy*, 1980, chapter 12. On local
     elections, see chapter 14 in J. Frears, *Political Parties and Elections
     in the French Fifth Republic*, 1977 and J. Hayward and V. Wright,
     'Governing from the centre: the 1977 French local elections',
     *Government and Opposition*, XII/4, Autumn 1977, pp. 433–54.

24   F. Mitterrand, op. cit., p. 568; cf. p. 423.

25   S. P. Huntington, 'Political Modernisation: America vs.
     Europe', *World Politics*, April 1966, pp. 378–9, 405–6.

26   Article in *Revue française de science politique*, April–June 1956, p.
     309, special issue on 'Aménagement du territoire'; cf. M. Debré,
     *La Mort de l'état républicain*, 1947. On the historical background to
     the development of regionalism, particularly the numerous
     Third Republic regional reform proposals in parliament, see the
     well documented study by M. Bourjol, *Les Institutions régionales de
     1789 à nos jours*, 1969.

27   Article in same issue of the *R.F.S.P.*, pp. 298–9.

28   Ibid., 'Administration de gestion, administration de mission',
     pp. 316, 321; cf. p. 325.

29   G. Delaunay, 'Plaidoyer pour une infante attendue', *Direction*,
     September 1964, pp. 825–6.

30   S. Hoffmann, 'Areal division of powers in the writings of French
     political thinkers', in A. Maas (ed.), *Area and Power. A Theory of
     Government*, 1959, pp. 121–2.

31   The best general study of the 1964 regional reform is C.
     Grémion, *Profession: décideurs. Pouvoir des hauts fonctionnaires et réforme
     de l'état*, 1979, Part 2. See also J. E. S. Hayward, 'From functional
     regionalism to functional representation in France, the Battle of
     Brittany', *Political Studies*, March 1969, p. 59 ff; cf. A.
     Baccigalupo, 'La participation des forces démocratiques à
     l'expérience française de planification régionale', *Canadian Journal
     of Political Science*, March 1972, pp. 1–27; P. Grémion, *La Mise en
     place des institutions régionales*, 1965, *passim*; P. Grémion and J.-P.
     Worms, 'La concertation régionale', *Aménagement du territoire et
     developpement régionale*, 1968, pp. 49–50; P. Grémion and J.-P.
     Worms: *Les Institutions régionales et la société locale*, 1968, *passim*; R.
     Mayer, *Féodalités ou démocratie?*, 1968, pp. 53, 60–7, 75.

32   *Journal officiel. Débats. Assemblée nationale*, 14 December 1968,
     p. 5466.

33 See Pierre Grémion, *Le Pouvoir périphérique. Bureaucrates et notables dans le système politique français*, 1976, part 1 and his 'Crispation et déclin du jacobinisme' in H. Mendras, *La Sagesse et le désordre. France 1980*, 1980, pp. 329–50.

34 *Le Monde*, 20 January 1982, p. 10.

35 M. Rocard, 'La région, une idée neuve pour la gauche' and P. Sadran, 'Les socialistes et la région' in the special issue of *Pouvoirs*, No. 19, November 1981, on 'Régions'. An opinion poll in October 1977 showed that while a majority of French people wanted greater power for municipalities (58 per cent) and regional councils (57 per cent) support was greatest among Socialist supporters (72 and 71 per cent respectively). See SOFRES, *L'Opinion française en 1977*, 1978, p. 232.

*Chapter 3    The Representative Mediators*

1 M. Crozier, *The Bureaucratic Phenomenon*, 1964, pp. 204–5.

2 J. Gretton, *Students and Workers*, 1969, p. 47.

3 L. Wylie, *Village in the Vaucluse*, 1961, p. 330.

4 All opinion data in this paragraph derived from SOFRES, *L'Opinion française en 1977*, 1978, pp. 173–4, 224–6, 230–2.

5 J. Mossuz-Lavau, *Les Jeunes et la gauche*, 1979, pp. 16–28, 33–5.

6 See P.G. Cerny (ed.), *Social Movements and Protest in France*, 1981.

7 F. Bourricaud, *Esquisse d'une théorie de l'autorité*, 1961, p. 313.

8 H.W. Ehrmann, 'French Bureaucracy and Organized Interests', *Administrative Science Quarterly*, vol. v, No. 4, 1961, p. 541; cf. 545–6.

9 Y. Weber, *L'Administration consultative*, 1968, p. 3 (quoting Chenot, who as a minister had access to the index in the prime minister's office), and G. Mignot and P. d'Orsay, *La Machine administrative*, p. 92; cf. J.-M. Diemer, 'L'administration consultative à l'échelle départementale', *Revue administrative*, 1964, p. 118 ff. See also G. Langrod (ed.), *La Consultation dans l'administration contemporaine*, 1972.

10 *La Vie bretonne*, July 1962, p. 11.

11 For a different view see G. Ross, 'Party and mass organization: the changing relationship of PCF and CGT' in D. Blackmer and S. Tarrow (eds), *Communism in Italy and France*, 1975, chapter 13. More generally, see J.-D. Reynaud, 'Trade unions and political parties in France: some recent trends', *Industrial and Labor Relations Review*, Jan. 1975, pp. 208–25.

12 On French business organizations see B. Brizay, *Le Patronat*, 1975, J. Bunel and J. Saglio, *L'Action patronale*, 1979, and J. Hayward 'Employer associations and the state in France and

Britain', in S.J. Warnecke and E. Suleiman (eds), *Industrial Policies in Western Europe*, 1975, chapter 5.

13  F.-H. de Virieu, *La Fin d'une agriculture*, 1967, pp. 73-4; cf. Y. Tavernier, 'Le syndicalisme paysan et la politique agricole du gouvernement', *Revue française de science politique*, September, 1962, p. 599 ff. and J.T.S. Keeler, 'The corporatist dynamic of agricultural modernization in the Fifth Republic' in W.G. Andrews and S. Hoffmann (eds), *The Fifth Republic at Twenty*, 1981, chapter 16.

14  M. Crozier, 'White-Collar Unions – the case of France', in A. Sturmthal (ed.), *White Collar Trade Unions*, 1966, pp. 121, 126.

15  H. Finer, *Representative Government and a Parliament of Industry. A Study of the German Federal Economic Council*, 1923, p. 229.

16  See J. Bridgford, 'The integration of Trade Union Confederations into the social and political system', in P.G. Cerny (ed.), *Social Movements and Protest in France*, chapter 3 *passim* and R. Mouriaux, *La CGT*, 1982.

17  H. Daalder, in J. La Palombara and M. Weiner (eds), *Political Parties and Political Development*, 1966, pp. 46, 54-6.

18  See especially F. Wilson, 'The Revitalization of French Parties', *Comparative Political Studies*, xii/No. 1, April 1979, pp. 82-103.

19  P. Ribes of the UDR, quoted in A. Campana, *L'Argent secret*, 1977, p. 54.

20  J. Hayward, 'Surreptitious factionalism in the French Communist Party', *Hull Papers in Politics*, No. 20, 1981; cf. O. Duhamel and H. Weber, *Changer le PC?*, 1979.

21  A. Guédé and S.-A. Rozenblum, 'Les candidats aux élections législatives de 1978 et 1981', *Revue française de science politique*, Oct.-Dec., 1981, pp. 994-5.

22  *Le Monde*, 7 February 1982, p. 5; cf. J. Elleinstein, *Le P.C.*, 1976, pp. 44-5, 63-4, 96-9.

23  J. Hayward and V. Wright, 'Governing from the centre: the 1977 French local elections', *Government and Opposition*, xii/4, Autumn 1977, pp. 446-8.

24  C. Peyrefitte, 'Religion et politique' in J. Jaffré *et al*, *L'Opinion française en 1977*, 1978, p. 120; cf. pp. 117-30. See also G. Michelat and M. Simon, 'Religion, class and politics', *Comparative Politics*, x/1, October 1977, pp. 159-86 and their book, *Classe, religion et comportement politique*, 1977.

25  R. Cayrol and J. Jaffré, 'Vers l'éclatement de l'électorat majoritaire?', *Le Monde*, 16 April 1981.

26  See P. Crisol and J.-Y. Lhomeau, *La Machine RPR*, 1977.

27  J. La Palombara, *Politics within Nations*, 1974, p. 111.

28 P. Loquet, *Les Commissions parlementaires permanentes de la V^e
République*, 1980, doctoral thesis, University of Lille II, p. 137; cf.
p. 269. See also J. Frears, 'Parliament in the Fifth Republic' in
W.G. Andrews and S. Hoffmann (eds), *The Fifth Republic at
Twenty*, 1981, p. 61.

29 Quoted by J.A.G. Griffith, *The Parliamentary Scrutiny of
Government Bills*, 1974, p. 7.

30 R. Cayrol *et al.*, 'Les députés français et le système politique', *Revue
française de science politique*, February 1975, p. 83; cf. pp. 81–2.
See also R. Cayrol *et al.*, *Le Député français*, 1973.

31 J. Frears, 'Parliament and the Fifth Republic', p. 60 and J.
Grangé, 'Attitudes et vicissitudes du sénat (1958–80)' in the
special issue of *Revue française de science politique*, XXI/1, February
1981, p. 74.

32 P. Williams, *Crisis and Compromise. Politics in the Fourth Republic*,
1964, p. 242; cf. R.K. Gooch, *The French Parliamentary Committee
System* (1935), 1969 edn, pp. 219–21.

33 J. Grangé, op. cit., p. 72. See also J. Hayward, 'Presidential
suicide by plebiscite: de Gaulle's exit, April 1969', *Parliamentary
Affairs*, XXII/4, Autumn 1969, pp. 290–8 and J. Mastias, *Le Sénat
de la V^e République: réforme et renouveau*, 1980.

34 N. Wahl, 'The French Parliament. From last word to after-
thought', in E. Frank (ed.), *Lawmakers in a Changing World*, 1966,
p. 52; cf. pp. 49–63.

*Chapter 4    Making and Implementing Government Policy*

1 'Un entretien avec M. François Mitterrand', *Le Monde*, 2 July
1981.

2 P. Avril, *Le Régime politique de la V^e République*, 1964, p. 205.

3 C. de Gaulle, *Memoirs of Hope*, 1971, p. 324; cf. pp. 31–2. For
the Bayeux speech, the de Gaulle press conference and the
Pompidou apologia, see M. Harrison, *French Politics*, 1969, pp.
28, 52, 75. On the de Gaulle presidency, see M. Anderson,
*Government in France*, 1970, chapter 2.

4 See note 1 above and press conference of 9 June 1982 reported
in *Le Monde*, 11 June 1982.

5 *L'Express*, 24 February 1975, quoted by O. Duhamel, *La Gauche
et la V^e République*, 1980, p. 276 note; cf. pp. 252–60, 284–9.

6 Reported in *Le Monde*, 20 April 1974 and quoted in O.
Duhamel, op. cit., p. 280 note.

7 Broadcast of 16 April 1974, published in a supplement to the
Socialist periodical *Le Poing et la rose*, April 1974, quoted in

Duhamel, op. cit., p. 279 note.

8 Broadcast of 12 December 1965 published in *Politique*, 1977, p. 432.

9 J.-L. Parodi, 'Sur deux courbes de popularité', *Revue française de science politique*, February 1971, p. 129 ff.

10 J. Hayward, 'France: the strategic management of impending collective impoverishment' in A. Cox (ed.), *Politics, Policy and the European Recession*, 1982, p. 124, reporting findings by J.-L. Parodi.

11 J.-L. Parodi and O. Duhamel, 'Chronique de l'opinion publique', *Pouvoirs*, No. 19, November 1981, p. 157 and No. 20, February 1982, p. 174.

12 Interview in *Le Monde*, 2 July 1981.

13 For example, see Y. Agnes, 'L'Etat-Giscard', *Le Monde dimanche*, 2 March 1980 and N.-J. Bergeroux, 'Etat ps: les nouveaux maîtres', *L'Express*, 22 January 1982, pp. 28–33.

14 This paragraph and the next two draw heavily upon Samy Cohen, 'Les hommes de l'Elysée' in *Pouvoirs*, No. 20, February 1982, pp. 87–100. See also Samy Cohen, *Les Conseillers du président. De Charles de Gaulle à Valéry Giscard d'Estaing*, 1980, especially chapters 4 and 5; M. Padovani, 'Comment fonctionne l'équipe Mitterrand', *Le Nouvel Observateur*, 25 July 1981, pp. 26–30.

15 Cohen, *Les Conseillers du président*, op. cit., p. 96, quoting an investigation reported in *Le Point*, 23 February 1976.

16 Cohen, *Les Conseillers du président*, op. cit., p. 92.

17 A. Rollat, 'La machine gouvernementale en fin de rodage – ii', *Le Monde*, 11 February 1982, p. 7.

18 A. Campana, *L'Argent secret. Le financement des partis politiques et des campagnes électorales*, 1976, p. 50; cf. pp. 49–53.

19 C. Debbasch, *L'Administration au pouvoir*, 1969, pp. 50–1; cf. pp. 44–56.

20 These figures were obtained from the secretariat-general to the government. For alternative figures, see J.-L. Bodiguel, 'Les réunions interministérielles' in F. de Baecque and J.-L. Quermonne (eds), *Administration et politique sous la V<sup>e</sup> République*, 1981, 2nd edn 1982, pp. 141–3.

21 J.-L. Quermonne, 'Un gouvernement présidentiel ou un gouvernement partisan?' in *Pouvoirs*, No. 20, February 1982, p. 77.

22 J.-L. Bodiguel, 'Les réunions interministérielles', p. 151. See also A. Delion, 'Les conseils et comités interministérielles', *Actualité juridique, droit administratif*, June 1975, pp. 268–76.

23　J. Hayward, 'Mobilizing private interests in the service of public ambitions: the salient element in the dual French policy style?' in J.J. Richardson (ed.), *Policy Styles in Western Europe*, 1982, pp. 120-1. See also Ezra N. Suleiman, *Elites in French Society. The Politics of Survival*, 1978, chapter 6 *passim*.

24　C. Grémion, 'Le milieu décisionnel central' in de Baecque and Quermonne (eds), *Administration et Politique sous le V<sup>e</sup> Republique*, 1982, p. 224; cf. pp. 219 ff.

25　B. Gournay, 'L'influence de la haute administration sur l'action gouvernementale dans la V<sup>e</sup> République' in de Baecque and Quermonne, (eds), ibid., p. 241; cf. pp. 238-48.

26　Quoted in J.H. McArthur and B. R. Scott, *Industrial Planning in France*, 1969, p. 286. For opinion poll evidence, see SOFRES, *Les Français et l'Etat*, 1970, pp. 90-3.

27　Professor Wallon, quoted in J.-J. Ribas, *L'Ecole nationale d'administration et la formation des fonctionnaires*, 1946, p. 81. See Terry Shinn, *Savoir Scientifique et Pouvoir Social. L'Ecole Polytechnique, 1794-1914*, 1980, on the nineteenth-century foundations of the model for the ENA, and E. N. Suleiman, *Elites in French Society*, p. 41.

28　Emile Boutmy, quoted by T. B. Bottomore, *Elites and Society*, 1964, p. 82.

29　See J. Siwek-Pouydesseau, *Le Personnel de direction des ministères*, 1969, p. 73, based on calculations for twelve ministries.

30　F. de Baecque, 'L'interpénétration des personnels politique et administratif' in de Baecque and Quermonne (eds), op. cit., p. 22 ff.

31　For details see the 1982 edition's additional material in de Baecque and Quermonne, op. cit., pp. 361-86.

*Chapter 5　Public Order and Civil Liberties*

1　*Traité de droit constitutionnel* (1911, 3rd edn 1927), vol. II, pp. 756-7.

2　Whilst Georges Vedel, *Droit administratif*, is the leading contemporary exponent of the Hauriou view, André de Laubadère, *Traité elémentaire de droit administratif*, 5th edn 1970, vol. I, pp. 41-51, 554, is closer to Duguit's standpoint.

3　Commission du Bilan (Bloch-Laîné), *La France en mai 1981. Forces et faiblesses*, 1982, pp. 302, 308 and chapter 24 *passim*. See also J.R. Frears, *France in the Giscard Presidency*, 1981, chapter 11.

4　SOFRES, *Les Français et l'Etat*, 1970, pp. 55-6, 66-8.

5　L. Favoreau, 'Le Conseil constitutionnel, régulateur de l'activité normative des pouvoirs publics', *Revue du droit public*, 1967, p. 62; cf. pp. 5-120; M. Duverger, *Institutions politiques et droit constitutionnel* (1963 edn), pp. 643-4.

6   See the special issue of *Pouvoirs*, No. 13, 1980, on 'Le Conseil Constitutionnel', especially the articles by Jean Rivero, Danièle Loschak and René de Lacharrière. See also the testimony of a former president of the Constitutional Council, Léon Noël, *De Gaulle et les débuts de la V^e République, 1958-65*, 1976, pp. 191-2, 223-5, 291-3.

7   O. Duhamel, *La Gauche et la V^e République*, 1980, pp. 505-9. See also F. Mitterrand, *Le coup d'état permanent*, 1965, pp. 121-7 and his *L'Abeille et l'architecte*, 1978, p. 388, and M. Charasse, 'Saisir le conseil constitutionnel. La pratique du groupe socialiste de l'assemblée nationale, 1974-9' in *Pouvoirs*, op. cit., pp. 81-94·

8   L. Philip, 'Le Conseil constitutionnel juge électoral', *Pouvoirs*, op. cit., p. 69; cf. pp. 61-79.

9   G. Braibant, *Recueil Dalloz*, 1 July 1960, p. 692, quoted in J.P. Négrin, *Le Conseil d'Etat et la vie publique en France depuis 1958*, 1968, pp. 152-3.

10   On this and other aspects of the mediator's office, see especially F. Stacey, *Ombudsmen Compared*, 1978, chapter 6, as well as the mediator's annual reports.

11   This paragraph is based upon the interesting article by D. Clark, 'The City of Paris *Médiateur* – an Ombudsman *à la Française*' in *Local Government Studies*, forthcoming.

12   SOFRES, *L'Opinion française en 1977*, pp. 177-85.

13   See the comments by C. Laroche-Flavin (a pseudonym for a number of French judges), *La Machine judiciaire*, 1968, pp. 101-4; cf. pp. 90-1 and the testimony of a former police commissioner and senior official of the ministry of the interior writing under the pseudonym of J. Lantier, *Le Temps des policiers*, 1970, pp. 280-1, 289-90. More generally, see Jacques Robert, *Libertés publiques*, 2nd edn 1977, pp. 185-6, 201-2, 213-19.

14   P.M. Williams, *Wars, Plots and Scandals in Post-War France*, 1970, p. 3 ff. and chapter 6 for a discussion of the Ben Barka Affair. On the Casamayor Affair, which arose out of a judge's defence of the independence of the judiciary involving criticism of the minister's hushing up of the Ben Barka Affairs, leading to a reprimand by the high council of the judiciary which is supposed to protect judicial independence, consult C. Laroche-Flavin, op. cit. pp. 139-40.

15   Interview in *Le Nouvel Observateur*, 8 August 1981, pp. 34-5. On

the problem of judicial independence, see the special issue on justice of the review *Pouvoirs*, No. 16, 1981. For a more polemical view, see P. Boucher, *Le Ghetto judiciaire*, 1978.

16  Laroche-Flavin, op. cit. p. 29.

17  Y. Lévy, 'Police and policy', *Government and Opposition*, July–September, 1966, p. 507; cf. p. 491 ff.

18  L.-M. Horeau, 'Les gendarmes malades de la fiche', *Le Canard enchaîné*, 23 December 1981, p. 4.

19  J. Sarazin, 'La police en France', *Le Monde*, 20 November 1973, p. 14.

20  Reported in *Le Monde*, 13 November 1973, p. 13. More generally, see A. Angeli and R. Backmann, *Les Polices de la nouvelle société*, 1971, pp. 36–42 and R. Errera, 'Les libertés en France: les mots et les choses' in *Projet*, No. 119, November 1977, pp. 1063–4, cf. p. 1050 ff.

21  *Le Monde*, 2 April 1977; cf. Ibid., 18 February 1977.

22  'Un pavillon qui a des oreilles', *Le Canard enchaîné*, 2 December 1981. See also Ibid. 23 December 1981.

23  F. Mitterrand, *Politique*, 1977, pp. 300–5. See also SOFRES, *L'Opinion française en 1977*, p. 229.

24  D. Langlois, *Les Dossiers noirs de la police*, 1971, p. 164 and chapter 5 *passim*.

25  B. Chapman, *Police State*, 1971, p. 81; cf. p. 93.

26  See the official police figures in *La Criminalité en France en 1980*, 1981 and the report in *Le Monde*, 26 November 1981.

27  J. Lantier, *Le Temps des policiers*, 1970, p. 102; cf. chapter 3 *passim* on 'The police and the army'.

28  J.S. Ambler, *Soldiers Against the State. The French Army in Politics* (1966), 1968 edn, pp. 7–9, 25. Military personnel still cannot belong to a political party except for two weeks before an election in which they stand as a candidate. Officers require the permission of the ministry of defence to write articles on current military policy.

29  Quoted in Ibid., p. 41. See Jean Meynaud, *Technocracy*, 1968, and Suleiman, *Elites in French Society. The Politics of Survival*, 1978, pp. 119–203, 229–40.

30  See R. Pelletier and S. Ravet, *Le Mouvement des soldats*, 1976. More generally, see G. Harries-Jenkins, *Trade Unions in the Armed Forces*, 1976.

31  J.-F. Thery, 'Le statut des objecteurs de conscience en France et la jurisprudence du Conseil d'Etat', in Conseil d'Etat, *Etudes et documents*, No. 32, 1980–81, pp. 115–34. See also J. Robert, op. cit., p. 340–4.

32 A. de Laubadère, *Traité elémentaire*, vol. 3, pp. 304-8, and J. Robert, op. cit., pp. 451-2.

33 Speech by Raymond Marcellin, minister of the interior, reported in *Le Monde*, 27 July 1971.

34 See D. Pons, *H. comme Hersant*, 1977, and D. Périer Daville, *La liberté de la presse n'est pas à vendre*, 1978. More generally, see C. Bellanger *et al*, *Histoire générale de la presse française*, 1977, v.

35 Quoted in F.-O. Giesbert, *François Mitterrand*, 1977, p. 105; cf. pp. 103-7.

36 André Gérard, quoted in Ruth Thomas, *Broadcasting and Democracy in France*, 1976, p. 13. The Pompidou quotation comes from his 2 July 1970 press conference, reported in *L'Année politique 1970*, p. 430.

37 A. Peyrefitte, *Le Mal Français*, 1976, pp. 69-70, 74, 77 note.

38 J. Chevallier, 'Le problème de la réforme de l'ORTF en 1968', *L'Actualité juridique. Droit administratif*, April 1969, pp. 218, 224.

39 R. Kuhn, 'Government and Broadcasting in France: the resumption of normal service?', *West European Politics*, III/2, May 1980, pp. 210-16.

40 *Indice-Opinion* reported in *Le Nouvel Observateur*, 9 February 1981, p. 22.

41 Quoted by C. Colombani in 'L'information télévisée après le 10 mai-II', *Le Monde*, 17 January 1982. The figure for the 1974 dismissals was given in the National Assembly debate of 27 April 1982 by the minister of communication.

42 Mauroy quoted in *Le Monde*, 3 April 1982. For a possibly prophetic, pessimistic view in 1977 of what the Socialists would do to broadcasting, see R. Errera, op. cit., p. 1070.

43 R. Kuhn, op. cit., p. 205; cf. p. 206.

44 M. Crozier, 'France's cultural anxieties under Gaullism. The Cultural Revolution revisited' in Andrews and Hoffmann (eds), *The Fifth Republic at Twenty*, 1981, pp. 382-3 and chapter 22 *passim*.

*Chapter 6   Economic Policy: By Whom and How It Is Made*

1 P. Huvelin, quoted in L. Stoleru, *L'Impératif industriel*, 1969, pp. 151-2.

2 S. Cohen, *Les Conseillers du président*, 1980, pp. 76-7. Levêque, as head of *Crédit Commercial de France*, one of the banks nationalized in 1982, led a bitter but forlorn resistance campaign in defence of private business. Cohen reports that the 1958 devaluation of the franc and other economic reforms imposed by de Gaulle on

Pinay, were based upon the advice of the president's economic adviser, Roger Goetze, working directly with the budget division of which he was a former director. Ibid., p. 92.

3   F.-L. Closon and J. Filippi (eds), *L'Economie et les finances*, 1968, pp. 131-60.

4   See P. Lalumière, *Les Finances publiques*, 1970, p. 404; cf. p. 401 ff., and J. Rivoli, *Le Budget de l'Etat*, 1969, p. 23.

5   F. Bloch-Laîné, *Profession: Fonctionnaire*, 1976, p. 104; cf. p. 115.

6   See the perceptive comments by J. Zysman, 'The interventionist temptation: financial structure and political purpose' in Andrews and Hoffmann, *The Fifth Republic at Twenty*, 1981, chapter 15, and S.S. Cohen, J. Galbraith and J. Zysman, 'Rehabbing the labyrinth: the financial system and industrial policy in France' in S.S. Cohen and P.A. Gourevitch (eds), *France in the Troubled World Economy*, 1982, chapter 3.

7   F. Bloch-Laîné and P. de Vogüé, *Le Trésor public et le mouvement général des fonds*, 1960, pp. 169-70; cf. Closon and Filippi, op. cit., p. 196.

8   Quoted in Bloch-Laîné and P. de Vogüé, op. cit., p. 167; cf. Bloch-Laîné, *Profession: Fonctionnaire*, pp. 113-14 and Lalumière, op. cit., pp. 371-5. On the relations between the Treasury and Bank of England, see R.A. Chapman, *Decision Making*, 1968, chapter 5.

9   J.G.S. Wilson, *French Banking and Credit Structure*, 1957, p. 296; cf. p. 285 ff. For a very critical assessment of the Bank of France and of the National Credit Council see J. Saint-Geours, *Pouvoir et finance*, 1979, pp. 109-11.

10  F. D'Arcy, 'La Société centrale pour l'equipment du territoire', in *Aménagement du territoire et développement régional*, vol. II, 1969, pp. 80-6, 101-3.

11  F. Bloch-Laîné, Postface to R. Priouret, *La Caisse des dépôts*, 1966, pp. 426, 429; cf. p. 396 ff. See also P. Lalumière, op. cit., pp. 334-6.

12  F. Bloch-Laîné, *Profession: Fonctionnaire*, p. 129; cf. pp. 128-43 generally on the *Caisse*. See also P. Beaudeux, 'Monsieur 200 milliards', *Expansion*, November 1973, pp. 139-43 and G. Dusart, *La Caisse des dépôts et consignations*, 1980.

13  J.G. Padioleau, *Quand la France s'enferre. La politique sidérurgique de la France depuis 1945*, 1981, pp. 133-6.

14  J.H. McArthur and B.R. Scott, *Industrial Planning in France*, 1969, pp. 321-4; cf. J. and A.-M. Hackett, *Economic Planning in France*, 1963, pp. 65-8.

15  S.S. Cohen, *Modern Capitalist Planning. The French Model*, 1969,

pp. 101–3; cf. pp. 112–15, and Bloch-Laîné, *Profession: Fonctionnaire*, pp. 108, 111–12.

16 B. Pouyet, *La Délégation à l'aménagement du territoire et à l'action régionale*, 1967, pp. 8, 59–63, 118–26, 134–5. See also F. Essig, *DATAR. Des régions et des hommes*, 1979, and S. Biarez, ' "Aménagement du territoire" in France: state interventionism or regulation', *West European Politics*, v/3, July 1982, pp. 270–86.

17 F. de Baecque, *Qui gouverne la France?* 1976, p. 125. See D.M. Green, *Economic and Financial Decision-Making in the Fifth French Republic*, University of London Ph.D. thesis, 1976, pp. 309–17. See also G. Lord, *The French Budgetary Process*, 1973, *passim* for the traditional practice.

18 The minister of education was M. Sudreau, September 1962, quoted in P. Lalumière, op. cit., p. 448; the agriculture minister, M. Edgar Faure, in his *Ce que je crois*, 1971, p. 20.

19 See E. Faure, 'Quand le dormeur s'éveillera', *Le Monde*, 16 November 1971; cf. R. Charvin, 'L'évolution du rôle des commissions des finances', *Revue de science financière*, January–March 1969, p. 122 ff. On parliament and the 1968 budget, see P.M. Williams and M. Harrison, *Politics and Society in de Gaulle's Republic*, 1971, pp. 314–21.

20 P. Lalumière, op. cit., p. 226; cf. p. 204 ff.

21 On INSEE, consult F.-L. Closon and J. Filippi, op. cit., chapter 3.

22 J. Hayward, 'From planning the French economy to planning the French State: the Priority Action Programmes of the 1970s' in V. Wright (ed.), *Giscard and the Giscardians*, 1983.

23 Ibid., and *Le Canard enchaîné*, 10 September and 17 September 1980. See also J. Boissonnat, 'Le budget contre le Plan', *L'Expansion*, 5 September 1980, pp. 60–6.

24 J. Hayward, 'France: the strategic management of impending collective impoverishment' in A. Cox (ed.), *Politics, Policy and the European Recession*, 1982, pp. 129–30.

25 P. Mendès France, *A Modern French Republic*, 1962, especially chapters 5–9.

26 See the 1959 Declercq Report 'Pour une planification démocratique' republished in *La CFDT*, 1971, pp. 64–96. See also J.-P. Oppenheim, *La CFDT et la planification*, 1973.

27 On the role of the ESC in Plan preparation, see J.E.S. Hayward, *Private Interests and Public Policy*, 1966, p. 65 ff. On the role of parliament, see P. Corbel, *Le Parlement français et la planification*, 1969, pp. 163–78, 278–81.

28 For a thorough critique of pre-1982 planning, see the report of

the Bloch-Laîné *Commission du Bilan, La France en Mai 1981*, 1981, chapter 6.

29 Report of the *Commission de réforme de la planification*, March 1982. See also *Plan intérimaire: stratégie pour deux ans 1982–1983*, 1981, pp. 46–7.

30 See J. Hayward in V. Wright (ed.), *Giscard and the Giscardians*, 1983.

31 Cour des Comptes, *Rapport du president de la République suivi des résponses des administrations, 1964*, 1966, pp. 33–4; cf. pp. 31–5, 142–5.

## Chapter 7    Elusive Autonomy: Education and Public Enterprise

1 Quoted in F. de la Fontainerie, *French Liberalism and Education in the Eighteenth Century*, 1971, pp. 17, 37.

2 Quoted by H. Taine, *Les Origines de la France contemporaine. Le régime moderne*, vol. 2, 1894, pp. 157–8. On the survival of regional dialects, see E. Weber, *Peasants into Frenchmen*, 1976, chapter 6.

3 *L'Unité*, 14 January 1977, reported in *Le Monde*, 15 January 1977, p. 9. See the more categoric commitment to 'nationalize' education in the PS–PCF–MRG *Programme commun de gouvernement*, 1972, Part 1, chapter 4.

4 Reported in *Le Monde*, 11 May 1982, p. 12.

5 SOFRES, *L'Opinion française en 1977*, p. 294; cf. p. 293.

6 W.D. Halls, *Society, Schools and Progress in France*, 1965, p. 3; cf. W.R. Fraser, *Reforms and Restraints in Modern French Education*, 1971, pp. 58, 120.

7 A. Darbel and D. Schnapper, *Les Agents du système administratif*, 1969, p. 94 ff., esp. pp. 102–3 and 158. See also J. Marceau, *Class and Status in France. Economic Change and Social Immobility, 1945–1975*, 1977, chapter 5 *passim*; J. Fournier, *Politique de l'education*, 1971, pp. 43–9; P. Bourdieu and J.-C. Passeron, *LesHéritiers*, 1964, esp. appendix 1; P. Bourdieu, 'La transmission de l'héritage-culturel', in Darras, *Le Partage des bénéfices*, 1966, p. 387 ff., p. 409 ff; P. Bourdieu and J.-C. Passeron, *La Reproduction. Eléments pour une théorie du système d'enseignement*, 1970, p. 176 ff. and appendix.

8 R. Gilpin, *France in the Age of the Scientific State*, 1968, p. 111; cf. p. 86 ff.

9 See J. Hayward, *The One and Indivisible French Republic*, 1973, pp. 200–3, and J. Minot, *L'Entreprise education nationale*, 1970, pp. 197–209, 332–3.

10 R. Duclaud-Williams, 'Centralization and Educational

Change: la Réforme Haby', *British Journal of Political Science*,
forthcoming, which critically examines some propositions
advanced in M.S. Archer, *Social Origins of Educational Systems*,
1979. On Fifth Republic France, see especially Archer, pp. 356–
83 and 651–69.

11    J.-L. Crémieux-Brilhac (ed.), *L'Education nationale*, 1965, p. 315.
See also J.M. Clark, *Teachers and Politics in France*, 1967.

12    C. Frankel, in OECD *Reviews of National Policies for Education.
France* 1971, p. 27; cf. M. Crozier, *The Bureaucratic Phenomenon*,
1964, pp. 239–43, and M. Crozier, *La Société bloquée*, 1970,
p. 145 ff.

13    J. de Chalendar, *Une loi pour l'université*, 1970, pp. 235–45; cf.
pp. 31, 122–4, 164–5. See also P.M. Williams and M. Harrison,
*Politics and Society in de Gaulle's Republic*, 1971, pp. 326–31. For a
hyper-pluralist assessment, see J. Fomerand, 'Policy formulation
and change in Gaullist France. The 1968 Orientation Act of
Higher Education', *Comparative Politics*, October 1975, pp. 59–89.

14    J. Capelle, *Tomorrow's Education – The French Experience*,
1967, pp. 210, 208.

15    E.N. Suleiman, *Elites in French Society, The Politics of Survival*,
1978, pp. 84–7; cf. pp. 53–5, 62–5. See also W.D. Halls,
*Education, Culture and Politics in Modern France*, 1976, chapter 16.
For an assessment of French education in 1981, see the report of
the Bloch-Laîné Commission, chapter 19.

16    R.F. Kuisel, *Capitalism and the State in Modern France. Renovation
and Economic Management in the Twentieth Century*, 1981, pp. 202–
13.

17    F. de Gravelaine and S. O'Dy, *L'Etat EDF*, 1978, p. 43.

18    N.J.D. Lucas, *Energy in France. Planning, Politics and Policy*, 1979,
p. 139; cf. pp. 9, 140–50.

19    Ibid., pp. 23–5, 32, 144–7.

20    Ibid., pp. 26–7, 33, 56–8, 141, 153, and Gravelaine and O'Dy,
op. cit., pp. 259–61. See also *Rapport sur les entreprises publiques*,
1968. Known as the Nora Report, it was presented to the
Government in April 1967 but not published until the autumn
of 1968. The appendices, examining particular public
enterprises, were not published.

21    Lucas, op. cit., p. 186; cf. pp. 120–1 and 125–32 on energy
planning. On the close links between EDF and CGT see
Gravelaine and O'Dy, op. cit., chapter 10.

22    See the 1980 SOFRES poll reported by A. Lancelot, 'Le service
public industriel et commercial devant l'opinion' in *Le Service
public industriel et commercial dans la société française aujourd'hui*, May

1980, Rouen colloquium, in *Le Monde's* 'Dossiers et documents', October 1980, p. 24.

23 P. Dreyfus, *La Liberté de réussir*, 1977, p. 27; cf. chapter 1 *passim*.

24 J. Sheahan, *Promotion and Control of Industry in Post-War France*, 1963, p. 123; cf. pp. 116–25, 197–8, 208. For more critical views, see P. Naville *et al.*, *L'Etat entrepreneur, La cas de la Régie Renault*, 1971, and J. Frémontier, *La Forteresse Ouvrière: Renault*, 1971.

25 M. Debré, *Au service de la Nation*, 1963, pp. 258–60.

26 Nora Report, op. cit., p. 80; cf. B. Chenot, *Les Entreprises nationalisées*, 1959, pp. 98–105.

27 On the problem of a tripartite board, see M. Byé, in M. Einaudi *et al.*, *Nationalization in France and Italy*, 1955, pp. 98–104; cf. pp. 29–31, and A. de Laubadère, *Traité elémentaire de droit administratif*, 5th ed., 1970, vol. 3, pp. 545, 560–1.

28 N. Delefortrie-Soubeyroux, *Les Dirigeants de l'industrie française*, 1961, pp. 120–1; P. Lalumière, *L'Inspection des finances*, 1970, pp. 128, 154–8; D. Granick, *The European Executive*, 1962, chapters 5 and 19 *passim*; B. Chenot, op. cit., pp. 108–11, 118–19; A.G. Delion, *L'Etat et les entreprises publiques*, 1958, pp. 78–80, 156–8; P. Birnbaum, *Les Sommets de l'état*, 1977, pp. 148–50.

29 J. Baumier, *Les Grandes Affaires françaises*, 1967, p. 193; cf. p. 185 ff. See also Gravelaine and O'Dy, op. cit., p. 258. The danger of a nationalized industry '*République de techniciens*', was pointed out by Camus' *Combat* as early as 14 February 1944. See A. Werth, *France 1940-1955*, 1956, p. 231.

30 Lucas, op. cit., p. 163; cf. pp. 20, 28, 157–8.

31 PS, PCF and MRG, *Programme commun de gouvernement*, 1972, part 2, chapter 2.

32 Quoted in A.G. Delion and M. Durupty, *Les Nationalisations 1982*, 1982, p. 206; cf. pp. 5–9. For more detailed statements of the case for nationalization, see, from Socialists: A. Boublil, *Le Socialisme industriel*, 1977, and two party publications, *L'Agression. L'Etat Giscard contre le secteur public*, 1980, and *Socialisme et industrie*, 1980. From the Communist standpoint, see H. Seğre *et al.*, *Les Entreprises publiques en France*, 1975, and (by a future minister) A. le Pors, *Les béquilles du capital. Transferts Etat-Industrie: critère de nationalisation*, 1977, especially chapter 8.

33 Delion and Durupty, op. cit., pp. 118–21, 139–40. On the 1977 PCF–PS argument on nationalization, see O. Duhamel, *La Gauche et la V^e République*, 1980, pp. 382–8.

34 Delion and Durupty, op. cit., p. 190; cf. pp. 189–92.

35 C. Debbasch, *L'Elysée dévoilée*, 1982, p. 96; cf. p. 57.

36    Delion and Durupty, op. cit., pp. 178-86.
37    Ibid., p. 193; cf., pp. 173-7.
38    Ibid., pp. 165-72.


*Chapter 8    National Independence and International Mission*

1    C. de Gaulle, *Memoirs of Hope*, 1971, p. 39; cf. pp. 36, 48.
2    F.S. Northedge, *The Foreign Policies of the Powers*, 1968, p. 37.
3    C. de Gaulle, op. cit., pp. 28-9.
4    M. Couve de Murville, *Une politique étrangère, 1958-69*, 1971,
     pp. 9-10.
5    P. Rouanet, *Pompidou*, 1969, p. 99; cf. R. Buron, *Le Plus Beau des
     Métiers*, 1963, pp. 219-21.
6    P. de Forges, 'Les Secrétaires généraux de ministères', Colloquium
     of the Institut Français des Sciences Administratives, *Les
     Superstructures administrations centrales*, 1973, pp. 106, 109-13, 119.
7    See S.K. Panter-Brick, '*La Francophonie* with special reference to
     educational links and language problems' in W.H. Morris-
     Jones and G. Fischer (eds), *Decolonisation and After. The British
     and French Experience*, 1980, chapter 14.
8    C. de Gaulle, op. cit., pp. 291 and 289; cf. p. 290.
9    A. Grosser, *French Foreign Policy under de Gaulle*, 1967, p. 143.
10   S. Cohen, *Les Conseillers du président*, 1980, p. 115 and chapter 6
     *passim*.
11   C. de Gaulle, op. cit., pp. 182, 194-5; cf. M. Couve de Murville,
     op. cit., pp. 292-8, 347 ff., and PEP, *France and the European
     Community*, Occasional Paper No. 11, January 1961, pp. 10-12,
     26-35. On Franco-German relations, see A. Grosser, *French
     Foreign Policy under de Gaulle*, chapter 5 and pp. 90-5.
12   Pompidou interview in *L'Express*, 4 September 1967, p. 9.
13   L. Scheinman, in R.S. Jordon (ed.), *International Administration*,
     1971, pp. 219-20; cf. p. 194 note; cf. J. Dromer, 'Le Comité
     Interministériel pour les questions de Coopération Economique
     Européenne', in the Institut Français des Sciences
     Administratives symposium on *La Coordination administrative en
     matière économique et sociale*, 1967, pp. 33-9.
14   M. Couve de Murville, op. cit., p. 303; cf. pp. 301-4.
15   H.S. Wallace, 'The impact of the European Communities on
     national policy-making', *Government and Opposition*, autumn
     1971, p. 537; cf. p. 523 ff. See also P. Gerbet, 'La préparation de
     la décision communautaire au niveau national français' in P.
     Gerbet and D. Pepy (eds), *La Décision dans les communautés*

*européennes*, 1969, pp. 195–205; J. Baillou and P. Pelletier, *Les Affaires etrangères*, 1962, pp. 174–6, 339, 345–51.

16  E. L. Morse, in W. L. Kohl (ed.), *Economic Foreign Policies of Industrial States*, 1977, p. 83; cf. p. 90.

17  M. Couve de Murville, op. cit., p. 449.

18  J. de St Jorre, *The Nigerian Civil War*, 1972, pp. 211–12; cf. p. 323. See also G. Chaffard, 'Foccart et les fonds secrets', *Le Nouvel Observateur*, 3 November 1969, pp. 52–8.

19  S. Cohen, op. cit., p. 168 and chapter 8 *passim*.

20  M.-C. Smouts, 'Bilateral relations and world diplomacy: Franco–African relations on trial at the UN' in Morris-Jones and Fischer (eds), op. cit., chapter 15.

21  G. de Carmoy, *The Foreign Policies of France, 1944–1968*, 1970, pp. 232–40; A. Grosser, op. cit., pp. 35, 46–50 and chapters 3 and 4. See also E. A. Kolodziej, *French international policy under de Gaulle and Pompidou*, 1974, p. 259 ff.

22  G. Destanne de Bernis, 'Some aspects of the economic relationship between France and its ex-colonies' in Morris-Jones and Fischer (eds), op. cit., p. 123 and chapter 5 *passim*.

23  See J. Poirier and J. Touscoz, 'Aid and Co-operation: French official attitudes as seen in the Jeanneney, Gorse and Abelin Reports' in Morris-Jones and Fischer (eds), op. cit., chapter 9. See also R. Robarts, *French Development Assistance: a Study in Policy and Administration*, 1974, esp. pp. 19–25, 33–4, 51–3 and 68–71, and M. Kahler, 'International response to economic crisis: France and the Third World in the 1970s' in Cohen and Gourevitch (eds), *France in the Troubled World Economy*, 1982, p. 80; cf. pp. 76–96. More generally, see G. de Lusignan, *French-Speaking Africa since Independence*, 1969.

24  C. Debbasch, *L'Elysée dévoilée*, p. 31; cf. pp. 30–2. On French military intervention in Africa, see S. Cohen, op. cit., pp. 166–7 and J. R. Frears, *France in the Giscard Presidency*, 1981, pp. 112–17.

25  Quoted in F. Ray Willis, *The French Paradox. Understanding Contemporary France*, 1982, p. 59. See also J. B. Wright, 'Francophone Black Africa since Independence', *Conflict Studies*, No. 130, May 1981, p. 3.

26  General de Monsabert, quoted by B. Chantebout, *L'Organisation générale de la défense nationale en France depuis la fin de la Second Guerre Mondiale*, 1967, p. 177; cf. p. 98 ff.

27  B. Chantebout, ibid., p. 224; cf. p. 192 ff.

28  P. de Forges, op. cit., pp. 104, 108–9, 117–18.

29  R. Gilpin, *France in the Age of the Scientific State*, 1968, p. 264; cf. pp. 257–81, 291–5, and B. Chantebout, op. cit., p. 426. See also

W.L. Kohl, *French Nuclear Diplomacy*, 1971, pp. 202-4.

30  G. Thayer, *The War Business. The International Trade in Armaments*, 1969, p. 270; cf. pp. 269-77. See also J. Stanley and M. Pearton, *The International Trade in Arms*, 1972, pp. 31-2, 85, 94-6, 117, 126-7, 171-7, 196 ff., and Stockholm International Peace Research Institute (SIPRI), *The Arms Trade with the Third World*, 1971, chapter 6.

31  Bloch-Laîné Report, *La France en Mai 1981*, IV, p. 78. See also E.A. Kolodziej, 'French disarmament and arms control policy: the Gaullist heritage in question' in Andrews and Hoffmann (eds), *The Fifth Republic at Twenty*, 1981, pp. 424-6 and Kolodziej, 'France and the arms trade', *International Affairs*, January 1980, pp. 54-72.

32  L. Scheinman, *Atomic Energy Policy in France Under the Fourth Republic*, 1965, pp. 215, 212; cf. pp. XVI-VII, 94-5, 210-15. On parliament and the nuclear force in 1960, see J.S. Ambler, *The Government and Politics of France*, 1971, pp. 188-91.

33  N.J.D. Lucas, *Energy in France. Planning, Politics and Policy*, 1979, pp. 28, 164; cf. pp. 29 ff. and 74-90.

34  W. Mendl, *Deterrence and Persuasion. French Nuclear Armament in the Context of National Policy, 1945-69*, 1970, p. 200; cf. pp. 144, 155, 181-4, 188-200, and Scheinman, op. cit., pp. 66, 97.

35  Mendl, op. cit., pp. 61, 77; cf. p. 78 ff., and C. de Gaulle, op. cit., p. 204.

36  On the attitudes of the PCF and PS before taking office, see M.M. Harrison, 'Consensus, confusion and confrontation in France: the Left in search of a defence policy' in Andrews and Hoffmann (eds), *The Fifth Republic at Twenty*, 1981, chapter 25, and S. Serfaty (ed.), *The Foreign Policies of the French Left*, 1979, *passim*.

37  SOFRES, *L'Opinion française en 1977*, p. 148.

*Chapter 9    The Constraints on Political Will*

1  J. Hayward, 'Mobilizing private interests in the service of public ambitions: the salient element in the dual French policy style?' in J. Richardson (ed.), *Policy Styles in Western Europe*, 1982, pp. 111-12.

2  E. Weber, *Peasants into Frenchmen. The Modernization of Rural France, 1870-1914*, 1977, p. 97 and chapter 7 *passim*.

3  Ibid., p. 493 and chapter 29 *passim*.

4  J. Hayward, 'Mobilizing private interests . . .', op. cit. p. 116.

# Further Reading

*General*

For an invaluable historical perspective, Alexis de Tocqueville's *The Old Régime and the French Revolution* (1856, 1955 English version, Double-day, Garden City, New York) is still unequalled. Eric Cahm has provided a very broad documentary history in *Politics and Society in Contemporary France, 1789-1971* (1972, Harrap, London). The best study of the 1946-58 period is Philip Williams' *Crisis and Compromise: Politics in the Fourth Republic* (1964, Longmans, London). On social, economic and political change, Stanley Hoffmann *et al.*, *France: Change and Tradition* (1963, Gollancz, London) is still worth reading but should be supplemented by Hoffmann's thought provoking essays, *Decline or Renewal? France since the 1930s* (1974, The Viking Press, New York) and William G. Andrews and S. Hoffmann (eds), *The Fifth Republic at Twenty* (1981, State University of New York Press, Albany) or the shorter paperback version, *The Impact of the Fifth Republic*. Michalina Vaughan *et al.*, *Social Change in France* (1980, Martin Robertson, Oxford) is a useful review but gives excessive stress to the omnipresence of the state. For a policy emphasis, backed by judiciously selected readings, Douglas E. Ashford, *Policy and Politics in France. Living with Uncertainty* (1982, Temple University Press, Philadelphia) provides a more integrated policy treatment than Philip G. Cerny and Martin A. Schain, eds, *French Politics and Public Policy* (1980, F. Pinter, London).

On the early years of the Fifth Republic, the testimony of Charles de Gaulle's *Memoirs of Hope* (1971 English version, Weidenfeld and Nicolson, London) should be supplemented by other sources, notably Philip Williams and Martin Harrison, *Politics and Society in de Gaulle's Republic* (1971, Longmans, London), who carry the record judiciously to the Pompidou succession. Anthony Hartley's *Gaullism: The Rise and Fall of a Political Movement* (1972, Routledge and Kegan Paul, London) sums up the de Gaulle era; while P. Rouanet's *Pompidou* (1969, Grasset, Paris) provides a subtle analysis of his career up to his election as president. For relevant background information on France, the

301

definitive' edition of John Ardagh's *France in the 1980s* (1982, Penguin, Harmondsworth) has his customary sureness of touch. Henri Mendras (ed.), *La Sagesse et le désordre. France 1980* (1980, Gallimard, Paris) is a rather disappointing series of essays compared with the less pretentious Vincent Wright (ed.), *Conflict and Consensus in France* (1979, Cass, London). J.R. Frears, *France in the Giscard Presidency* (1981, G. Allen & Unwin, London) provides a wide ranging study of the French political system from 1974–81, but Vincent Wright (ed.), *Giscard and the Giscardians* (1983, G. Allen & Unwin, London) is more penetrating and critical. See also the Bloch-Lainé Report *La France en mai 1981* (1982, La Documentation Française, Paris) with five volumes of more detailed reports. For Mitterrand's pre-presidential reflections see his *The Wheat and the Chaff: the Personal Diaries of the President of France, 1971–78* (1982, Weidenfeld and Nicolson, London), while Denis MacShane, *François Mitterrand. A political odyssey* (1982, Quartet Books, London) includes a useful but too literal translation of Mitterrand's 1981 presidential election programme as an appendix.

## Local and regional politics and administration

For an excellent worm's eye view of rural France, one should consult Laurence Wylie's *Village in the Vaucluse* (1957, Harvard University Press, Cambridge, Mass.), while Yves Mény, *Centralisation et décentralisation dans le débat politique français, 1945–69* (1974, L.G.D.G., Paris) is a judicious review of this controversial subject. Two useful discussions of French and British experience are provided by Jacques Lagroye and Vincent Wright (eds), *Local Government in Britain and France. Problems and Prospects* (1979, G. Allen & Unwin, London) and Douglas E. Ashford, *British Dogmatism and French Pragmatism. Central-Local Policymaking in the Welfare State* (1982, G. Allen & Unwin, London), the latter being genuinely comparative. The most valuable theoretical and empirical study of French regional and local politics is Pierre Grémion, *Le Pouvoir périphérique. Bureaucrates et notables dans le système politique français* (1976, Seuil, Paris) while Sidney Tarrow, *Between Center and Periphery. Grassroots Politicians in Italy and France* (1977, Yale University Press, London) explores some challenging trans-Alpine contrasts. Howard Machin, *The Prefect in French Public Administration* (1977, Croom Helm, London) is a masterly treatment of the pre-1982 prefect in the local and regional context, while Peter Gourevitch, *Paris and the Provinces. The politics of local government reform in France* (1980, G. Allen & Unwin, London) has a more political emphasis. For a stimulating set of essays on the regions prior to 1982, see the special issue of *Pouvoirs*, No. 19, November 1981.

## Further Reading

### Interest groups, parties and parliament

Jean Meynaud's *Les Groupes de pression en France* (1957, A. Colin, Paris) still remains the only full-length general description of French interest groups. For a description of the participation of the major interest groups in a functionally representative third chamber, see Jack Hayward's *Private Interests and Public Policy. The Experience of the French Economic and Social Council* (1966, Longmans, London), while their relations with the civil service are admirably discussed in H.W. Ehrmann's 'French bureaucracy and organized interests', *Administrative Science Quarterly*, v, no. 4, 1961. For a recent general study, see Frank L. Wilson's 'Alternative models of interest intermediation: the case of France', *British Journal of Political Science*, 12/2, April 1982, while some of the more peripheral groups are discussed in Philip G. Cerny (ed.), *Social Movements and Protest in France* (1982, F. Pinter, London). On French business, see Bernard Brizay, *Le Patronat* (1975, Seuil, Paris) and Jean Bunel and Jean Saglio, *L'Action patronale* (1979, PUF, Paris). For a Franco–British comparison, see J. Hayward, 'Employer associations and the state in France and Britain' in Steven J. Warnecke and Ezra N. Suleiman (eds), *Industrial Policies in Western Europe* (1975, Praeger, New York). On French trade unions, see George Ross, *Workers and Communists in France* (1981, University of California Press, Berkeley), René Mouriaux, *La CGT* (1982, Sueil, Paris) and Edmond Maire and Jacques Julliard, *La CFDT d'aujourd'hui* (1975, Seuil, Paris). For a comparison of French and British trade unions' industrial role, see the perceptive study by Duncan Gallie, *In Search of the New Working Class* (1978, Cambridge University Press, Cambridge), especially part four, while his 'Trade Union ideology and workers' conceptions of class inequality in France' in Jack Hayward (ed.), *Trade Unions and Politics in Western Europe* (1980, Cass, London) assesses the influence of trade unions on French workers. For a Franco–Italian comparison, see Peter Lange, George Ross and Maurizio Vannicelli, *Unions, Change and Crisis: French and Italian Union Strategy and the Political Economy, 1945–80* (1982, G. Allen & Unwin, London).

Peter Campbell's *French Electoral Systems and Elections since 1789* (2nd edn 1966, Faber, London) provides the best succinct description of France's many experiments with electoral systems, while Philip Williams' *French Politicians and Elections, 1951–1969* (1970, Cambridge University Press, Cambridge) gives one the feel of what the elections were actually like. For a thorough study of particular elections, see Howard R. Penniman (ed.), *France at the Polls. The Presidential Election of 1974* (1975, American Enterprise Institute, Washington, D.C.) for the first Giscard–Mitterrand duel, and Howard R. Penniman (ed.), *The French National Assembly Elections of 1978* (1980, American Enterprise

303

Governing France

Institute, Washington, D.C.). For a thorough piece of electoral sociology, see the inappropriately entitled (for a book that appeared in 1981), *France de gauche vote à droite* (Presses de la Fondation Nationale des Sciences Politiques, Paris) by Jacques Capdevielle *et al.*, while Guy Michelat and Michel Simon's *Classe, religion et comportement politique* (1977, Presses de la Fondation Nationale des Sciences Politiques, Paris) is a superb analysis of French voting behaviour. The most comprehensive studies in English are J.R. Frears, *Political Parties and Elections in the Fifth French Republic* (1978, Hurst, London) and David S. Bell (ed.), *Contemporary French Political Parties* (1982, Croom Helm, London), the most up to date and useful being Frank L. Wilson, *French Political Parties under the Fifth Republic* (1982, Praeger, New York).

As far as particular parties are concerned, the right is less fully covered than is the left. However, there are two useful books with an historical emphasis: Malcolm Anderson's *Conservative Politics in France* (1974, G. Allen & Unwin, London), and the heavily revised new edition of René Rémond, *Les Droites en France* (1982, Aubier, Paris). On the left, there are a great many books on the PCF. Particularly to be recommended are Ronald Tiersky, *French Communism, 1920–72* (1974, Columbia University Press, New York) and Olivier Duhamel and Henri Weber (eds), *Changer le PC?* (1979, PUF, Paris). For comparative treatments, see Donald L.M. Blackmer and Sidney Tarrow (eds), *Communism in Italy and France* (1975, Princeton University Press, Princeton) and Peter Lange and Maurizio Vannicelli (eds), *The Communist Parties of Italy, France and Spain: Postwar Change and Continuity* (1981, G. Allen & Unwin, London). On the Socialist Party, the most comprehensive coverage is provided by George A. Codding and William Safran, *Ideology and Politics. The Socialist Party of France* (1979, Westview Press, Boulder, Colorado). Jean-François Bizot, *Au parti des socialistes* (1975, Grasset, Paris) provides a readable study of the party in transition, while Paul Bacot, *Les Dirigeants du parti socialiste* (1979, Presses Universitaires de Lyon, Lyon) provides a more academic treatment. On the far left, see Charles Hauss, *The New Left in France: The Unified Socialist Party* (1978, Greenwood Press, Westport, Conn.). On the left in general, Olivier Duhamel's monumental thesis on *La Gauche et la Ve République* (1980, PUF, Paris) shows how far attitudes to the institutions had evolved before 1981, while R.W. Johnson, *The Long March of the French Left* (1981, Macmillan, London) provides an idiosyncratic and racy account of post-war developments. For a more conventional treatment see Neill Nugent and David Lowe, *The Left in France* (1982, Macmillan, London), but the special issue of *Pouvoirs* on 'La gauche au pouvoir', No. 20, February 1982, provides a better early description and assessment of the post-1981 left-wing government.

304

Further Reading

Philip Williams' excellent, succinct study of *The French Parliament, 1958–1967* (1968, G. Allen & Unwin, London) has not yet been super-seded, although the *Revue française de science politique's* special issue on 'Le Parlement français sous trois présidents, 1958–1980' has a very full bibliography on the Fifth Republic parliament. On the social origins and political careers of French deputies, see Roland Cayrol *et al.*, *Le Député français* (1973, A. Colin, Paris).

*The Executive*

The seminal analysis of the values and behaviour characteristic of the French style of authority has been provided by Michel Crozier in *The Bureaucratic Phenomenon* (1963, English version 1964, Tavistock Publications, London). For a modified version of this approach, see Michel Crozier and Erhard Friedberg, *Actors and Systems. The Politics of Collective Action* (1980, Chicago University Press, Chicago) and Michel Crozier *et al.*, *Où va l'administration française?* (1974, Editions d'organisation, Paris). Somewhat dated general discussions of the executive in English are those of Malcolm Anderson, *Government in France: An Introduction to the Executive Power* (1970, Pergamon, Oxford) and F.F. Ridley and J. Blondel, *Public Administration in France* (1964, 2nd edn 1969, Routledge and Kegan Paul, London). For a conceptual and institutional comparative examination of the state in Britain, France and Italy, see Kenneth Dyson, *The State Tradition in Western Europe* (1980, Martin Robertson, Oxford). Two contrasting studies of the presidential *entourage* are worth consulting: an outsider's more comprehensive view by Samy Cohen, *Les Conseillers du président. De Charles de Gaulle à Valéry Giscard d'Estaing* (1980, PUF, Paris) and an acute participant observer's description by Charles Debbasch, *L'Elysée dévoilé* (1982, A. Michel, Paris). Despite the socio-cultural clichés, the astringent anecdotes based upon his experience as a minister make Alain Peyrefitte's *Le Mal Français* (1976, Plon, Paris) worth reading.

For the most authoritative general studies of the higher French civil service and their formative *grandes écoles*, see Ezra Suleiman, *Politics, Power and Bureaucracy in France* (1974, Princeton University Press, Princeton) and *Elites in French Society. The Politics of Survival* (1978, Princeton University Press, Princeton). On the products of two of the most important *grandes écoles*, see Jean-Claude Thoenig, *L'Ère des technocrates. Le cas des ponts et chaussées* (1973, Editions d'organisation, Paris) and Jean-Luc Bodiguel, *Les Anciens Élèves de l'ENA* (1978, Presses de la Fondation Nationale des Sciences Politiques, Paris). One learns much from the personal testimony of the father figure of the more imaginative members of the higher civil service, François Bloch-Laîné,

*Profession: Fonctionnaire* (1976, Seuil, Paris), while insights that attempts at administrative innovation provide into the working of French government are to be found in Catherine Grémion, *Profession: décideurs. Pouvoir des hauts fonctionnaires et réforme de l'état* (1979, Gauthier-Villars, Paris). Much is also to be learned from Francis de Baecque and Jean-Louis Quermonne (eds), *Administration et politique sous la V<sup>e</sup> Republic* (1981, 2nd edn 1982, Presses de la Fondation Nationale des Sciences Politiques, Paris).

## Public order and civil liberties

For a general review of the subject, see Jacques Robert, *Libertés publiques* (2nd edn 1977, Editions Montchrestien, Paris). Roger Errera's *Les Libertés à l'abandon* (3rd edn 1975, Seuil, Paris) documents the inroads on civil liberties made by successive governments. See also Errera's 'Les libertés en France: les mots et les choses' in *Projet*, November 1977, pp. 1050-70. For a general critique of the judicial system by an anonymous group of French judges, consult C. Laroche-Flavin, *La Machine judiciaire* (1968, Seuil, Paris). On the Council of State, it is still worth reading C.J. Hamson's classic, *Executive Discretion and Judicial Control: An Aspect of the French Conseil d'Etat* (1954, Stevens, London). Margherita Rendel's *The Administrative Functions of the French Conseil d'Etat* (1970, Weidenfeld and Nicolson, London) draws mainly on examples prior to the Fifth Republic, so one should also consult J.-P. Négrin, *Le Conseil d'Etat et la vie publique en France depuis 1958* (1968, Presses Universitaires de France, Paris), which is more useful than the more ambitious study by M.-C. Kessler, *Le Conseil d'Etat* (1968, A. Colin, Paris). On the Constitutional Council, see the excellent special issue of *Pouvoirs*, No. 13, 1980.

In a class by itself is the sinisterly entertaining collection of articles by Philip Williams entitled *Wars, Plots and Scandals in Post-War France* (1970, Cambridge University Press, Cambridge). This sets the scene for an insider's pseudonymous study of the political organization and utilization of the police by J. Lantier, *Le Temps des policiers* (1970, Fayard, Paris) and a collection of articles by two well-informed left-wing journalists, R. Backmann and C. Angeli, *Les Polices de la nouvelle société* (1971, Maspero, Paris). On the domestic role of the French military, the best study is J.S. Ambler's *Soldiers Against the State: The French Army in Politics* (1966, 1968 edn Doubleday, Garden City, New York). On the perennial problem of state radio and television, see Ruth Thomas, *Broadcasting and Democracy in France* (1976, Bradford University Press, London). On political interference, see the testimony of Arthur Conte, *Hommes libres* (1973, Plon, Paris).

*Economic policy*

The best general introduction remains Andrew Shonfield's *Modern Capitalism. The Changing Balance of Public and Private Power* (1965, Oxford University Press, London) although a more up-to-date assessment is provided by Stephen S. Cohen and Peter A. Gourevitch (eds), *France in the Troubled World Economy* (1982, Butterworths, London). A useful official review of the French economy just before 1981 is Jean-Pierre Pagé (ed.), *Profil économique de la France* (1981, La Documentation Française, Paris). For a dated but still useful description of the finance ministry, consult F.-L. Closon and J. Filippi (eds), *L'Economie et les finances* (1959, Presses Universitaires de France, Paris). On the working of financial control, see Pierre Lalumière's *Les Finances publiques* (1970, A. Colin, Paris), the same author having earlier studied *L'Inspection des finances* (1959, Presses Universitaires de France, Paris). On the budget the best study is still Guy Lord's *The French Budgetary Process* (1972, University of California Press, Berkeley).

On state intervention in industry the key work remains J.H. McArthur and B.R. Scott, *Industrial Planning in France* (1969, Harvard University Press, Cambridge, Mass.). More limited in empirical scope but theoretically suggestive is John Zysman's *Political Strategies for Industrial Order. State, Market and Industry in France* (1977, University of California Press, Berkeley). On French planning in the 1970s see Jacques Freyssinet, Jean-Marie Martin and Lucien Nizard (eds), *Planification et société* (1974, Grenoble University Press, Grenoble) the swan song of pre-1980s French planning, and the relevant chapters in two comparative collections: Jack Hayward and Michael Watson (eds), *Planning, Politics and Public Policy: the British, French and Italian experience* (1975, Cambridge University Press, Cambridge) and Jack Hayward and Olga Narkiewicz (eds), *Planning in Europe* (1978, Croom Helm, London). On a 1970s experiment in planning that has influenced the new style planning of the 1980s, see Jack Hayward's 'From planning the French economy to planning the French state' in Vincent Wright (ed.), *Giscard and the Giscardians* (1983, G. Allen and Unwin, London). The minimal role of parliament is exhaustively treated in P. Corbel, *Le Parlement français et la planification* (1969, Editions Cujas, Paris). On the main agency shaping regional planning, see B. Pouyet, *La Délégation à l'aménagement du territoire et à l'action régionale* (1967, Editions Cujas, Paris) and a study by a former head, François Essig, *DATAR, des régions et des hommes* (1979, Stanké, Paris).

*Education and public enterprise*

There are useful discussions of French education in W.R. Fraser, *Reforms and Restraints in Modern French Education* (1971, Routledge and Kegan Paul, London), W.D. Halls, *Education, Culture and Politics in Modern France* (1976, Pergamon, Oxford) and chapter 6 of D.L. Hanley *et al.,Contemporary France. Politics and Society since 1945* (1979, Routledge and Kegan Paul, London). The most penetrating discussion available is in the OECD *Reviews of National Policies for Education, France* (1971, OECD, Paris). Education policy is also dealt with in J. Fournier's *Politique de l'éducation* (1971, Seuil, Paris). One may also consult J.M. Clarke, *Teachers and Politics in France: A Pressure Group Study of the Fédération de l'Education Nationale* (1967, Syracuse University Press, Syracuse, New York) and A.B. Fields, *Student Politics in France: A Study of the Union Nationale des Etudiants de France* (1970, Basic Books, New York). A judiciously inconclusive discussion of the eight main explanations of the May 1968 events is provided by P. Bénéton and J. Touchard, 'Les interpretations de la crise de mai–juin 1968', *Revue française de science politique*, XX, no. 3, June 1970, while Jacques de Chalendar provides an insider's testimony on the preparation of the 1968 University Guidelines Act in *Une loi pour l'université* (1970, Desclée de Brouwer, Paris).

The best discussions of public enterprise: Maurice Byé, in M. Einaudi *et al., Nationalization in France and Italy* (1955, Cornell University Press, Ithaca, New York), André G. Delion's *L'Etat et les entreprises publiques* (1958, Sirey, Paris), Bernard Chenot's *Les Entreprises nationalisées* (1959, Presses Universitaires de France, Paris), and *Rapport sur les entreprises publiques* – the Nora Report – (1968, La Documentation Française, Paris) are now rather out of date. They should therefore be supplemented with André G. Delion and Michel Durupty, *Les Nationalisations 1982* (1982, Economica, Paris). On the role of nationalized industries in the making of energy policy, see the well-informed and penetrating study by N.J.D. Lucas, *Energy in France. Planning, Politics and Policy* (1979, Europa Publications, London).

*Foreign and defence policy*

For a (dated) description of the foreign ministry one should consult J. Baillou and P. Pelletier, *Les Affaires étrangères* (1962, Presses Universitaires de France, Paris). Alfred Grosser has provided masterly discussions of the content of French foreign policy under the Fourth and Fifth Republics in *La Quatrième Republique et sa politique extérieure* (1961, A. Colin, Paris) and *French Foreign Policy under de Gaulle* (1965, English edn 1967, Little, Brown, Boston). One may also consult Herbert Tint,

*French Foreign Policy since the Second World War* (1972, Weidenfeld and Nicolson, London). For an official apologia, see Maurice Couve de Murville's *Une politique étrangère, 1958–1969* (1971, Plon, Paris) while Guy de Carmoy's *The Foreign Policies of France, 1944–1968* (1970, Chicago University Press, Chicago) and Edward A. Kolodziej, *French International Policy under de Gaulle and Pompidou. The Politics of Grandeur* (1974, Cornell University Press, Ithaca, New York), provide a more critical assessment of Gaullist policy abroad. See also Michael M. Harrison, *The Reluctant Ally: France and Atlantic Security* (1981, Johns Hopkins, Baltimore). The ideological aspects of de Gaulle's foreign policy are dealt with in Philip G. Cerny's *The Politics of Grandeur* (1980, Cambridge University Press, Cambridge), while a pre-1981 examination of *The Foreign Policies of the Left*, edited by Simon Serfaty (1979, Westview Press, Boulder, Colorado) allows comparison to be made with post-1981 performance. For a brief, general review of French foreign and defence policy, see F. Roy Willis, *The French Paradox. Understanding Contemporary France* (1982, Hoover Institution Press, Stanford, California). W.L. Kohl's *French Nuclear Diplomacy* (1971, Princeton University Press, Princeton, New Jersey) closely links foreign and defence policy, as does Wolf Mendl's *Deterrence and Persuasion: French Nuclear Armament in the Context of National Policy, 1945–1969* (1970, Faber, London). Lawrence Scheinman skilfully disentangles the threads of clandestine policy-making in *Atomic Energy Policy in France under the Fourth Republic* (1965, Princeton University Press, Princeton, New Jersey). On defence policy generally consult Lothar Ruhl, *La Politique militaire de la V$^e$ Republic* (1976, Presses de la Fondation Nationale des Sciences Politiques, Paris).

# Index

*Index*

*Index*